Political Survival

Politicians and Public Policy
in Latin America

California Series on Social Choice and Political Economy
Edited by Brian Barry, Robert H. Bates, and Samuel L. Popkin

Political Survival

Politicians and Public Policy
in Latin America

Barry Ames

University of California Press

Berkeley / Los Angeles / London

University of California Press
Berkeley and Los Angeles, California

University of California Press, Ltd.
London, England

© 1987 by
The Regents of the University of California

Library of Congress Cataloging-in-Publication Data

Ames, Barry.
  Political survival.

  (California series on social choice and political
economy)
  Bibliography: p.
  Includes index.
  1. Latin America—Politics and government—1948–
2. Politics, Practical. 3. Government spending policy—
Latin America. I. Title. II. Series.
JL976.A44 1987   320.98   86-24921
ISBN 0-520-05974-3 (alk. paper)

Printed in the United States of America

1 2 3 4 5 6 7 8 9

To my mother and late father

Contents

Tables and Figures

Tables

Figures

Acknowledgments

Not surprisingly, I have accumulated a great many debts in the course of this project. Robert Bates and Peter McDonough read more than one version of the entire manuscript. In addition to important insights, they supplied the kind of encouragement that motivates constant efforts to sharpen one's thinking and writing. Barbara Geddes read the manuscript for the press and made extremely thoughtful and helpful critiques. Samuel Popkin, an editor of the California Series on Social Choice and Political Economy, pushed me to improve the organization and readability of the text. Barbara Nunberg gave the whole manuscript an exceptionally careful reading, tightening it intellectually and editorially.

My colleagues at Washington University supported me in this work for a very long time. Their faith that it might finally amount to something was crucial. John Sprague told me so many times that my work constituted a research program that I finally believed him and began to see how it all tied together. He, John Kautsky, and Victor Le Vine read the manuscript in various drafts and made many useful suggestions. David Felix and Peter Schwartz helped with particular chapters. John Woolley read numerous versions of the conclusion and aided me to see more clearly the connections between my work and that of others.

Many Latin Americanists were generous with their time and interest. Gaston Fernandez commented on the whole manuscript, and John Bailey and Charles Gillespie read major portions. In Brazil the University Research Institute of Rio de Janeiro let me use their facilities, and their journal *Dados* published an early version of Chapter 4. I also had many useful conversations with José Murilo de Carvalho, Walder de Góes, Glaucio Soares, Edson Nunes, and David and Gloria Vetter. Without David Fleischer and his assistants the survey of Brazilian deputies would not have been possible. I learned a great deal about politics in the Brazilian

Northeast from Teresa Haguette, Jardelino de Lucena Filho, Yves Chaloult, Rejane de Vasconcelos Carvalho, and Maria Antonio Alonso de Andrade. The Research and Documentation Center of the Getúlio Vargas Foundation allowed me to use their oral histories, and Robert Packenham let me examine his interviews with Brazilian deputies of the 1960s. Many former members and staffers of the Brazilian Congress patiently explained to me how things really worked.

A project of this type is impossible without considerable financial assistance. From 1976 to 1978 I was supported by the Tinker Foundation, and during this period I received office space and computer support from the Latin American Center at Stanford University. Ed Goff, then of Washington University, wrote computer routines for archiving and accessing Latin American budget data. My fieldwork in Brazil was supported by the American Philosophical Society and by the National Science Foundation, Grant SES-8209454.

In the era of word processors I typed the whole manuscript myself, but Jean D'Wolf ably did the tables.

Introduction

This is a book about the coalition-building strategies of political leaders in Latin America. Strategic coalition theory begins with the assumption that leaders want to hold onto their jobs. *Why* they want power is not at issue. In their own minds, leaders may seek power in order to assist certain social or ethnic groups, to improve the well-being of all citizens, to enjoy the trappings of office, or to get rich. None of these goals is attainable unless executives can maintain a grip on their offices. Mindful of the high frequency of unscheduled leadership changes in the region, Latin America's executives seek bases of support that will sustain them in office. The central focus of this book is the use by political leaders of public policy, especially public expenditures, as a weapon for survival.

The centrality of public spending in this analysis of the coalition-building efforts of executives does not mean that other kinds of policy have no importance. Indeed, Chapter 5 analyzes four other policy areas along with spending. But because political actors think of expenditures as rewarding or penalizing different groups and regions, and because they care intensely about allocations, the budgetary process is inevitably a key arena of political conflict. Between groups and over time, budgetary politics is inherently a politics of winners and losers.

The first part of this book builds a theory that focuses on no particular country or group of countries. It does not explain, for example, why Argentina spent more in the 1950s on education than Brazil, or why Mexico spent less in the 1960s on the military than Colombia. Instead, the theory explains variations in public spending patterns among "administrations." Why did Ecuador's Velasco Ibarra spend more on public works in his second term than in his first term? Why did he spend more than Kubitschek in Brazil or Arias in Panama?

To put this another way, the units of analysis—the "cases"—are the terms of office (or certain years within terms of office) of individual presidents. If a series of administrations has a common set of institutional relationships, these administrations constitute a "regime." Brazil between 1964 and 1984 was a military regime with five different administrations. Post-1934 Mexico has been a civilian regime with nine administrations, and post-1945 Argentina has had a number of regimes and various administrations.

Everyday political discourse labels administrations with the names of their chief executives: the Thatcher government, the Reagan administration, the Geisel years, and so on. In such usage the term "administration" includes the chief executive plus his or her inner circle of advisers, and it excludes legislatures and political parties. In this book I use the names of executives in just this everyday sense. Each executive has some trusted confidants. Whether every decision is made personally by the executive is irrelevant. In essence, I ignore the inevitable differences and disagreements that occur between presidents and their closest advisers.

What governments do, the policies of governments themselves, are outputs. What these outputs lead to, their consequences for society, are outcomes. Government expenditures on education are an output; declining illiteracy is an outcome. In this book I am concerned only with outputs. Whether programs in public works are actually worth their cost is beyond the scope of my analysis. Whether social expenditures really improve the physical quality of life more under one administration than under another is an important question, but it will not be answered here.

To disregard the ultimate consequences of spending is not to deny their importance, but public expenditures are significant in and of themselves. Changes in outcomes usually presuppose changes in spending. Expenditures, in other words, are generally a necessary but not sufficient condition for other kinds of change. Spending allocations are also important just because political forces fight over them. Political actors care about allocations, so it is profitable for leaders to manipulate programs as a way of rewarding or punishing friends or enemies.

Because administrations are generally short-lived, and because I stress executives' efforts to secure their jobs, I devote most of my attention to determinants of strategy that fluctuate in the short run. In turn, factors that change gradually—economic dependence on advanced countries, for example—do not figure explicitly in the analysis. This is not to argue that dependence has no effect on political actors, for surely national economic vulnerability affects the choices open to executives. But such phenomena are virtually immutable from one year to the next or from one administration to its successor. They get overwhelmed in the decision-making calculus of political actors faced with immediate threats of military revolt, major strikes, or rising inflation.

Explaining Public Expenditures

What are the basic elements of a model of expenditure policy? In this book the distribution of public expenditures is viewed as a consequence of three clusters of causes: the constraints other political actors place upon the leader; the executive's own preferences; and the limitations of scarce financial resources.

The constraints other political actors place upon a leader constitute a structure of political influence. A structure is a set of linked institutions that create claims, either formal or informal, to participate in policy formation. Political structures regulate *access* to the executive. Access equals influence. Certain actors, such as a legislature with the right to approve a national budget, have influence rooted in law. Some actors affect policy through personal ties to the executive. Others trade information for influence. Groups such as investors affect policy because their cooperation is crucial to the attainment of leaders' economic goals (Lindblom 1977).

Latin Americanists have thought a great deal about the characteristics of influence structures that affect policy outputs. One comprehensive list of such structures includes the nature and intensity of societal cleavages, the nature of the electoral system, the level of citizen participation in politics, the potential for coercion, the competence of administrators, the method of selection of the executive, the military presence in the executive, and the strength of the legislature and political parties (Remmer 1978). Much more progress, however, has been made in *identifying* these basic factors than in evaluating their joint impact on policy. Though statistical estimations are common, the dimensions evaluated are generally restricted to a few factors: competitive versus noncompetitive party systems, military versus civilian executives, and so on.

Failure to assess the joint effects of structural characteristics on policy has particularly serious consequences in view of the inherent difficulty of modeling the second cluster of causes, the preferences of executives. Preferences are of two kinds: survival and substantive. Survival behavior is designed to ensure holding onto the office itself. Substantive preferences—those the executive can implement if he or she maintains office—include everything else. Substantive preferences describe beneficiaries from government programs, favored regions, the future of the society, etc.

It is not easy to measure substantive preferences. The public statements leaders make, for example, mix substantive with survival preferences. Before making such statements, leaders calculate how others will react, what is possible, and who can be swayed. "True" substantive preferences become, in effect, unknowable.

I avoid the problem of identifying substantive preferences by assuming that at certain times the predominant interest of leaders is the maintenance of office. Driven by survival motives, executives examine the competing claims made upon them and estimate the cost of attracting new supporters. This calculus leads to a set of policies executives hope will ensure their tenure. If, as observers, we can make the same calculation of coalitional possibilities executives make, we can evaluate their actual strategic behavior.

The third element affecting outputs is the constraint of scarce economic resources. If executives had perfect understanding of the future, they would incorporate resource constraints into their preferences; that is, the rank they assign to each objective would be higher or lower depending on its cost. Executives obviously lack such timely and complete knowledge of resource flows—indeed, even their information about near-term resources is uncertain. Moreover, executives with fixed terms of office can choose to postpone paying their bills. They can act, in effect, as if they were much less constrained by resource scarcity. As a result, the way executives incorporate resource constraints into preferences is not always the same, and it makes sense to treat economic resources as a separate influence.

The Plan of the Book

Part I of this book analyzes cross-national time series of expenditures. This multinational statistical approach offers important virtues. Since the number of cases in Part I is very large—more than a hundred separate administrations and almost six hundred annual observations—we can evaluate the effects on spending of any potential influence while holding other factors constant. And since the range of relevant political characteristics is much wider across seventeen countries than within one, we can assess factors appearing infrequently in any single nation.

Part II takes the theory developed in Part I and applies it to a pair of Brazilian cases. Without denying the strengths of the cross-national analysis, these single-country applications have virtues of their own. In the analysis of public expenditures, the focus on a single country allows us to examine the *local* distribution of policy outputs, especially the distribution of public works. Moreover, we can analyze political actors below the level of the chief executive more systematically, and we can consider nonbudgetary policies that may be especially important in a particular country.

The Conclusion summarizes the main points of the analysis and discusses the place of strategic coalition approaches in the study of comparative politics. Problems of coalition formation, particularly during leadership transitions, turn out to be central in a number of diverse studies. Scholars utilizing more traditional modes of analysis, especially modes that stress the primacy of social class, need to pay more attention to short-run survival motivations, because the policy manipulations executives undertake during crises have effects reaching far beyond the crises themselves.

Part I: The Theory of Survival Coalitions

Part I develops and tests a set of propositions that constitute a theory of survival coalitions. Fundamental to this theory is the notion that political leaders cannot attain their substantive goals unless they hold onto their jobs. In the turbulent politics of developing nations, leaders can never take tenure for granted. Political survival must be actively pursued by manipulating public policy to construct supporting coalitions. Public expenditures are central to survival coalitions. No arena of policy involves so many actors so intensely as public expenditures. Claims on the budget come from job-seekers, economic groups, social classes, and regional interests, and the annual changes in programs unambiguously record winners and losers.

Chapter 1 explores budgetary politics in seventeen Latin American countries between 1947 and 1982. It does so in the simplest way possible, by adding together all the various programs and categories making up the annual central government budget in each country. Latin American executives use the budget to reward old followers and recruit new ones, to keep bureaucrats happy and the military at bay. Because their resources are limited, executives spend most when their vulnerability is greatest, notably near elections and just after military coups. The chapter demonstrates that a small set of causal conditions adequately explains fluctuations in total public spending. These conditions include the occurrence of elections or military coups, the coming to power of an opposition party, support by a political party with a working-class base, and the rise or fall of potential budgetary resources. Leadership transitions lead to two expenditure cycles, one for elected governments and another for military governments. Incumbent executives respond to approaching elections by increasing real outlays, whereas newly elected leaders reward their followers just after taking office. Military governments coming to power via coups behave like newly elected civilian governments, raising expenditures in their own search for popularity.

Chapter 2, "Survival Strategies and Expenditure Trade-offs," broadens the concept of political transitions developed in Chapter 1. During certain periods—crisis points—in the tenure of each administration, the executive's hold on office is weakest. At these crisis points we expect survival preferences to dominate substantive preferences completely. All policies—certainly expenditure policies—are devoted to survival. The executive tries to determine the mix of budgetary trade-offs that will maximize support. Will raising public sector salaries ensure the support of the bureaucrats? Will expanding health care increase working-class support? Will construction projects in a certain town guarantee the support of the local boss? Because expenditure programs such as education, health, and public works affect individual social groups and regions differently, the executive builds a survival coalition through *budgetary trade-offs:* boosting some programs, cutting others, leaving still others unchanged.

Chapter 3, "With Time to Breathe," examines the policies of administrations surviving their immediate crises. It begins by considering the effects of expenditures on long-term survival. Did expenditures help stave off military overthrow? Were electoral challenges overcome? The chapter then considers one of the oldest problems students of comparative politics face: How do military and civilian governments differ in their spending on the armed forces? Finally, Chapter 3 extends the central argument of the book to begin an assessment of overall patterns of spending in administrations managing to overcome their survival crises. Five programs—education, health, public works, agriculture, and the military—are ranked according to their gains or losses from one administration to the next. This multiprogram comparison enables us to determine which programs lose when a selected program gains, and it is used to evaluate the explanatory power of such regime characteristics as civilian versus military executive and competitive versus noncompetitive party system.

1. The Politics of Public Spending

Public expenditures in Latin America rarely move up or down as smoothly as they do in advanced industrial nations. Consider Figure 1, which traces total central government spending in Argentina, Bolivia, and Peru. In Argentina spending is remarkably volatile, with sudden leaps succeeded by gradual declines. Bolivia reflects the turmoil of a revolution, the consolidation of a new regime, and even a huge infusion of aid from the United States. Expenditures in Peru follow a much smoother course, but then in four years total spending triples. These three nations are representative of Latin America's diversity. Indeed, the seventeen countries analyzed in this chapter illustrate just about every pattern of spending imaginable. Despite the apparent differences among these patterns, are the processes that generated them roughly similar? Are these processes in some sense "political"?

This chapter establishes the political quality of public spending—political in the sense that expenditures are instruments that Latin American leaders utilize in their quest for security. The chapter focuses on *total* central government spending rather than individual programs precisely to demonstrate that the whole budget, not just a few key programs, responds to the political needs of leaders.

The chapter is divided into two main sections. The first, devoted to creating a theory of expenditure fluctuations, emphasizes executives' *motivations* to build political support through government expenditures and the *constraints* within which such efforts operate. Expenditures respond to an electoral cycle, to the bargaining power of constituents, and to a military cycle. Moreover, economic, bureaucratic, and ideological considerations all constrain spending. The chapter's second section evaluates this theory with a regression model pooling overall central government spend-

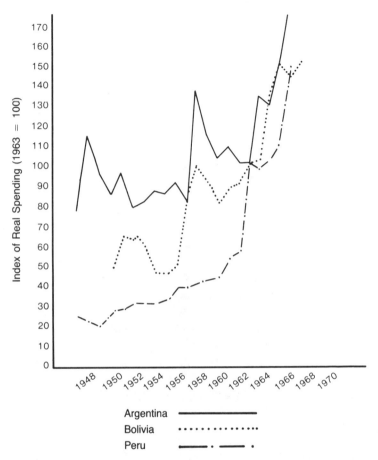

Figure 1. Central Government Public Spending in Three Selected
Latin American Nations

ing for seventeen countries between 1947 and 1982.[1] The results
of this statistical test are then illustrated in more depth through
a brief discussion of individual countries. Appendix A at the back

1. The seventeen are Argentina, Bolivia, Brazil, Chile, Colombia, Costa Rica,
Ecuador, El Salvador, Guatemala, Honduras, Mexico, Nicaragua, Panama, Paraguay, Peru, Uruguay, and Venezuela. The absence of sufficient data led to the
exclusion of Haiti and the Dominican Republic, and Cuba was excluded because
its budget after the Cuban Revolution is not comparable to the others.

of the book discusses problems of data quality and sources, operationalization, left-out variables, time-series regression, and interpretation of results.

The Functions of Public Spending

Sometimes we think of government as a referee or a broker responding to different kinds of pressures. In all societies, however, and particularly in developing nations, it is appropriate to view the government as an institution with its own preferences, usually in harmony with certain private interests and in conflict with others. This does not mean government always seeks the "public interest"; indeed, a government's policies may coincide with no interests but those of its leaders.

Executives are almost always interested in maintaining office, and the power of the purse has long been crucial in their search for security. In the pluralist regimes of advanced industrial societies, political elites maximize their chances of reelection by coordinating economic policy decisions with the election calendar—that is, by reducing unemployment and maximizing per capita income near the date of the vote.[2] Latin American governments, burdened with volatile and open economies and lacking adequate technical advice, utilize spending somewhat differently. They spend to recruit and retain followers. Historically, Latin America has been a region of bloated and politicized bureaucracies, with substantial proportions of the work force dependent on government largesse. In Brazil, for example, the proportion of the working population in bureaucratic posts increased steadily during much of the twentieth century. According to Daland (1972:4) changes of regime rarely led to "throwing the rascals out." Instead, they were moved to innocuous positions, their places taken by new shifts of rascals. In Chile, Parrish (1970:18) found that the increase in bureaucratic employment between 1940 and 1968 was more than ten times the increase in population. New administrations regarded nearly all middle and upper bureaucratic posts as spoils, but displaced bureaucrats, as in Brazil, maintained their

2. The notion of the "political business cycle" was made popular by Nordhaus (1975) and Tufte (1978). For an excellent review of this literature, see Alt and Chrystal (1983).

jobs and salaries. The consequence, of course, was a cyclically expanding government payroll.

Though leaders may believe the economic objectives they are pursuing will benefit the nation as a whole, specific policies can rarely be explained without considering political effects. Kahil (1973:330) demonstrates that in post–World War II Brazil the goal of winning the allegiance of the urban masses—while still serving other key groups—was as important as the goal of industrialization. For Kahil, the support-maximizing aspects of Brazilian policy help illuminate the incoherent and often inflationary nature of economic choices, and they explain the creation of hundreds of thousands of public sector jobs through the launching of grandiose projects.

The political implications of expenditures extend beyond ensuring that one's followers have government jobs. Because endemic inflation so often plagues Latin American economies, salary adjustments for civil servants and military personnel become critical economic issues—not only for government employees themselves but also for economies dependent upon the purchasing power of these employees. The transfer of funds to other levels of government may also further the political interests of central government executives. In Mexico, for example, the authoritarian regime responds to election results by manipulating its allocations to individual states, sometimes rewarding supportive states and sometimes bolstering states where the opposition is threatening (Coleman and Wanat 1973:18).

Job creation, maintenance of real wages, intergovernmental transfers—these goals all make sense in competitive governments. Latin America, however, is hardly a pluralist paradise. Is this an argument about a nonexistent world? It is not. Recent authoritarian experiences in the region notwithstanding, elections in the years since World War II have been frequent and significant. Between 1945 and 1982, administrations in Latin America ended their terms with elections in eighty-two instances and with military coups in fifty-one cases. Moreover, even in polities like Mexico, where the opposition only dreams of winning, elections play a vital role for lower-level politicians trying to demonstrate their political skill. Last—and this is crucial—military and civilian regimes often feel the same insecurities. Latin America's Pinochets and Stroessners, with their substitution of massive repression for any sort of popular legitimacy, are really quite exceptional.

The Electoral Cycle

Because budgetary resources are limited, executives must allocate spending when and where it is most needed. The concern of leaders for their own survival is greatest just before and just after elections. New jobs must be created to recruit additional followers; salaries must be improved to keep old supporters satisfied. In Chile, this process turned the final years of most presidencies into "administrative fiascos, with programs completely subjected to electoral considerations" (Cleaves 1974:24). But the election might not relieve the pressure, for once in office an administration has to satisfy the demands of its new supporters for a piece of the public pie. As a result, we can expect administrations seeking reelection and administrations newly elected to increase total expenditures in the year of the election and in the year immediately after.

Constituency Pressures

The claims faced by executives go beyond the cyclical demands imposed by elections. One such claim stems from the preferences of the voters to whom a party appeals and from whom it receives support. It matters little whether leaders and supporters agree on many issues, although such agreement is likely. Leaders respond to party constituencies because they desire reelection.

Parties with constituencies among the poor are less likely to be fiscally conservative.[3] Support from lower-middle and lower-class voters usually requires commitment to expanded social welfare and infrastructure projects, and demands for such programs tend to increase with the entrance of new participants into the political process. Latin American political systems (like most political systems) generally accommodate the claims of new entrants without injuring the interests of older "power contenders" (Anderson

3. Fiscal conservatives may believe that prosperity and electoral success result from balanced budgets, or their desire for limited spending and low inflation may outweigh the desire for electoral victory. At the national level in the United States, Democrats have traditionally been less conservative fiscally than Republicans. European socialist parties are obviously less conservative than center or rightist parties (Kirschen and others 1964).

1967), so spending for welfare and infrastructure rarely leads to compensatory decreases in other areas. Fiscal conservatism becomes impossible.

Obviously the nature of political parties varies greatly across Latin America. A leftist party in Bolivia behaves politically quite unlike a leftist party in Argentina. The issue, however, is not just the absolute degree of "leftism" of any party but also its representation of groups previously excluded from political participation. In Latin America, political parties mobilizing formerly excluded groups should be more likely to increase expenditures.

No formula exists to determine which administrations have enjoyed the support of such parties. After a thorough search of the monographic literature on Latin American politics, I concluded that incumbent administrations in twelve nations enjoyed the backing of parties with bases in the working class or lower middle class:

Argentina, 1948–1955	El Salvador, 1950–1956
Bolivia, 1952–1964	Guatemala, 1951–1953
Brazil, 1952–1963	Nicaragua, 1980–1982
Chile, 1965–1973	Panama, 1969–1975
Colombia, 1959–1962, 1967–1970, 1975–1982	Peru, 1964–1975
Costa Rica, 1963–1966, 1971–1977	Venezuela, 1959–1968, 1974–1978

A variable called "leftbase" indicated the presence or absence of a supportive working-class party. When an administration has the backing of such a party, expenditures should increase.

Insecurity: New Executives
and Electoral Margins

The security of executives is usually proportional to the length of time they hold office. Newly elected executives are the most insecure. As Lipset demonstrated for Saskatchewan's socialist government (1968:296–298), insecurity encourages budgetary expansion. Administrations seek to reward favored groups, but they avoid penalizing opponents.

Unfortunately for new leaders, their lack of control over legislatures and bureaucracies often thwarts their desire to spend and, as the ends of their terms near, personal authority declines. Cleaves, for example, notes that Chilean presidents begin their terms with considerable legitimacy and status but little understanding of program implementation. With time comes experience, but once lesser political leaders begin jockeying for positions in the administration of the next president, executives lose the ability to manipulate programs (Cleaves 1974:22).

In sum, inexperience increases incentives to spend, but it denies the skills necessary for implementation. The net effect of these tendencies depends on the executive's ability to acquire necessary information and the speed at which authority declines. The variable "nonincumbent" measures the spending of executives serving their initial terms in office, but we can make no explicit prediction of its consequences for overall spending.

Insecurity also results from close elections. A term in office provides an opportunity to use the public treasury to widen the electoral gap between followers and opponents. In a case like Mexico, by contrast, executives lack serious opposition, so they are free to play the role of statesman, deferring the claims of job-seekers. Survivors of close elections have no such luxury. The closer the previous election, the greater should be the incentive to spend.

Just as the constraint of ignorance counterbalances the incentive of inexperience, the absence of political support checks the expansionary motivation of close elections. Executives surviving close elections often confront hostile legislatures. Even worse, close elections most often occur in countries like post-1958 Venezuela, where the legislature wields meaningful authority over fiscal matters. Why should the opposition support an executive's efforts at political machine building? In effect, the closer the electoral margin, the more limited is the executive's ability to spend.

Given this ambiguity in the margin–spending relationship, I made a number of attempts to assess the impact of electoral closeness on expenditures. Initially, the difference between the percentages of the vote received by the two leading presidential contenders defined the variable "margin." Preliminary tests of this variable in the complete model produced insignificant coefficients—that is, the size of the electoral margin had no impact on spending. I then examined the possibility that extremely large and extremely small margins might both depress spending. That hypothesis, too, yielded insignificant results. Finally, close elections (those with differences of less than ten percentage points) were identified with a dummy variable, but it is impossible to make a definitive prediction.

The Military Coup Cycle

Military takeovers in Latin America are normal events. Coups occur most often in the midst of economic difficulties. Prior to a coup, real government spending has usually declined, because in periods of stagnation and inflation tax collections shrink, new foreign investments diminish, and foreign loans become difficult to secure. Declining expenditures may themselves contribute to coups, because spending cuts hurt the economic interests of the armed forces (Villanueva 1969).

Once in power, the victorious military faction justifies its coup by noting the economic distress, corruption, and subversion it inherited. Attempts will be made to rectify the various ills and injustices, with the junta taking credit for any prosperity that follows. Sometimes the new government is temporarily successful, but in reality the military's success is as likely to be mere luck, because coups tend to occur just at the bottom of economic slides (Merkx 1969; Needler 1974).

Upward readjustments in military salaries need not be accompanied by compensatory cuts in other programs. In fact, the limited evidence available, especially my study of the post-1964 Brazilian military (Ames 1973), indicates that newly installed officers act like newly installed civilians—that is, they increase overall spending to win friends and reward followers. If the economy turns upward, the military benefits from rising revenues, and its greater vigor in the collection of taxes further increases available resources.

After the initial boost, military regimes allow spending to decline. The military relies more on coercion than on freely given support, so its sense of security gradually increases without the rapid loss of authority suffered by civilian regimes. The military is also more autonomous from social forces relying on government programs, and its preferences are generally conservative. Finally, military regimes seldom face truly open electoral challenges. Sometimes military regimes allow controlled elections, and sometimes they accept elections when the economy proves unmanageable or when the prestige of the armed forces falls sharply (as in Argentina after the Malvinas conflict). But such regimes really worry about countercoups by dissident military factions. Military governments try to prevent their own ouster by co-opting or repressing potential troublemakers. Transfers of recalcitrant officers to distant regions, bribes of cash or appointments abroad, forced retirements or assassinations—such efforts minimize the probability of countercoups.

This logic suggests a cycle of spending in military administrations: The year in which the coup occurs should be associated with a decline in spending; the first year after the coup should witness a surge; subsequent years should be associated with declines. At the same time, students of recent Latin American politics know that austerity is not always the dominant motif of military regimes. In certain cases—Panama after 1968, Brazil between 1968 and 1973, Peru from 1968 until 1975, and Argentina between 1969 and 1973—the military expanded the scope of government activities rather sharply. What caused these expansions?

Quite different starting points lead to fiscal expansionism. Leftist or reformist military regimes inevitably expand the role of the government. They reject the orthodoxy of "getting the prices right" as a developmental strategy, and they use welfare and job creation programs as carrots to co-opt restive working-class and middle-class supporters. In Brazil, by contrast, overall economic policy during the first years of military rule was a gradualist version of orthodox austerity and restraint. Perhaps these orthodox policies were necessary to reduce wages and increase investor confidence, but they failed to lift Brazil from the stagnation precipitating the coup in the first place. Between 1968 and 1973, however, the government became much more aggressive and the growth rate soared. After 1973 economic growth slowed, but the regime continued its expansionist tendencies, because it feared the disruptive effects of a recession on its program of gradual democratization. (Chapter 5 treats this topic at more length.)

In Argentina between 1966 and 1970, President Onganía attempted to control expenditures and "rationalize" government activities. These policies were partly successful in restoring GNP growth, but their social costs led in 1969 to the violent outburst known as the "Cordobazo." In its aftermath Onganía fired the minister of the economy, and in 1970 Onganía's military colleagues removed the president himself. As the military regime began a gradual withdrawal, it returned to budgetary expansion as a way of relieving social tensions.[4]

Is there a general rule in these stories of right-wing regimes becoming big spenders?[5] Certainly the cases have many common characteristics. Both Argentina and Brazil had relatively sophisticated economies in which the government had long played a high-profile economic role. Technocrats in both military regimes were ideologically less purist than Chile's neoliberal "Chicago Boys." Both regimes switched policies when austerity programs failed.

With so few examples, it is easy to inflate a couple of anecdotes into a principle, but the key appears to be *sequence*. After early surges in spending, right-wing military regimes face various options. In relatively simple economies, the military is fiscally conservative. In more complex economies (where the government is inevitably a major economic force), the military remains antistatist and conservative as long as the economy performs acceptably. If the economy falters, the military seems willing to replace a failed economic team with one committed to expansionist policies. The only exception is Pinochet's Chile, where neoliberal economists were so well entrenched in policy-making positions that failures led to more rigorous application of the same policies. (See the conclusion to this book.)

Long-lasting military regimes in each of these categories are actually rather scarce, so the entire scenario cannot be included in a statistical model. Instead, the model evaluates the first four years of military government—four years in which the initial jump should be followed by a declining trend. The final section of the chapter examines individual cases for clues about the behavior of the long-term regimes.

The Constraint of Domestic Resources

Comparative quantitative research on public expenditures was really born with studies of the policy outputs of the fifty United

4. The best source on Argentina in this period is William C. Smith, "Crisis of the State and Military-Authoritarian Rule in Argentina" (1980). A similar story might be told, with the ideological directions reversed, in Peru with the changeover from Velasco Alvarado to Morales Bermúdez.

5. Clearly fiscal expansion is not merely a characteristic of the so-called bureaucratic-authoritarian regimes. Spending in Brazil did rise during the heyday of bureaucratic authoritarianism, but in Argentina expenditures shrank during the installation phase of the 1966–1969 BA state and expanded only after its collapse. Chile under Pinochet steadily reduced public spending, and Panama and Peru fail to qualify as bureaucratic-authoritarian regimes. See O'Donnell (1973).

States. This literature emphasized the primacy of the social and economic environment as a determinant of demands for governmental services. Urbanization and industrialization were thought to have created both the need for an expanding social welfare sector and the wealth to pay for that expansion. This argument, which assumes that political systems process the demands generated by the socioeconomic environment into outputs, makes less sense in Latin America. True, over the long run social changes increase the demands on political leaders, but the adoption of policies in areas such as social security can be explained much better as a result of a pattern of diffusion from wealthy to poor countries than as a response to demands made by populations at certain economic levels (Collier and Messick 1973). Besides, in Latin America the public sector has always been large in relation to levels of national wealth, because government has provided the employment opportunities lacking in perennially weak economies.

Latin America lacks the industrialization–demand creation mechanism that in the United States translates resources into expenditures, but it does not follow that the empirical linkage will disappear as well. Economic growth should still lead to increased public spending, not necessarily because growth increases societal needs—most leaders already believe needs are enormous—but simply because growth increases resources, giving the government the ability to respond to ongoing problems, and because the sheer level of economic development creates expectations about the kinds of services government ought to provide.

The economies and tax structures of Latin America are much more heterogeneous than those of the fifty United States. Latin American nations earn substantial income from import and export taxation, and they remain vulnerable to sudden shifts in commodity prices. Rather than measuring the revenue base of these seventeen nations with a single indicator, the analysis separates the export-dependent countries from the more diversified. The former tend to have tax structures geared to exports, while the latter collect more revenue from taxes on personal income, property, and sales. Colombia, for example, collected more than 50 percent of its taxes in the 1960s from income and property and about 25 percent from imports and exports. Honduras collected less than 20 percent of its taxes from income and property and almost 50 percent from imports and exports (Instituto Americano de Estatística 1971). In the model of public spending used in this chapter, the gross domestic product (GDP) served as the measure of domestic resources for the seven countries in which the percentage of revenue raised from direct taxes was at least 45 percent of total taxation. For the ten countries in which direct taxes were less than 45 percent of the total, income received from exports measured domestic resources.[6] When resources expand, one can predict that public expenditures should rise.

The Constraint of International Resources

Because Latin America depends so heavily on export earnings, balance of payments positions are critical. Levels of international reserves, including gold holdings, International Monetary Fund (IMF) drawings, and foreign exchange reserves, function as important signals of the health of the import–export balance and as indicators of future restraints on growth. When reserves drop (or when debt/reserve ratios grow too large), countries may reduce expenditures. Such cuts can be part of attempts to right the financial ship without resorting to the IMF, or the IMF may impose them as a "conditionality" for the extension of its assistance.

Information on the health of the reserve position is not available to Latin American executives quickly enough to allow instant adaptation in spending. Instead, changes in the current reserve position generally affect economic plans one year later.[7] In preliminary tests of the model, measures of reserves had no significant effects on spending. It seemed plausible, however, to wonder whether executives might respond only to large changes in reserves. This possibility was operationalized by creating two dummy variables, one for increases in reserves greater than 50 percent and the other for decreases greater than 50 percent. We can expect spending to move in the same directions as these large fluctuations in reserves.

When a country borrows from the IMF, it proceeds through a series of credit lines, or "tranches," each with more stringent conditions. In the higher tranches, the IMF may require the borrower nation to agree to a formal program of economic reform. Since

6. The GDP-measured countries are Argentina, Brazil, Chile, Colombia, Peru, Mexico, and Panama. The export-measured countries include Bolivia, Costa Rica, Ecuador, El Salvador, Guatemala, Honduras, Nicaragua, Paraguay, Uruguay, and Venezuela. The data come from the IMF's *International Financial Statistics*.

7. Because reserves are a function of the aggregate size of the economy, the actual indicator is the ratio of reserves to the GDP.

such programs almost always call for fiscal austerity, the existence of an IMF program should be associated with declines in public spending.[8]

At times, grants from the United States have constituted an important source of revenue in Latin America. After the CIA helped overthrow Guatemala's President Arbenz in 1954, the U.S. government sought to use aid to make Guatemala a showcase of democracy and capitalism. In Bolivia in the late 1950s, the United States supplied up to 40 percent of the central government's budget (Wilkie 1971). And in Chile between 1964 and 1970, Washington's interest in the Frei administration led to another sharp increase in economic aid.

The potential impact of foreign aid depends upon its size relative to the country's economy. Each nation's gross domestic product was therefore used to deflate annual U.S. grants. So adjusted, we can expect grants to be positively and significantly related to spending.

Incrementalism in Public Spending

In the short run, decision makers have only a limited ability to affect the level of overall spending. Once started, programs develop their own momentum. Earmarked taxes often fund government-owned enterprises and autonomous agencies. Retirement pensions may be untouchable. Dubious projects begun in the distant past continue receiving public funds. As a result, levels of spending change in small increments and the potential influence of political factors is therefore reduced.

In the United States, "incrementalist" theories explain why there are limits on the short-run flexibility of expenditures (Wildavsky 1964).[9] These theories argue that spending in prior years is the best predictor of current spending. Previous spending is not, however, likely to dominate the statistical explanation of Latin American expenditure movements as it does in the United States:

8. For analyses by IMF economists of the effects of IMF programs on countries' behavior, see Reichmann and Stillson (1978) and Kelly (1982). The programs analyzed by the IMF economists were used here as well.

9. Early expenditure analysts argued that changes in expenditures are incremental because decision makers have limited cognitive ability and high motivation to avoid conflict. But Gist (1977) and others discovered that the most controllable programs in the U.S. federal budget are those that conform least to the incremental model.

Latin American budgets are legally much more manipulable in the short run than those of the United States, political structures are less institutionalized, and resource fluctuations are greater. Still, although incrementalist influences will not overwhelm political and economic effects, we should see a significant positive effect. We can expect spending in any year to be positively related to spending in the previous year.

The Diffusion of "Developmentalism"

In an attempt to promote economic development and prevent repetitions of the Cuban Revolution, a host of international agencies expanded their activities in Latin America in the 1960s. For the United Nations, the period became known as the "Development Decade." With the help of the UN, the Alliance for Progress, and the international lending institutions, a new generation of technically trained administrators encouraged their governments to take a more active role in economic management. More resources became available, and (partly through international efforts to improve tax systems) more revenue was squeezed out of existing resources.

Demands for government allocations *within* Latin American nations also grew. As Latin American societies became more competitive politically, and as more groups pressed their demands, political dialogue moved slightly to the left (Schmitter 1971b; Anderson 1967). Everyone became, in Albert Hirschman's words, a "card-carrying developer."

If this change in the political climate led to increases in public spending, how was the spending financed? A substantial share of the expansion of the late 1960s came from international and domestic borrowing, as Latin America spent roughly 15 percent more than it took in. A few countries, particularly Argentina, Chile, and Peru, at times ran up deficits equal to 25 percent of tax receipts. The consequence of continual deficits was a heavy burden of debt service. In 1965, service payments on external debts averaged 9 percent of the value of exports for all of Latin America. By the late 1960s, Argentina, Chile, and Peru were spending one-sixth of their export receipts to service external debts, and in 1971 service payments required 13.5 percent of exports for Latin America as a whole (Ruddle and Barrows 1974:520–521). Such levels of debt service pale in comparison, of course, with the burden of debts accumulated after the 1973 and 1979 oil shocks. Were pre-1973 levels of debt service seen as a drag on spending? Apparently not. Debts could simply be pushed forward, postponed to be paid by future administrations. After 1973, of course, the cumulative burden of debt made its cost unbearable even to incumbent leaders.

In the more advanced economies, increased government intervention was linked to policies of import substitution. Although import substitution led to a brief period of rapid expansion, growth eventually slackened. Politicians, unfortunately, were late in recognizing the boom's end. They continued through the sixties to spend heavily on projects of little merit, finally contributing to inflation and, in the end, a decline in the rate of growth (Hirschman 1968).

This expected jump in spending was a sudden (or discontinuous) shift in the middle sixties rather than a gradual increase over the whole post–World War II period. After some experimentation, the period from 1965 to 1975 was selected as best representing the Development Decade. In this period we expect spending to rise.

Analysis

The first section of this chapter linked, one by one, a series of political and economic factors to movements in central government public expenditures. Table 1 summarizes these hypothetical linkages. To measure the independent effect of each factor, the individual linkages must now be evaluated together. The appropriate technique for such statistical evaluation is multiple regression. So that data from seventeen countries can be evaluated jointly, we must convert the monetary variables to constant local currency (using the price deflators of the IMF) and then to 1963 U.S. dollars. Next we index the constant dollar figures so that 1963 equals 100. An index is also used for the annual ratio of reserves to GDP, and U.S. aid grants are measured as percentages of GDP. All other variables are dichotomous "dummies," taking the value of 1 if a condition exists and 0 if it does not. The dependent variable—total central government spending for each year—aggregates all types of expenditures: ministerial budgets, decentralized agencies, debt payments, bond purchases, and so on.

Table 2 presents the results of the multiple regression. In the

Table 1. *Summary of Hypotheses*

Independent Variables	Predicted Effect of Independent Variable on Total Spending
"Political" Variables	
Election$_t$	Increase
Postelection$_t$	Increase
Leftbase$_t$	Increase
MarginLow$_t$	Unclear
Nonincumbent$_t$	Unclear
Coup$_t$	Decrease
Postcoup$_t$	Increase
Postcoup + 1$_t$	< Postcoup$_t$
Postcoup + 2$_t$	< Postcoup + 1$_t$
Postcoup + 3$_t$	< Postcoup + 2$_t$
"Setting" Variables	
Spending \$$_{t-1}$	Increase
Resources \$$_t$	Increase
Reserves \$$_{t-1}$	Increase
IMF Agreement$_t$	Decrease
Grants$_t$	Increase
Development$_t$	Increase

case of the monetary variables, the coefficients should be interpreted as the number of percentage points the index of spending changes when the indexed variable changes one percentage point. In the case of the dichotomous dummy variables, the coefficients measure the percentage change in spending when the selected condition is present.

The results fit the theory well. The model explains more than 90 percent of the variance of total spending in the seventeen countries, and the explained variance is not less than 70 percent in any country. In general, the coefficients are substantial and carry the appropriate signs. When a hypothesis forecast the *order* of a series of coefficients, the results are supportive.

Domestic and International Resources, the Effect of Prior Spending, and the Development Decade

Consider the context in which support-maximizing budget makers operate. Increases or decreases in resources, whether domestic

Table 2. *Multiple-Regression Estimates: Public Spending in Latin America*

Independent Variable	Parameter Estimate	Standard Error	T Statistic
Intercept	−8.975	2.15	−4.174
Election$_t$	6.267	2.21	2.830
Postelection$_t$	−7.569	2.81	−2.690
Leftbase$_t$	8.082	2.29	3.534
MarginLow$_t$	−3.275	3.35	−.976
Nonincumbent$_t$	16.482	3.82	4.309
Coup$_t$	−4.270	2.81	−1.518
Postcoup$_t$	2.243	3.10	0.723
Postcoup + 1$_t$	−1.619	3.42	−0.472
Postcoup + 2$_t$	−3.769	4.05	−0.932
Postcoup + 3$_t$	−0.029	4.82	−0.006
Spending \$$_{t-1}$	0.922	0.02	43.783
Resources \$$_t$	0.201	0.03	6.913
Reserves Up$_{t-1}$	10.338	3.52	2.944
Reserves Down$_{t-1}$	−2.562	2.71	−0.945
IMF Agreement$_t$	−0.253	2.07	−0.122
Grants$_t$	25.733	120.61	0.213
Development$_t$	1.669	2.67	0.625

Note: R^2 = 0.93; DF = 595.

or international, were expected to lead to parallel movements in total spending. In the case of domestic resources, the hypothesis proved correct: When domestic resources rose or fell 1 percent, spending rose or fell an additional one-fifth of 1 percent. Changes in international reserves, however, had a more complex effect. Preliminary tests revealed that only large movements in reserves had any effect on spending, but we expected *symmetrical* effects—that is, large movements up or down should stimulate parallel changes up or down in expenditures. In fact, big improvements in reserves did encourage executives to spend more, but big declines elicited only weak and statistically insignificant cuts.[10] Leaders prefer to increase spending, so good news motivates them more than bad news discourages them.

Contrary to our expectation, recourse to the International Mon-

10. Between 1947 and 1982, changes from one year to the next of 50 percent or more occurred forty-two times in our seventeen countries.

etary Fund did not affect spending. The really draconian phase of IMF intervention began, of course, just after the end of this analysis. Ignoring the IMF may no longer be easy, but the major debtors still seem willing to try. Through 1986, neither Brazil nor Peru met any of the IMF's fiscal deficit targets. Mexico made progress in 1983 and 1984, but the fiscal floodgates reopened for the 1985 congressional election (Bagley 1986).

Aid from the United States was expected to have a positive impact on spending, but the size of aid grants is extremely variable between countries and over time in the same country, so statistical verification is difficult. In fact, the regression revealed no consistent link between grants of aid and spending. In certain cases— Bolivia in the late fifties, Guatemala after the overthrow of Arbenz, El Salvador during its civil war, Chile under Frei—U.S. aid undoubtedly added to overall spending. The small amounts received by other countries produced no measurable effects.

The weight of past spending had, as expected, a smoothing effect on current spending. Increases or decreases of 1 percent in spending in the previous year led to increases or decreases of 0.92 percent in the current year. The statistical reliability of this result is especially noteworthy. Past fluctuations in spending have a constant impact on current spending regardless of time or country. Indeed, the weight of the past is the most *consistent* variable in the model.

The years from 1965 to 1975 were expected to be a time of higher spending. They were not. In an estimation made when data were available only through 1971 (Ames 1977), post-1964 expenditures rose about 9 percent. After the energy crisis, however, spending increases in the oil-importing nations shrank so much that the overall 1965–1975 results are insignificant.[11] The Development Decade, in the end, was something less.

The Electoral Cycle, Constituency Pressures, Insecurity, and the Military Cycle

The political aspect of the budget was strongly and unequivocally confirmed. Executives respond to political incentives and constraints with substantial changes in overall spending.

11. Because of other improvements in the model, these earlier results are not perfectly comparable.

Is there an electoral cycle? Because governments running for reelection sought to buy support, spending before electoral tests rose more than 6 percent.[12] For *postelection* spending, however, the prediction of increased spending proved quite wrong. Spending actually declined by the same amount it had risen the previous year. Note, however, that nonincumbent administrations increased spending more than 16 percent. Since most incumbents lost or could not run, newly elected administrations were typically non-incumbents as well. The huge nonincumbent effect swamped the postelection effect—that is, the few incumbent leaders or parties who were reelected immediately began lowering their expenditures, perhaps to deter inflation. Newly elected leaders postponed that readjustment while they constructed their own bases of support.

Did the *size* of the electoral victory affect spending? No unequivocal prediction could be made earlier in the chapter, because the stimulative effect of a close election might be countered by the depressive effect of the executive's political weakness. The results reflect the evenness of these opposing forces: Actual spending bore no relation to the *size* of the electoral victory.

This model attributes no special significance to the nature of the election itself, that is, to its importance in legitimizing and constituting national authority. Still, Latin American elections vary considerably. Mexico, for example, has regular but hardly competitive presidential elections. In El Salvador, elections have at times appeared open, but clearly certain competitors are never allowed to win. In Colombia, elections between 1958 and 1974 simply ratified an agreement between the major parties mandating alternation in office. In other countries, including Costa Rica, pre-1973 Chile, post-1958 Venezuela, pre-1972 Uruguay, and pre-1964 Brazil, elections were true determinants of leadership. Is the electoral–budgetary cycle in such cases heightened? In other words, does the *openness* of the election stimulate spending? In order to evaluate this possibility, I examined competitive elections separately. Their electoral cycle coefficients, however, differed little from the aggregated elections whose coefficients are reported in Table 2.

12. If we experiment with the electoral cycle by adding dummy variables for the second year before an election, it becomes even more evident that the jump in spending occurs typically just one year before the contest.

In addition to the cyclical effects of elections, pressure from working-class constituencies was expected to boost overall spending. In administrations supported by parties with working-class backing, total spending increased more than 8 percent. In essence, even modest class polarization of the party system raised the cost of retaining office. Naturally such polarization affects some government programs more than others. In the next chapter we shall examine the consequences of class polarization on trade-offs *between* programs; here it is important to note merely that demands for certain programs are not matched by compensatory cuts in others. Working-class demands are accommodated at the cost of overall budgetary expansion.

Is there a military coup cycle? The results are not extremely solid statistically, but they clearly move in the right directions. Coups occur during economic recessions, at times when overall spending is shrinking.[13] Because military regimes initially bring order, better tax collection, and higher public sector salaries (especially for the armed forces), and because military regimes seek to buy popularity, expenditures rise more than 6 percent from the year in which a coup occurs to the first subsequent year. Then declines set in, lasting until the fourth year of military government. Military governments, in other words, behave for one year like civilians. Then their sense of security increases, and they begin to emphasize austerity and orthodoxy.

What about the bureaucratic-authoritarian cases and the few left-leaning military regimes? If these regimes truly followed distinctive courses, courses not captured by our theory, the model should systematically err in its prediction of their expenditures. The spending of expansionist administrations should be underpredicted, and the spending of orthodox regimes should be overpredicted. Instead, the model does quite well with all variants. In Brazil the model's prediction of the overall spending of Presidents Costa e Silva and Médici was off by less than 2 percent, and even President Geisel's expenditures were within 3 percent of the estimate. Argentina's General Videla, whose neoliberal experiment foundered on its inability to cut the size of the government, actually spent 4 percent *less* than the model predicted. Pinochet in

13. In a study of fiscal responses to business cycles in Latin America, I found that the countercyclical use of expenditures is relatively rare; indeed, it is common for diverse regimes in Latin America to *cut* spending during recessions.

Chile and Velasco Alvarado in Peru, ideologically farthest apart of all the military leaders of the 1970s, were both within 1 percent of the model's prediction. In these cases the factors included in the model explain spending quite well, so we can conclude that bureaucratic authoritarianism is not characterized by a distinctive approach to public spending. Indeed, the only consistent errors in predicting the spending of military regimes came with regard to the populist caudillos of the late 1950s: Odría (Peru), Rojas Pinilla (Colombia), and Pérez Jiménez (Venezuela). Each spent considerably more than the model's prediction. *Populist* authoritarianism, in other words, was truly the missing factor in the model.

Some Deviant Cases

Any statistical model fits some cases better than others. An examination of poorly explained cases can help us identify important factors left out of the original theory. Table 3 includes the 40 administrations (out of 102) deviating most (either underspending or overspending) from the model's prediction.[14] A number of cases were extreme for quite idiosyncratic reasons. Paz Estenssoro's first-term underspending in Bolivia resulted from the general chaos following the 1952 revolution, and the overspending of Paz's second term and the subsequent administration of Siles Zuazo were made possible largely by huge infusions of U.S. aid. Colombia's Ospina Pérez confronted the beginning of the *violencia* that wracked his country and nearly became a civil war. In Guatemala, foreign grants substantially inflated the budget of President Castillo Armas. And in Nicaragua, the Sandinista government faced an enormous rebuilding task after the departure of Somoza.

These exceptional cases aside, do any patterns appear? Among the overspenders, such leaders as Gálvez, Arévalo, Figueres, Lleras Restrepo, Odúber, Belaúnde, and Roldós were all elected as "reformists," and nearly all triumphed in quite competitive elections. Although a few underspenders (Betancourt, Orlich, and Leoni) could claim to be reformists as well, most democratically elected underspenders were conservatives like Galo Plaza, Manuel Prado, or Mário Echandi. The overspending of liberals reflects preferences beyond political survival, preferences about programs and about the beneficiaries of government policy.

14. Each of these administrations held power at least two years.

Table 3. *Administration Residuals*

"Maximum Overspenders"

1. Alemán (Mexico)	11. López Portillo (Mexico)
2. Paz, 1961–1964 (Bolivia)	12. Gálvez (Honduras)
3. Siles Zuazo (Bolivia)	13. Arévalo (Guatemala)
4. Ruiz Cortines (Mexico)	14. Figueres, 1953–1958 (Costa Rica)
5. Ospina Pérez (Colombia)	15. Pacheco (Uruguay)
6. Lemus (El Salvador)	16. Lleras Restrepo (Colombia)
7. Pérez Jiménez (Venezuela)	17. Odúber (Costa Rica)
8. FSLN (Nicaragua)	18. Belaúnde, 1963–1968 (Peru)
9. Luis Somoza (Nicaragua)	19. Roldós (Ecuador)
10. Castillo Armas (Guatemala)	20. Banzer (Bolivia)

Zero Deviance from Prediction

21. Barrientos (Bolivia)	31. Betancourt (Venezuela)
22. Prado (Peru)	32. Sánchez Hernández (El Salvador)
23. Osorio (El Salvador)	33. Illía (Argentina)
24. Rivera Carballo (El Salvador)	34. Onganía (Argentina)
25. Robles (Panama)	35. Galo Plaza (Ecuador)
26. Valencia (Colombia)	36. Ibañez (Chile)
27. Gestido (Uruguay)	37. Leoni (Venezuela)
28. Méndez Montenegro (Guatemala)	38. Orlich (Costa Rica)
29. Echandi (Costa Rica)	39. Chaves (Paraguay)
30. Díaz Ordaz (Mexico)	40. Paz, 1952–1956 (Bolivia)

"Maximum Underspenders"

Note: Presidents are listed in order of their deviation from the model's prediction, from the greatest overspender (Alemán) to the greatest underspender (Paz, 1952–1956).

Comparing overspenders with underspenders also confirms the argument that the competitiveness of elections rarely determines budgetary pressure. Mexican elections are hardly examples of effective competition, but Mexico placed three administrations among the top overspenders. Costa Rica, with very competitive elections, and Colombia, where elections were much less competitive, each placed presidents at both extremes of the spending spectrum. Competition may increase incentives to spend, but it denies executives the power to do so.

When compared to the other executives from his country, an

administration like that of Chile's Carlos Ibañez seems quite anomalous. Total spending for all other Chilean presidents—Alessandri, Frei, Allende, and Pinochet—fell within 3 percent of the model's prediction. Why did Carlos Ibañez underspend by almost 22 percent? In a nation whose political parties were the most class-specific in Latin America, Carlos Ibañez was elected "above party." Chosen because of his great personal popularity and owing election to no single social group, Ibañez envisioned a kind of Peronist future for Chile. He found it easy to avoid spending, but Peronism was inappropriate in a polity where the party system accurately reflected social cleavages. Ibañez's Peronist strategy failed, and his administration became unpopular in practically all quarters (Bray 1967).

The two widely separated terms of Peru's Fernando Belaúnde Terry illustrate the complexity of the relationships among incentives, constraints, and ideological preferences. In his first administration (1964–1968), Belaúnde confronted a strong labor movement and a hostile legislature dominated by the opposition *apristas*. Labor's power—particularly its potential for violence—could compel favorable wage settlements and bring down governments (Payne 1965). In 1967, for example, Belaúnde's budget included a wage increase for public employees of only 10 to 15 percent. The unions reacted strongly, and the *apristas*—political allies of labor—backed them. Though APRA had claimed to be a "sound money" party, it would not support Belaúnde in imposing new taxes and it refused to oppose the unions' wage demands. As the deficit rose, Belaúnde overspent the model's prediction by nearly 8 percent. His term was abruptly ended in 1968, however, by military ouster. In 1980 the military withdrew and Belaúnde was reelected to the presidency, but the economy was in disarray as inflation and the foreign debt soared. After an initial boost to the budget, Belaúnde opted for orthodox economic policies. Overall spending in his second term fell below the model's prediction by nearly 4 percent. Why spending policy was so different remains to be explained: The structure of politics had changed; the economy had changed; perhaps even Belaúnde himself had changed.

Finally, these deviant cases suggest that sequence matters. In 1958 Colombia's two parties signed a formal power-sharing agreement. This agreement specified alternation in the presidency, equality in the legislature and bureaucracy, and heavy majorities to pass legislation. Such an agreement could work only if the two parties were relatively close on substantive issues. In terms of our model, however, President Guillermo León Valencia *underspent* by more than 12 percent, while his successor, Carlos Lleras Restrepo, *overspent* by nearly 9 percent. The key to Lleras's reversal of Valencia's policies lies precisely in the requirement of party alternation. Lleras sought to undo the destabilizing effects of Valencia's conservative economic policies. Realizing that his party could not succeed itself, Lleras spent heavily in order to commit the next president to his programs (*Latin America* 1967:111–152). Since the spending of Misael Pastrana, Lleras's successor, matched almost exactly the model's prediction (neither under- nor overspending), Lleras must surely have felt vindicated.

This cursory look at the model's under- and overpredictions provides confirmation that the model works. It is also an exercise in speculation—an exercise that leaves plenty of puzzles and clues for further exploration.

Conclusion

This chapter has sought a plausible, *general* explanation of total central government expenditures in Latin America. The model developed here sees the government neither as a mere referee for the conflicts of social groups nor simply as a representative of some dominant economic interest. Instead, the model emphasizes the survival motivations of political leaders. Public expenditures, as an instrument for the realization of leaders' goals, become political expenditures.

Most Latin American leaders would like to satisfy every demand for public money, but they cannot: In poor and volatile economies, resource constraints are ever present. Fluctuations in the gross domestic product and in exports exert a powerful influence on spending. But the pressure to spend must be intense, because leaders ignore whenever possible such economic warnings as falling international reserves and IMF agreements.

Spending cannot, in this difficult economic environment, rise constantly, so executives husband their resources for use against the strongest threats. Some leaders must accommodate the demands of working-class constituencies for job creation and social programs. Others face the cyclical threat of elections. Before elections, spending rises as incumbents try to ensure electoral success, and after elections spending rises again if a new leader has attained the presidency.

The importance of elections in constituting national authority was not a factor in the size of spending increases. Why do elections of varying significance elicit similar expenditure responses? One answer is that the more important the election, the more likely it is to be close and the tougher will be opposition to the executive's attempts to buy victory. Another answer is that achieving the widest possible margin of victory may be important even when an election obviously will not be close. Mexico's PRI cannot lose, but the campaign is taken seriously by a host of lower-level politicians on their way up.

Finally, what about Latin America's many authoritarian governments? In light of the repressiveness of a Stroessner in Paraguay or a Pinochet in Chile, is the political function of public spending irrelevant? It is not. Classifying governments as authoritarian and nonauthoritarian oversimplifies: In reality few governments are so secure that the budget is not a tool for increasing support. Military governments may opt for austerity once they feel safe, but in their first year in power they cover their political bases.

Aggregate spending remains, however, a blunt political instrument. Guiding expenditures to serve political needs requires precise strategic calculations on the part of executives. The next chapter elaborates this model of Latin American political survival by disaggregating total spending into the specific programs that bind together the executive's survival coalition.

2. Survival Strategies and Expenditure Trade-offs

This chapter analyzes the strategies chosen by Latin American executives to guide the allocation of public expenditures into individual programs. The central question is whether executives adopt allocation policies increasing their chances for survival in office. Since the choice of an appropriate policy depends on each country's political and social environment, the first section of the chapter explores the conditions executives consider when they frame their strategic approaches. The second section evaluates five strategies available to Latin American political leaders. Each strategy stresses specific programs of public expenditures, and each strategy is directed at a specific political target—the military, bureaucrats, local interests, receivers of direct transfer payments, or specific social classes. The third section treats the economic context of allocations, focusing on the relationship between expenditure strategies and changes in the rates of economic growth and inflation.

What Counts in the Calculus of Survival?

The executive's problem is one of coalition formation.[1] In building survival coalitions, the key choices of Latin American leaders revolve around two sets of factors: the sites, currencies, and sizes of winning coalitions and the conditions governing the prices paid to secure allies.

1. Of the vast literature in coalition theory, I have found particularly useful the essays by Leiserson, Kenworthy, and De Swann in Groennings and others (1970).

Site, Currency, and Size:
The Dimensions of Winning Coalitions

Since most research on the formation of political coalitions has concentrated on the United States and Western Europe, we know most about coalition processes in legislatures and cabinets. In these sites votes are the major currency, and the influence wielded by political actors depends on the number of votes they command. In Latin America, by contrast, multiple sites and currencies are the rule, and political forces losing in one arena may not accept the decision. Legislatures, if they exist, are only one of many arenas of decision making. Other sites include international financial agencies, transnational corporations, military headquarters, bureaucracies, and even the streets. Currencies of influence include violence (or the potential for violence), the ability to unseat a government by force, the market power of investors, and the potential to block or advance the implementation of programs.

Scholars have often noted the failure of Latin American nations to agree on the dominant currency of authority. In an attempt to apply coalition analysis to Latin America, Eldon Kenworthy (1970) offers a "dual currency" model in which coercion and popularity are the dominant power resources. Coercion, mostly in the hands of the military, is a resource of the upper and upper middle classes. Popularity, defined as the ability to elicit support from large numbers of people across occupational strata, is a currency more available to middle-class and working-class groups.

Kenworthy's dual currency model is a good beginning, but its restriction to coercion and popularity is too narrow. The centrality of entrepreneurs, for example, comes from their roles as investors and employers.[2] The mere threat of organized disruptive behavior by entrepreneurial elites is often sufficient to derail government efforts at reform, and even where economic competition is too fierce for entrepreneurs to collude, government policies that frighten investors lead to economic decline. In the same way, the bargaining power of organized labor extends beyond getting out the vote. Labor's ability to disrupt economic activity can bring down governments by encouraging military intervention.[3] In es-

---

2. See Lindblom (1977), a liberal restatement of this long-argued Marxist position.
3. This argument is made by Payne (1965).

sence, coalition formation in Latin America is more than a two-arena game. Latin American coalitions involve multiple sites and currencies, and battles fought in one site remain indecisive as long as a major political force finds better odds elsewhere.

What determines coalition size? Suppose we distinguish, along with Kenworthy, between "reigning" and "ruling." If leaders merely want to preserve the status quo—that is, to reign—they require smaller coalitions that need not include every currency. But when leaders want to effect change—to rule—they must develop larger coalitions including more of the major currencies. The more a program demands active support—rather than mere acquiescence—the larger the coalition necessary to ensure its success.

Whether leaders choose to rule or reign is surely no accident. Reformist leaders representing middle-class or working-class groups need the power to rule. Leaders representing higher-status groups are usually content to hold the line, to reign. Beginning in the middle 1960s, however, military regimes representing industrial and agro-export elites came to dominate Brazil, Argentina, Uruguay, and Chile. Not content merely to reign, these regimes attempted to transform the political and economic structures of their societies. The nature of each regime's program determined the minimum size of its support coalition. In Chile, Pinochet adopted a program of shrinking the state, a program that commanded so little domestic support the regime had to rely on heavy doses of coercion. In Brazil, on the other hand, the Geisel administration tried hard after the 1973 oil crisis to attract the support of the domestic bourgeoisie, because without its support the regime's ambitious plans for promoting capital goods production could not succeed.

The Costs of Coalition Building

Putting together a coalition requires determining which political actors are potential participants. A society's cleavages define its political actors. Totally latent cleavages create no political demands. Cleavages become manifest through organization. Organized interests, represented by political actors, constitute the bases of conflict, the building blocks of the executive's political world.

Once having identified the society's cleavages and relevant political actors, the executive divides them into allies and adversaries. Allies are those who contributed support at the executive's accession to power (or at some other critical test); adversaries are those who were opposed. The executive can convert old adversaries into new allies, but conversions may come at the cost of losing some previous allies. Old supporters defect because resources—in the form of control over programs—are transferred to the new re-cruits.[4] The executive therefore seeks to minimize expected losses and maximize expected gains. The crucial elements in this tactical equation include the bargaining resources and unity of potential coalition members, the nature of intermediate organizations like political parties, and the motivating issues themselves.

The resources with which political actors bargain have no fixed or absolute weight. Instead, the perceptions of other actors deter-mine the weight of each actor's resources. The military, for ex-ample, can always threaten to overthrow the government, but such a threat will be taken much more seriously in Argentina than in Mexico, simply because coups occur much more frequently in Ar-gentina and because other political forces might support a take-over. Similarly, the pre-1973 Chilean legislature paid more atten-tion to working-class groups than did the Colombian legislature, because in Chile the parties divided along class lines and repre-sented every major social group, while in Colombia the elite-dom-inated National Front largely excluded labor.

The fundamental point is simple: Rules and structures translate interests into bargaining resources at particular sites. In industrial countries, legislatures and bureaucracies are the main sites. In Latin America, legislatures are sometimes important and bureau-cracies always so, but claims are also pressed through personal and family connections, demonstrations, elections, strikes, and in-surrections. When executives are aware of these bargaining sites, they can estimate the value of any potential coalition participant to their chances of surviving and implementing a program.

Executives often find it useful to divide or disaggregate political forces. If the executive can split a once-united group, and if one of the new subgroups dominates the other, cheaper coalitions be-come feasible. Thus an executive seeking to cut wages may try to deal separately with labor's leaders. If the leaders will accept

---

4. Net distributable political-economic spoils may increase as a consequence of a new coalition that increases productivity, gross output, or foreign aid, but such increases are uncertain. To induce a political actor to accept future for present rewards requires a premium.

bribes to counsel workers against striking, it will be much easier
to ignore the interests of the workers themselves.

The Importance of Intermediate Organization.   The notion of *organized* interests implies intermediate authority between the executive and the population itself. The strength of such intermediate
organizations varies tremendously, from structures thoroughly
dominating followers to those safely ignored by executives. In the
former case, organizational leaders may have a direct "charismatic" authority over followers, an authority based on personal
dependence. At the other extreme, an organization such as a political party may exist only at elections and there may be little
agreement between party leaders and followers even on basic issues.

The effects of intermediate organizations on coalition formation
depend on two factors: the nature of group loyalties and the ease
of entry of new competitors. The more intense the links between
allies and the executive, the easier it is to woo the opposition
without losing the allies' support. Conversely, the more intense a
group's loyalties to an adversary, the more difficult it is for the
executive to pursue them. Desertion of old allies usually pays only
if the executive can keep a significant part of their support. In a
case like Mexico, for example, since competition with the ruling
Institutionalized Revolutionary Party (PRI) is very difficult in the
first place, defection of allies from the ruling coalition is nearly
impossible. As a result, Mexican presidents can adopt policies that
are contrary to the interests of important members of the coalition.[5]

Ideological Distance.   Coalition theorists recognize the concept of
ideological distance. Coalition partners must not be ideological
opposites, and coalitions form more easily among political actors
with shared interests. Still, such simple rules obscure the richness
of political life. Ideological distances change with the passage of
time. When import substitution in Chile, Argentina, and Brazil had
reached a point where an emphasis on economic stabilization be-

5. The recent electoral gains by the opposition PAN in Mexico only reinforce
this argument. Though by 1985 the PRI had lost a significant percentage of its
electoral share, it was not close to losing control of the mechanisms of policy
making, and it did not suffer the defection of important members of its coalition.

came imperative, populist coalitions of industrialists and urban laborers were no longer possible, because each side came to see its interests as quite opposed to those of the other (O'Donnell 1973). Moreover, if issues are perceived as zero sum—if IMF help is contingent upon a slowing of land reform or if the army hinges its support on repression of workers—then certain alliances are ruled out.

Divisibility and Symbolism. Executives seek to avoid zero-sum situations, so they resort to divisibility and symbolism. Perhaps they can divide a peasant movement by conceding bureaucratic jobs to its leaders or providing a few symbolic gifts of land for the masses. Perhaps the executive can announce grandiose plans for education and health care or the arrival of Peace Corps volunteers. Symbolic policies are promises. Even though real benefits are postponed, executives expect prompt rewards from the grateful recipients of symbols.

Promises made to one group imply costs for another. Even though costs, like real benefits, are postponed, why do those on the cost-paying side of promises not see their long-term implications and penalize the executive accordingly? Perhaps they realize promises are subject to future renegotiation that will lower their cost or even void the deal entirely. Beneficiaries of promises should come to the same conclusion and hold back their rewards as well, but they often do not, particularly if they are poor. Such groups may be victims of an "ideological hegemony" preventing them from comprehending the consequences of political action.[6] Symbolic outputs satisfy those with the clout to compel a better outcome but insufficient understanding to demand more than promises.

Suppose, however, that political actors refuse to accept symbols in place of material allocations. If a demand must be met with an immediate material response, then its benefits ought to be as spe-

6. In an interesting paper on public opinion in authoritarian Brazil, Geddes and Zaller (1985) found that people of lower education tended to increase their support of the regime's policies as their information increased. Because the media in this period (1972–1973) were controlled so strictly that only government-sponsored information penetrated, the situation was truly one of ideological hegemony. Rapid economic growth satisfied most people, and comparisons with the (mostly verbal) excesses of the old pluralist regime favored the armed forces.

cific and its costs as diffuse as possible.[7] If costs are spread out
so much that each person's share is very small, individuals may
not be able to perceive them at all. When this happens, the executive maintains a level of perceived rewards higher than the level
of perceived penalties. As Lowi's work suggests (1964), executives
prefer distributive "rivers and harbors" policies, which carry specific benefits and diffuse costs, to redistributive policies like progressive income taxes, which have clear and specific costs as well
as benefits.

Information gathering is a task essential to the formation of a
survival coalition. Some questions—the nature of a society's cleavages or the bargaining resources of different political forces—are
so obvious they hardly need asking. Other kinds of information,
such as the specific demands a political actor makes as the price
of adherence, need to be repeatedly and explicitly sought. Queries
concerning the intensity of loyalties or the willingness to accept
symbolic rewards may be unanswerable until the executive com-
mits real political resources. Coalition formation is always uncertain and experimental. If, as Kenworthy suggests, reigning requires
a smaller coalition than ruling, it is no surprise that ambitious
programs often give way to mere continuance in office.

Applying Coalition Theory
to Budget Allocations

The range of strategies available to executives depends upon
the elements crucial to coalition formation. Individually, these elements reflect the great diversity of Latin American politics. Barriers
against entry to political competition, for example, vary from
practically impregnable to nearly nonexistent. People may harbor
intense loyalties to political parties, to individual leaders, or to
neither. Effective budgetary control by legislatures varies from substantial to practically none. And, finally, the techniques used by
executives to manipulate followers range from direct personal control to payoffs to powerful intermediaries.

Still, shared historical, cultural, and political roots combine to
produce a limited number of coalition patterns. Each pattern cor-
responds to one of five strategies of budgetary allocations: pacify
the military, recruit bureaucrats, target local interests, increase di-

---

7. On this subject see Echols and Rundquist (1979).

rect transfer payments, and reward social strata. This correspondence—coalition patterns to budgetary allocations—exists even though economists find it difficult to attribute the costs and benefits of public expenditures to individual groups or social classes. (See Selowsky 1979 and Webb 1977.) Public expenditures are central to survival behavior because politicians and other political actors struggle over allocations *as if* their incidence were clear.

The remainder of this chapter is devoted to explaining these strategies and determining whether political leaders actually implemented them.[8] Before we can begin that task, however, the strategies must be "operationalized"—that is, they must be defined precisely. Three steps are critical: choosing the appropriate survival-maximizing strategy for each country in each year, defining the concept of political crisis, and measuring expenditure trade-offs. (Additional details of a methodological nature will be found in Appendix B at the back of the book.)

Choosing the Right Strategy. For each year within each country in this study, it was necessary to decide which strategies would be appropriate (or "optimal") for an executive trying to survive. Choosing strategies requires judging the bargaining resources of various political groups. How can bargaining resources be measured? On occasion voting results or survey responses might serve as indicators, but such data are quite scarce. At the same time, Latin Americanists have little trouble agreeing that political parties have reflected class cleavages more in Argentina than in Uruguay, more in Chile than in Colombia. They agree as well that military coups were more likely in pre-1964 Brazil than in post-1948 Costa Rica. Indeed, Latin Americanists would probably agree on the recent status of practically any country on any of these dimensions. Because such a consensus exists, it was possible to use a "sophisticated coder" methodology—a technique relying on the Latin Americanist literature and frequent consultation with country experts. In essence, the analysis used the monographic literature for

8. Note, however, that leaders are likely to pursue multiple strategies simultaneously. The military, for example, may be pacified while transfers are increased. Bureaucrats may be recruited while local interests are targeted. But it would be difficult to recruit bureaucrats, target local interests, and increase transfers all at the same time, because these expenditure categories alone would exhaust the whole budget. Moreover, many theoretically possible strategies, as we shall see, prove unrealistic in practice.

each country as a basis for judgments about changing social and political conditions. These judgments were translated into dummy variables; that is, they took the value 1 if a strategy was optimal and 0 if it was not. Consultants for each country (an average of two or three and at least one per country) verified and corrected the preliminary codings. These classifications are still open to debate, of course, so Appendix B contains a complete listing.

The Concept of the Political Crisis.   Political leaders have many goals they would like to pursue, but budgetary resources are always in short supply. Because survival is not the sole objective of political leaders, the devotion of budgetary resources to survival strategies is likely to be greatest when leaders are most vulnerable—that is, during political crises. Two kinds of events, elections and military coups, define crises. If an incumbent president or party is competing in an election, then we can expect the year just prior to the event to reflect the executive's allocational response. After an election, the winners seek to secure their positions with their own modifications of spending.[9] In the case of coups, a different pattern of shifts is predicted. Since the incumbent executive does not plan for a coup, we expect no prior budgetary movement, but a newly installed military regime (unless it envisions itself as merely a caretaker) faces the same coalition-building problem as civilians, even to the point that it may need to increase the military budget to prevent a countercoup by disgruntled officers. The first year in which a new regime has budgetary control is thus defined as a year of political crisis.[10]

Measuring Expenditure Trade-offs.   Budgetary programs (public works, education, foreign relations, and the like) are competitors for scarce resources. A program's competitive success is measured

9. Only presidential elections are included here. In Chapter 3 I consider midterm elections. If the outcome of the election is quite certain, it is not considered to provoke a crisis unless the election serves—as in Mexico—recruitment and mobility functions. If the regime holding power is not competing (when, for example, a military caretaker government is holding an election), no fiscal effect is expected. If an election is scheduled late in the year, spending should change in that same year. If the election occurs early in the year, trade-offs should be felt in the previous year.

10. This aggregation of elections and coups simply means that both events are expected to yield *some* kind of survival behavior. It does not imply that civilian and military regimes will adopt the same strategies.

by its share of total final expenditures—that is, the percentage of total spending allocated to it. Hence the military share of total expenditures is the ratio

$$\frac{\text{Army} + \text{Air Force} + \text{Navy} + \text{Other Military Allocations}}{\text{Total Expenditure for All Programs}}$$

and public works[11] would be the ratio

$$\frac{\text{Communications} + \text{Transportation} + \text{Public Works} + \ldots}{\text{Total Expenditure for All Programs}}$$

Since the arguments of this chapter are framed in terms of expected *movements* in shares, the dependent variables (what we are trying to explain) are typically the percentage changes between two consecutive years in some program's share of the central government budget. If, for example, executives try to keep the military happy during a year of political crisis, the change in military allocations between that year and the previous year should be significantly greater than the change in other years.

These strategic hypotheses predict more than just a high growth rate in the share of a given program. Indeed, growth in one specific program comes at the expense of other specific programs. To express this trade-off, annual rates of change were first calculated for each of two programs and then the difference between these rates was taken. If A_t is the military share of the budget at time t, for example, and B_t is the public works share at time t, then the military–works trade-off is

$$\text{Mil–Works}_t = \frac{A_t - A_{t-1}}{A_{t-1}} - \frac{B_t - B_{t-1}}{B_{t-1}}$$

Five Strategies of Budget Allocation

Pacify the Military

Conditions Favoring Military Pacification. For most contemporary Latin American executives the threat of military overthrow

11. In some countries ministries such as communications are "high tech" compared to traditional pork barrel programs such as public works. Overall, however, no consistent distinction of this type can be made in Latin America. As a result, this measure is not as sharp as one would like.

is very real. Whether the chief executive is a civilian or a soldier, a wary eye and ready checkbook are indispensable. In all post-1945 Latin America, only Mexico and Nicaragua have been entirely free of overt military intervention.

The probability of coups varies across countries and across time. In a pioneering study of intervention, John Fitch argues that the military acts as a "monitor of the political scene, intervening when, in its judgment, a 'national crisis' exists." Officers' perceptions of the level of crisis depend on the

> military's ratings of the constitutionality of governmental actions, the officers' personal ties or antagonisms toward the government, public opinion toward the government, government attentiveness to the institutional needs of the armed forces, government policy toward any perceived "communist threat," the level of public disorders, and the need for socioeconomic reforms (1977:160).

These "triggers" of crises have changed over the years. As the level of military professionalism has increased, the social backgrounds of the officers have become less important than their institutional interests. Professionalization has also raised the military's confidence in its own ability to govern while lowering its opinion of the abilities of civilians. The threat of communism became much more important as a trigger after the Cuban Revolution, because military officers generally believed that a coup against Batista would have prevented the rise of Fidel Castro (Fitch 1977:160–164).

These observations refer to the perceptions of individual officers, but coups are not made by individuals. Coups occur when a minimum number of officers agrees on their desirability. The formation of that minimum involves more than just a hard core of conspirators expanding until enough moderates join to guarantee victory. Successful conspiracies form in different ways and act with varying strengths.

Faced with such uncertainty, the executive assesses the probability of a coup. A leader knows coups are more likely if (1) the military has a tradition of intervention, (2) the economy is declining, (3) mass disorder is increasing, (4) the military's financial requests have not been met, and (5) there is ideological conflict between the executive and the officer corps.

Direct budgetary rewards are a logical response to the military threat. If the armed forces' primary motivation is simply their own institutional enrichment, the executive can spread the costs of meeting their claim over various nonmilitary programs. If, on the other hand, the military not only wants more for itself but less for its enemies, then its budgetary gain should be accompanied by specific cuts in programs the officers dislike.[12]

Evaluating the Strategy.   Table 4 shows what happens during periods of political crisis. When the military pacification strategy is appropriate, the military's share of the budget rises. The big losers are programs in health, welfare, police, and foreign relations (although foreign relations is too small to contribute much to the military). Education yields lesser amounts, and public works and pensions defend themselves quite well. The success of public works is probably due to the substantial number of cases, especially in Central American countries like El Salvador and Honduras, where military leaders combined construction projects with payoffs to the armed forces. Pension programs in Latin America are often treated as entitlements, so they are less subject to short-term manipulation.[13]

Table 4 applies only to conditions of political crisis. In noncrisis years the same regressions produce no significant trade-offs. Did these executives, all of whom were vulnerable to coups, turn against the military when the crisis abated? They did not. Note that military budget shares gradually decline in about three-fourths of our seventeen countries, and remember that this decline is sharpest in administrations with little to fear from the military. For the *vulnerable* governments in Table 4, on the other hand, the absence of shifts to or from the military budget in noncrisis years means that the armed forces still have enough strength to neutralize the trend against them.

Figure 2 illustrates the response of military spending to political

12. An emphasis on budgetary reward is not meant to imply that no other strategies are available. A leader may try to maintain a base of support in one faction of the armed forces as a way of minimizing overall weakness vis-à-vis the military. Such an approach would clearly not preclude a simultaneous budgetary reward.

13. The only budget category with the wrong sign is transfer payments. Official classifications separating transfers from other kinds of spending happen to be quite weak, perhaps the weakest of any budget category. Measurement error is thus a distinct possibility.

Table 4. *The Military Pacification Strategy During Political Crises*

Shift to Military From	b	$\rho < |T|$	R^2	N
Health	0.1105	0.0002	28	80
Welfare	0.0757	0.0257	15	73
Police	0.0689	0.0014	23	121
Education	0.0305	0.1143	17	123
Public Works	0.0358	0.331	13	116
Agriculture	0.0445	0.19	28	97
Foreign Relations	0.0888	0.0001	25	119
Pensions	0.0452	0.210	73	17
Transfers	− 0.1981	0.08	15	49

Note: Each row represents a separate equation in which the trade-off is regressed on the strategy dummies for years of crisis. Thus

$$\triangle \text{ Mil } - \triangle \text{ Health} = A + b \text{ (military dummy)} + c \text{ (bureaucratic dummy)}$$
$$+ d \text{ (regional dummy)} + \cdots$$

The dependent variables in these equations are the rates of change of the military share minus the rates of change of the program in the left column. Here b and ρ refer to the coefficient and significance level of the military pacification dummy when all other strategy dummies are included in the equation. For clarity the signs have been reversed, since logs of numbers less than 1 are negative. The coefficients are unstandardized. R^2 and N refer to statistics for the complete regression equations; that is, all strategy dummies are included.

crises in Brazil.[14] The increment in the military budget share in 1951, the first year of the elected government of Getúlio Vargas, was strongly positive. The military had removed Vargas in 1945, so upon his return to office Vargas was attentive to his military support. In 1956, the first year of Juscelino Kubitschek's rather insecure administration, the military share shrank, but this decline was reversed by 1957. In 1962 and 1963, João Goulart bucked the negative trend in the increments the armed forces had received after 1957, but their shares continued to shrink, and that shrinkage may have contributed to the collapse of his administration. In 1965, 1967, and 1970, military presidents began terms.[15] In the first two cases the military share jumped immediately, and in the last—Médici's government—it gained in the second year. In all,

14. Except in Figure 5, the horizontal dotted lines on each plot represent a zero rate of change. Points above and below the line represent positive and negative percentage increments, respectively. Since the data are differences of logged shares, the actual scale on the vertical axis has been omitted.

15. The coup initiating Brazil's twenty-year period of authoritarian rule occurred March 31, 1964, but the first full year in which the generals had budgetary control was 1965.

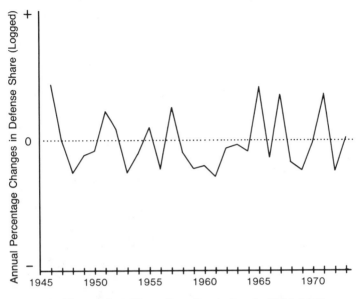

Figure 2. Changes in Military Spending in Brazil: 1946–1973

of six administrations for which military pacification was crucial, the military share rose immediately in three cases, rose in the second year in two, and rose not at all (though the trend was up) in the soon-to-be-ousted Goulart administration.

Recruit Bureaucrats

Conditions Favoring Recruitment of Bureaucrats. Bloated bureaucracies in Latin America date from colonial times, and public employees have long constituted a larger fraction of the politically active population than in industrial countries. The importance of government employees becomes even greater when ethnic or linguistic divisions cut the size of the politically relevant population. In the early 1960s, for example, Peru's teachers (plus their immediate relatives) received about 3 percent of the nation's personal disposable income and constituted 6 to 8 percent of the total number of voters (Kuczynski 1977). When bureaucrats constitute a large fraction of the politically significant population, their pay becomes a pivotal public issue.

Table 5.   *The Bureaucratic Strategy: Estimated Share of Allocations Devoted to Salaries in Crisis and Noncrisis Situations*

Strategy	Political Crisis[a]		No Political Crisis[b]	
	b^c	$\rho < \|T\|$	b	$\rho < \|T\|$
Pacify Military	0.051	0.38	0.015	0.75
Recruit Bureaucrats	0.131	0.02	−0.012	0.81
Increase Transfers	0.037	0.03	−0.019	0.78
Reward Local Interests	−0.150	0.02	0.007	0.90
Reward Social Strata				
Dominant Classes	−0.010	0.92	−0.015	0.85
Intermediate Classes	−0.005	0.90	0.012	0.86
Subordinate Classes	−0.097	0.58	0.041	0.84
Multiclass	−0.012	0.85	0.019	0.82

[a]$N = 93$; $R^2 = 15$; $\rho = 1.65$; Prob $> F = 0.11$.
[b]$N = 196$; $R^2 = 0.06$; $\rho = 1.36$; Prob $> F = 0.21$.
[c]Here b and ρ refer to the coefficients and significance levels of the individual dummies in a single regression.

Bureaucratic recruitment is directed toward political activists. It works best when layers of intermediate leaders control the mass base supporting the executive. Just as Lyndon Johnson's War on Poverty benefited well-placed activists more than the poor, so a bureaucratic recruitment strategy rewards labor leaders more than factory workers, teachers more than pupils. By contrast, bureaucratic recruitment is less useful when intermediate organizations are weak or absent—that is, when the relationship between leaders and followers is direct and personal.

A bureaucratic strategy may be implemented either by enlarging the size of the bureaucracy or by increasing public sector salaries. The executive's problem is to determine when such tactics would be effective. Surely one important datum is the size of the bureaucracy relative to the politically relevant population. If the number of government employees is large, perhaps compared to the actual or potential electorate, then bureaucratic recruitment makes sense.[16] The feasibility of emphasizing the bureaucracy de-

16. An interesting statistic from Costa Rica is provided by Oscar Arias Sánchez (1976). The percentage of federal deputies whose fathers were public employees rose as follows: 1920–1922, 6.3 percent; 1942–1944, 13 percent; 1953–1958, 18.9 percent; 1966–1970, 20 percent.

Table 6. *Gains and Losses to Public Works Programs When Bureaucratic Recruitment Strategy Is Optimal*

	Program Benefiting	
Trade-off Between Programs	*Noncrisis*	*Crisis*
Works–Defense	Works	Defense
Works–Education	Works	Education
Works–Health	Neither	Works
Works–Foreign Relations	Works	Foreign Relations
Works–Welfare	Works	Welfare
Works–Police	Works	Police
Works–Agriculture	Works	Agriculture
Works–Labor	Labor	Labor
Works–Pensions	Works	Pensions

pends also on the absence of alternative power bases. If there are strong regional cleavages—that is, if executives must appease local or regional bosses—then a bureaucratic emphasis would be *counterproductive,* because bureaucratic rewards cannot easily be limited to a specific geographic area.

Evaluating the Strategy. Since bureaucratic strategies affect wages and salaries, the most straightforward test of the approach is the change in the percentage of the whole budget devoted to personnel. Table 5 shows that when the bureaucratic strategy is optimal during crises, the salary share of expenditures rises.[17] When, on the other hand, local or regional interests must be satisfied, salaries fall.

Public works, with its relatively low wage and salary component, is antithetical to bureaucratic recruitment. If an administration seeks to maximize bureaucratic support during a crisis, public works programs ought to suffer. Table 6 shows that public works does indeed decline vis-à-vis all major programs except labor and health.[18] The individual coefficients associated with all categories

17. Note that Table 5 presents results from a single regression in which all the strategy dummies are included.
18. Labor and health programs are typically among the smallest of central government ministries, so there is little payoff in squeezing them.

of Table 6 are quite low, however, and only the consistency and direction of the results lend credence to the argument.[19]

Figure 3, which charts percentage increments in the share of total expenditures devoted to government wages and salaries in Costa Rica, illustrates the bureaucratic recruitment strategy. Of the thirteen cases in which the salary share declined, only four— 1962, 1965, 1966, and 1970—occurred in preelection or post-election years, and the declines of 1966 and 1970 were quite small. Moreover, salaries rose before every election except the election of 1965.[20] Thus in Costa Rica salaries were more likely to rise near elections and more likely to fall between them.

Target Local Interests

Conditions Favoring a Local Strategy.   Fundamental cleavages often develop along geographic lines. In Ecuador, the landowners of the highlands (*sierra*) traditionally oppose the planters and bankers of the coast (*costa*). In Colombia two highly organized parties recruit and maintain intensely loyal followings down to the village level. When local cleavages manifest themselves in such arenas as elections and legislatures, executives need a suitable response.[21]

Such a response is found in pork barrel spending. Nothing distributes government largesse like public works. An executive can place a school, hospital, or dam just where it visibly rewards loyalists. The whole country bears the costs of the project, while carefully selected localities enjoy the benefits (including construction jobs).

If a society's major cleavages all fall along geographic lines, this strategy predicts an expansion of public works expenditures at the expense of every other program, but executives need not abandon

19. If we compare the salary components of these programs during crises and noncrises, no differences appear in the competitive strength of public works programs. This finding supports the hypothesis that each ministry's wage bill should maintain its relative position. But once again the results are consistent in direction rather than impressive in size.

20. In 1950, the beginning of the first nonprovisional government after José Figueres's uprising, no preelection effect is expected.

21. Local strategies are not necessarily appropriate for all political machines, just for those competitive at the local or regional level. Machines that are dominant nationally, such as Mexico's PRI, may require very different approaches.

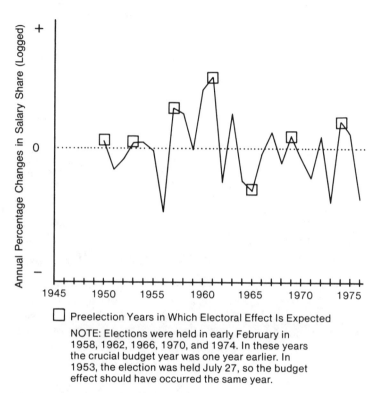

Figure 3. Share of the Budget Devoted to Wages and Salaries in Costa Rica: 1950–1976

public works strategies even if geographic cleavages combine with a horizontal cleavage such as social class. Government programs favoring certain social classes also include physical construction components. Both primary schools and universities are made from bricks and mortar, but the class backgrounds of the students attending these schools vary dramatically, so a political leader can

Table 7. *Tests of the Local Strategy During Political Crises*

Shift to Public Works From	$b^†$	$\rho > |T|^†$	$R^{2‡}$	$N^‡$
Military	0.110	0.007	13	116
Education	0.106	0.010	8	124
Health	0.107	0.006	15	71
Foreign Relations	0.113	0.001	11	124
Transfers	0.422	0.001	70	21
Welfare	0.106	0.013	15	83
Police	0.128	0.002	12	122
Agriculture	0.102	0.044	25	101
Labor	0.206	0.003	36	35
Pensions	0.176	0.007	29	48

†Here b and ρ refer to the coefficients and significance levels of the local interest dummy when all other variables are included in the equation.
‡Here R^2 and N refer to statistics for the complete regression equation. See Table 4.

use the school construction budget to appeal to class and local interests at the same time. Similarly, an airport or road project may serve military purposes as much as local interests.

Evaluating the Strategy. Table 7 provides unequivocal evidence for the local strategy. When local approaches are optimal during crisis periods, all other programs lose to the public works ministries. When local approaches are optimal during *noncrisis* periods, no program loses to public works. Executives reward local or regional interests only for the brief intervals when such rewards are most critical.

Figure 4 provides a concrete illustration of the local strategy. It relates the public works budget share in Ecuador to the shares of two competitors: the traditionally weak foreign relations ministry and the powerful military ministries. Politics in twentieth-century Ecuador has been dominated by José Maria Velasco Ibarra. Five times president but only once able to complete a term as scheduled, Velasco was truly a charismatic figure. His volatile temperament and his penchant for translating popular mandates into quests for dictatorial powers made his political survival continuously problematic. Only once, from 1953 to 1956, did Velasco complete an administration. In that term he tempered his enthusiasm for big construction projects with the realization that a military that had already removed him twice might repeat the favor. As Figure 4 demonstrates, Velasco increased public works in 1953 at the expense of foreign relations, but he favored the military over public works. Many factors contributed to his survival, of course, but his early pacification of the armed forces could not have hurt.

When Velasco returned to power in 1961, he ignored the military and, as Fitch (1977:198) and Pyne (1973) make clear, turned away from his Conservative party supporters altogether. Public works were favored over both the military and foreign relations. Velasco's administration collapsed almost immediately, and he was replaced by Carlos Julio Arosemena, the vice president. Arosemena reduced public works vis-à-vis the military, but the new president's overall budgetary strategy was puzzling. Why should a traditional ministry like foreign relations gain more than a politically important program like public works? The answer is that Ecuador's relations with Cuba had become the chief issue of his administration. Arosemena's efforts to steer a path of neutrality against U.S. efforts to isolate Cuba infuriated Ecuadorean conservatives, particularly in the military. The legislature, the bureaucracy, and the armed forces combined to block the president's initiatives, and the government drifted until his ouster after only eighteen months in office (Fitch 1977:55–64). In this case budgetary allocations reflect an uncaring and perhaps uncomprehending attitude toward survival.

In July 1963 a military junta with certain developmental pretensions replaced Arosemena. Public works grew more rapidly than foreign relations throughout the junta's rule, and works even gained initially against the military. After the armed forces withdrew in 1968, Velasco managed to win a fifth term in the presidency. He repeated his earlier strategy, with public works growing faster than both foreign relations and the military. The result was repeated as well—Velasco was overthrown again.[22]

22. Velasco's last ouster may not have been so clearly a result of his expenditure strategy. In 1972 he seemed almost to be inviting a coup in order to prevent a popular candidate from winning the next presidential election. Then, when the coup became inevitable, he tried to make common cause with the candidate. Too late.

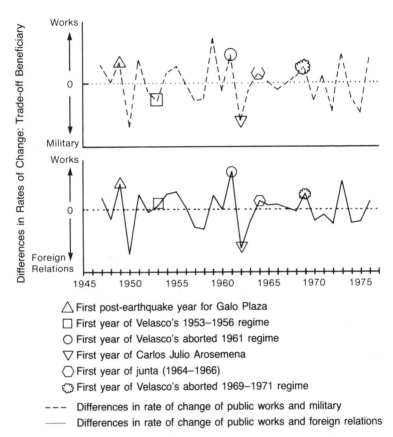

△ First post-earthquake year for Galo Plaza
☐ First year of Velasco's 1953–1956 regime
○ First year of Velasco's aborted 1961 regime
▽ First year of Carlos Julio Arosemena
◯ First year of junta (1964–1966)
✿ First year of Velasco's aborted 1969–1971 regime

- - - Differences in rate of change of public works and military
—— Differences in rate of change of public works and foreign relations

Figure 4. Public Works vs. the Military and Foreign Relations
in Ecuador: 1947–1976

Increase Transfers

Conditions Favoring a Transfer Strategy. When no intermediate organizations claim rewards and no stratum of activists demands jobs, instant cash becomes the logical strategy and transfers become the appropriate medium. A transfer strategy succeeds when weak political parties coexist with fiercely competitive leaders. Old parties disappear; new parties form; platforms hardly matter. The personal qualities of leaders, their charisma, attract followers. Miners, urban workers, and middle-class students may be barely organized but still intensely loyal to some political leader. Executives can buy their support with such programs as pensions, social security benefits, and university scholarships.

This strategy combines well with other approaches. An executive seeking working-class support can concentrate transfers in programs that benefit workers, such as health, rather than programs that benefit the middle class, such as education. Thus transfer payments retain class selectivity, but the recipient populations are much broader than those affected by specific programs.

In general, then, a transfer strategy succeeds when intermediate organizations are weak. When leaders seek to recruit masses rather than reward machines, when they desire immediate responses from broad populations, direct payments are an appropriate tactic.

Evaluating the Strategy.   The transfer strategy is the most difficult to evaluate, because the measures of transfer payments are quite weak. Classifications of transfers across countries are less consistent than classifications of specific programs, and in many cases data are missing. In Table 8a two measures of transfers (pensions and social security payments) reveal no signs of a transfer strategy.[23] In Table 8b, however, where the expenditures that governments themselves label as transfers are evaluated, the results are better. Here all the signs are in the predicted direction, and most of the coefficients are substantial. The most encouraging results come from Table 8c, which examines shifts from salaries to transfers in periods of crisis and noncrisis. Here the coefficients are substantial and appropriately signed. In general, however, the data are inadequate to confirm the existence of a transfer approach. Whether these provisional results would hold up with less ambiguous data is uncertain.

Reward Social Strata

Conditions Favoring a Reward Strategy.   Few Latin American societies qualify as "advanced industrial," but the social class cleav-

---

23. Social security programs doubtless have important political aspects (Mesa Lago 1978), but payments have generally followed a smooth upward path.

Table 8. *Tests of the Transfer Strategy*
(a) Government Contributions to Social Security Funds During Political Crises

Shift to Government Social Security Contributions From	b[†]	$\rho > |T|$[†]	R^2[‡]	N[‡]
Welfare	−0.176	0.07	37	23
Military	0.107	0.12	31	35
Police	−0.034	0.96	14	41
Foreign Relations	−0.082	0.32	7	41
Public Works	−0.100	0.28	11	40
Agriculture	−0.015	0.87	3	36
Education	−0.050	0.55	11	40

(b) Transfer Payments During Political Crises

Shifts to Transfers From	b[†]	$\rho > |T|$[†]	R^2[‡]	N[‡]
Police	0.123	0.06	46	21
Education	0.053	0.51	25	21
Public Works	0.285	0.01	70	21
Agriculture	0.072	0.49	35	21
Foreign Relations	0.103	0.08	63	21
Military	0.121	0.09	73	17

(c) Transfers vs. Salaries

Shift from Salaries to Transfers	b[†]	$\rho > |T|$[†]	R^2[‡]	N[‡]
Political Crisis	0.270	0.12	40	21
No Political Crisis	−0.105	0.08	14	53

[†]Here b and ρ refer to the coefficients and significance levels of the transfer dummy when all other variables are included in the equation.
[‡]Here R^2 and N refer to statistics for the complete regression equation. See Table 4.

ages that characterize Western Europe and North America are often critical in Latin America as well.[24] In such diverse countries as Nicaragua, Brazil, Chile, and Haiti, recent political conflicts have involved interclass struggles over the distribution of national

24. Some definitions: "Dominant classes" means upper and upper-middle groups—the bourgeoisie, big landowners, high-level professionals and managers,

wealth. How can we link the rise and fall of newly organized social forces to the evolution of public spending?[25]

Effective challenges to the power of traditional oligarchies in Latin America have occurred roughly in step with each nation's economic evolution. In Argentina and Uruguay, middle-class groups challenged the political power of the old oligarchy in the first quarter of this century. In Brazil the challenge started around 1930; in Bolivia it began in the forties. Working-class groups achieved substantial power later—in Argentina after 1945 and in Brazil around 1960. Beginning in the mid-1960s, however, the flow of political influence to lower-status groups proved quite reversible. In Brazil, Argentina, Uruguay, and somewhat later in Chile, coalitions of domestic and foreign bourgeoisies joined the armed forces to reassert their dominance. The political expression of this coalition, the "bureaucratic-authoritarian" regime, was modernizing in the sense of promoting greater economic integration with advanced industrial economies, but it was reactionary in the sense of promoting greater inequalities in the distribution of income. In budgetary terms this strategy implied, on the one hand, cuts in those social programs helping the middle and working classes and, on the other, boosts in military spending.

Dominant-Class Strategies. What policy choices further the interests of dominant classes? If a politician is simply the latest in a long line of leaders representing dominant groups, we expect little change. But when a leader represents the *reaction* of dominant classes against the challenge of subordinate groups, then the latter may lose some previously won benefits. Defenders of dominant classes will claim such retractions are in the public interest, part of the restoration of entrepreneurial optimism so necessary for economic stabilization and growth. Even in the days before IMF conditionalities, a Banzer, Castello Branco, or Pinochet would

---

and the like. "Intermediate classes" includes middle bureaucrats and professionals, shopkeepers, teachers, white-collar employees, and so on. "Subordinate classes" means the urban working class, marginal groups such as squatters, and the rural poor.

25. It might be objected that the attribution of the costs and benefits of public expenditures to individual social classes has proved to be quite a difficult problem for economists. This is undoubtedly true, but it is beside the point: Political actors fight over allocations *as if* their incidence were clear. See Selowsky (1979) and Webb (1977).

assume that entrepreneurial confidence required a reduction in "unproductive" public expenditures, notably those on education, health, labor, and land reform. Because reductions in social spending cannot be enforced without increases in the repressive capacity of the government, dominant-class trade-offs benefit military and police forces.

Dominant-class reactions differ fundamentally from the patrician, liberal-democratic style of a leader like Ecuador's Galo Plaza and from anachronisms like Somoza or Stroessner. Typical examples of aggressive defenders of upper-class interests include Onganía and Videla in Argentina, Banzer in Bolivia, the post-1964 Brazilian junta, Pinochet in Chile, and Castillo Armas, Peralta, and Arana in Guatemala. In these cases dominant groups reacted after subordinate classes had already mobilized and achieved victories. In other cases of dominant-class reactions, notably those of Odría in Peru, Pérez Jiménez in Venezuela, and Ospina Pérez in Colombia, popular mobilization was substantially lower. The administrations of Odría and Pérez Jiménez began as reactions against popular mobilization, but, not surprisingly, they soon turned to a "populist" style, emphasizing public works and social welfare spending. In Colombia the level of social mobilization was so low that a class strategy seems incongruous, but the feuds between Liberals and Conservatives temporarily polarized elites, and Ospina Pérez saw himself as preserving civilization against the mindless hordes. The ease with which Colombian elites accepted the National Front after the *violencia* and the repressive administration of Rojas Pinilla demonstrates that Ospina's strategy missed Colombian reality.

Intermediate-Class Strategies.   Conditions favorable to targeting the intermediate classes have existed in both Central and South America. In Chile, for example, political conflict has long revolved around class, with distinct political parties representing the left, center, and right in a well-defined ideological spectrum. From 1958 until 1964, Conservative Jorge Alessandri held Chile's presidency. He was succeeded by Christian Democrat Eduardo Frei. In *Class Conflict and Economic Development in Chile* (1978), Barbara Stallings argues that Alessandri defended the interests of the big bourgeoisie while Frei favored the smaller bourgeoisie. In terms of the overall economic consequences of Alessandri's and

Frei's policies her analysis is convincing. In terms of expenditures, however, their incentives were equally center-directed. Alessandri had little reason to fear a rightward defection of his conservative supporters, and he needed the backing of the centrist Radical party in the legislature. When his party lost support in the midterm legislative election of 1961, he was forced to move toward the electorally crucial center.

The term of another Chilean president, Gabriel González Videla (1947–1953), contrasts sharply with that of Alessandri. Elected with the support of the left, González Videla's first cabinet included three Communists. But personal beliefs and international financial pressure soon made González Videla a cold warrior. He removed the Communists and began a crackdown on labor. Moran's (1974) description gives the impression of a complete turn toward the dominant classes, but González Videla should have adopted an intermediate strategy. In Chile such a strategy would necessarily be more repressive than the same approach in a country like Peru, simply because the mobilization of the left was so much greater in Chile (Bowers 1958).

Fernando Belaúnde Terry in Peru and Arturo Frondizi in Argentina also followed intermediate strategies. Belaúnde combined an intermediate strategy with a regional approach. Frondizi began his term pursuing economic policies favorable to the Peronist support that had put him into office, but overall the policies of his administration reflected the interests of the intermediate classes supporting his branch of the Radical Civic Union (Zuvekas 1968).

In a number of Central American countries the overthrow of old Somoza-style dictators led to military-sponsored attempts at reform. Under such executives as Osorio and Rivera in El Salvador and Villeda Morales and López Arellano in Honduras, the scope of governmental activity grew. These administrations began infrastructural projects and attempted minimal social reform.[26] Until the early seventies political conflict in these societies was not organized along class lines; that is, the working class and peasantry had no legitimate mechanisms to articulate their interests. As a result, the resistance of the dominant classes could easily stymie military efforts to encourage a larger role for government. In El Salvador, where the replacement of subsistence farming with cap-

26. The best source on Central America in this period is Anderson (1967).

italist agriculture sharply increased social tensions, the political center became increasingly isolated as class conflict grew. Center-dominated reform proved illusory, giving way finally to civil war.

Subordinate and Multiclass Coalitions. Few administrations embark on a strategic defense of the interests of the subordinate classes alone. A generous definition of administrations pursuing subordinate-class strategies might include the pre-1951 government of Juan Perón in Argentina, the Popular Unity administration of Salvador Allende in Chile (1970–1973), the incompetent government of Teodoro Picado in Costa Rica, and the administrations of Juan José Arévalo and Jacobo Arbenz in Guatemala. All came to unhappy endings at the hands of military uprisings.[27]

Multiclass coalitions are more common. In Argentina, the post-1950 phase of Perón's government represented a broadening of its earlier targeting of subordinate classes, but transitions in this direction (subordinate to multiclass) have been rare. More often, multiclass strategies have immediately followed one of two conditions. One condition is simply the existence of plentiful resources. In Venezuela, the Democratic Action (AD) governments of Rómulo Betancourt and Raúl Leoni (1958–1968) took good care of the military, but thanks to oil resources AD was able to forge a multiclass alliance at the same time. In 1968 AD's split allowed its centrist opponents to take the presidency. The victory of the Christian Democrats might have led to an intermediate-centered strategy, but the central government budget could easily expand to accommodate new claimants, so expenditure policy remained substantially unchanged.

Multiclass coalitions have also followed a second route. If class-based mobilization is too weak to permit a strategy based on either the intermediate or subordinate classes alone, and if there has not yet occurred a successful challenge to upper-class domination, then such a challenge could come from an alliance of intermediate and subordinate classes. This condition was met in Bolivia, where the

27. Picado, it should be noted, was ousted not by his own military but by a popular rebellion led by José Figueres. Perón was overthrown after (but not because) his regime had shifted to a multiclass strategy. Arbenz differs from other leaders who followed working-class strategies, including his predecessor Arévalo, because he was oriented toward the rural poor rather than the urban working class. In terms of expenditures, increases in spending would be expected on rural electrification, roads, and the like.

first government of Victor Paz Estenssoro's National Revolutionary Movement (1952–1956) rapidly expanded benefits to its middle-class and working-class supporters while cutting spending on the military, a military closely associated with the previous regime.[28]

A setting quite different from Bolivia existed in Brazil in the early sixties. Because the government apparatus was already in the hands of challengers to traditionally dominant elements, the feasibility of coalitions depended upon the experience of that earlier set of challengers. The government of Juscelino Kubitschek (1956–1961) followed no class strategy, but it increased government intervention in the economy and it supported intermediate-class interests. Fortunately for Kubitschek, Brazil was in the heyday of import substitution, so he had the luxury of dividing an expanding pie. By the early sixties the mobilization of the subordinate classes was sufficiently advanced to make a multiclass alliance unavoidable but very costly. João Goulart tried to preside over such an alliance, but stagnation had replaced rapid growth and trade-offs were made over a shrinking pie. Economic and political chaos followed, and in 1964 the military ousted the democratic regime.

Evaluating Dominant-Class Strategies. For the dominant-class strategy the key trade-offs involve expenditures on the military and police versus those on education, health, agriculture, public works, and foreign relations. Table 9 shows that during crises military spending grows at the expense of education and health but not at the expense of public works and foreign relations.[29] Education and

28. Similar events probably also occurred in the late 1950s in Ecuador. See Fitch (1977).

29. Contrary to expectations, police and military spending did not move in parallel. One reason for this divergence is suggested by the police–military trade-off itself, which favors the police during noncrisis periods but shifts to the military during crises. This result might seem odd, because in the recent dominant-class reactions in the Southern Cone (Uruguay, Brazil, Argentina, and Chile), both police and military forces realized gains. The police share rose because police were taking a more active role in the repression of popular movements. But since World War II the military has generally borne the main burden of antiguerrilla and antipopular repression, so even police spending has been forced to yield to the military during crises. In addition, measurement error in the police indicator may blur its relationships with other categories. Our measure of police spending is less reliable than most categories because indicators of police spending sometimes include other programs. Moreover, the use of police forces as part of the repressive apparatus (rather than as traffic police) varies from country to country.

Table 9. Tests of Social Class Strategies

Expenditure Trade-off Categories	Estimated Parameter							
	Dominant Classes		Intermediate Classes		Subordinate Classes		Multiclass	
	Non-crisis	Crisis	Non-crisis	Crisis	Non-crisis	Crisis	Non-crisis	Crisis
Education (+) Military (−)	+0.024	−0.079[a]	−0.013	+0.017	+0.090[a]	+0.054	+0.028	+0.051[a]
Education (+) Police (−)	0.000	−0.003	−0.010	−0.021	+0.021	+0.067	+0.014	+0.013
Education (+) Agriculture (−)	+0.012	−0.052	+0.002	−0.035	−0.006	+0.400[a]	+0.004	+0.002
Education (+) Public Works (−)	−0.036	−0.037	+0.003	+0.028	+0.014	−0.029	+0.055[a]	−0.022
Education (+) Foreign Relations (−)	−0.018	−0.040[a]	−0.015	−0.011	−0.002	+0.003	−0.021	−0.010
Health (+) Military (−)	−0.006	−0.122[a]	−0.029	−0.022	+0.075	+0.023	−0.036	+0.029
Health (+) Education (−)	−0.033	−0.047	−0.009	−0.035	+0.006	−0.027	+0.005	−0.008
Health (+) Agriculture (−)	−0.008	−0.114[a]	−0.038	−0.140[a]	+0.034	+0.200	−0.002	−0.018
Health (+) Public Works (−)	−0.053[a]	−0.001	−0.021	−0.064[a]	−0.022	−0.039	+0.063	−0.061
Health (+) Police (−)	−0.040[a]	−0.091[a]	−0.028	−0.073[a]	+0.007	−0.059	+0.017	−0.011

Health (+) Foreign Relations (−)	-0.054^a	-0.071^a	-0.038^a	-0.068^a	-0.026	-0.045	$+0.023$	-0.042
Public Works (+) Military (−)	$+0.065^a$	-0.063	-0.025	-0.006	$+0.069$	$+0.087$	-0.033	$+0.074$
Public Works (+) Agriculture (−)	$+0.051$	-0.044	-0.017	-0.121^a	-0.019	$+0.400^a$	-0.063	$+0.031^a$
Public Works (+) Foreign Relations (−)	$+0.019$	$+0.003$	-0.017	-0.033	-0.011	-0.028	-0.032	$+0.009$
Public Works (+) Police (−)	$+0.037$	-0.013	-0.010	-0.053	$+0.012$	$+0.093$	-0.032	$+0.030$
Foreign Relations (+) Military (−)	$+0.047$	-0.037	0.000	$+0.040$	$+0.091^a$	$+0.062$	$+0.006$	$+0.079^a$
Agriculture (+) Military (−)	$+0.023^a$	-0.010	-0.001	$+0.100^a$	$+0.098^a$	-0.312^a	$+0.014$	$+0.047^a$
Police (+) Military (−)	$+0.041^a$	-0.076^a	-0.004	$+0.045$	$+0.068^a$	-0.011	$+0.014$	$+0.044$

Note: The numerical entry in each column represents the *b* associated with each class dummy when all other dummies are included in the equation. See Table 4.

[a] Probability level better than 0.10.

health are programs identified with intermediate and subordinate classes, while agriculture, public works, and foreign relations lack clear class beneficiaries.[30]

Figure 5, which traces 1945–1974 budget shares for four key programs in Brazil, illustrates a vigorous dominant-class reaction.[31] In 1965, the first full year in which the Castello Branco government controlled the budget, military spending reversed its long post–World War II slide (a slide common to most Latin American countries) and quickly moved to higher levels. Spending on police rose at an enormous rate in 1965 and 1966, maintained a very high level until 1969 (by which time an efficient and repressive police apparatus was in place), and never returned to pre-coup levels. Education and health programs, on the other hand, behaved quite differently. Education jumped in the first postcoup budget, when the military sought popularity through spending on primary schools, but then declined until 1970. Subsequent rebellions of middle-class youth stimulated an expansion of universities that led to an increase in the total education budget.[32] Health programs increased their budget share in 1966 but then went into a tailspin from which they did not recover until after 1974.

Evaluating Intermediate-Class Strategies. What happens when executives pursue such intermediate classes as teachers, white-collar employees, shopkeepers, or middle-level bureaucrats? According to Table 9, the key program is education. In crises, education gains against every program except police and agriculture.[33] Health programs, which are comparatively more important to the poor, lose to education, public works, police, and foreign relations. Public works programs generally suffer as well, only holding their own vis-à-vis the military and losing against everything else.

Many administrations pursuing an intermediate strategy face a military threat as well as a class cleavage. As a result, military

30. Foreign relations continues here as an example of a traditional program. The diplomatic service has always been an outlet for the career aspirations of upper-class gentlemen.

31. Note that these numbers do not (as they did in earlier figures) represent rates of change over time.

32. For an extended discussion of educational politics, see Ames (1973).

33. Neither exception is important. Both police and agriculture are much smaller than education, so small increases can have disproportionate effects on the overall trade-off. The loss to agriculture was largely a result of the long-term upward trend in agriculture spending in Chile.

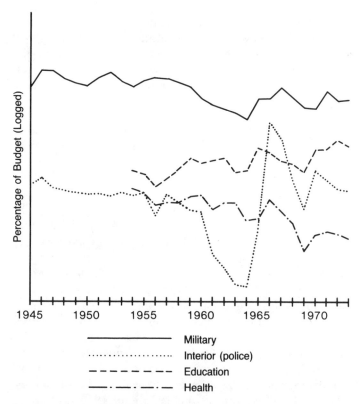

Figure 5. Budget Shares in Brazil: 1945–1974

pacification may accompany an intermediate-class strategy, and the total effect on military spending could be positive. The real winner, however, is education: Middle-class teachers and middle-class pupils indeed create a powerful constituency.

Evaluating Subordinate-Class Strategies.   Tests of the subordinate-class strategies produced less consistent estimates, but they did reveal the priorities of administrations involved in such approaches. In crises, education and health lose some of the edge they maintain over the military in noncrisis situations, and both education and health gain substantially against agriculture. Public works is favored over the military in both crisis and noncrisis situations. Health does well against education in noncrisis periods but loses during crises. Overall, then, subordinate-class strategies include some efforts to satisfy the military and social programs get a lower priority, but the key programs are those generating jobs.

Evaluating Multiclass Strategies. Leaders typically adopt multiclass approaches when they realize a subordinate-class strategy is no longer viable. Since these administrations usually face severe economic problems, and since economic instability can lead to military takeovers, they ought to seek immediate military support. Instead, administrations pursuing multiclass strategies generally make no such efforts or make them only *after* their initial survival crises. In Argentina and Bolivia, for example, Perón and Siles Zuazo lowered military spending upon beginning their terms but raised it each year thereafter.[34] João Goulart steadily lowered military spending. The fact that the military overthrew all three administrations helps us understand why multiclass strategies have as little success as strategies focusing on the subordinate classes alone.[35]

Figure 6, which charts the movements of military and health programs in Bolivia, presents an example of a multiclass strategy. The first government of Paz Estenssoro's National Revolutionary Movement (MNR) held office from 1952 until 1956. In four of the five years health programs gained more than the military. But the MNR could not sustain a multiclass approach—with its redistributive changes in policy outputs—when inflation was accelerating and the GNP was plummeting. The regime then turned to the social groups that had provided its original leadership. Paz's successor, Siles Zuazo, rebuilt the military while cutting social programs such as health. When Paz returned to office in 1960, he continued the new pattern with steady increments for the armed forces. Unfortunately for the MNR, Paz was unable to appease the generals. Colonel Barrientos overthrew the MNR in 1964, and the colonel's own effort at military pacification soon produced another healthy increment in the armed forces' budget (Mitchell 1977).

34. Note that in Perón's case this is the term beginning in 1951.
35. Oil-rich Venezuela is an understandable exception.

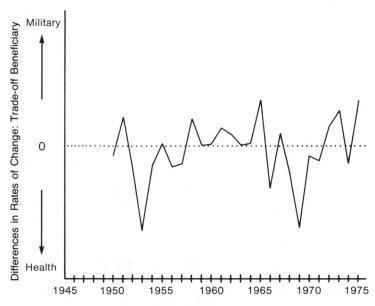

Figure 6. Military vs. Health Spending in Bolivia: 1950–1975

The Economic Context of Allocations

Thus far the discussion has emphasized the share of the budget allocated to certain programs. In principle, shares of spending can rise or fall regardless of movements in the gross domestic product (GDP), exports, or price levels. Still, the absence of a *necessary* connection does not deny the possibility of an empirical relationship. This section develops and tests some simple linkages between the health of the overall economy and trade-offs in budget shares.

Suppose we discover that whenever the GDP rises, the share of the budget going to the military declines. Why might that happen? Surely an increase in resources does not inevitably cause a decline in the military's budget share. When the GDP rises, however, the total budget is likely to rise, and a rising total budget makes it easier to cut the military's relative share without the political danger of an absolute cut.

Executives make three decisions related to budgets. They select a strategy, determine the total size of the budget, and decide program shares. Their first step is the adoption of a strategy; then they determine the size of the total budget and the size of each program. Decisions to expand or contract the total budget can only be understood in the context of the resource base. A political milieu in which the total budget grows while resources shrink is very different from a milieu in which the total grows while resources grow. In the former case allocation policy is aggressive and risks fiscal and political strain; in the latter it proceeds from a secure and expanding base.

Strategies and Global Increases

When a strategy calls for expanding a certain program, do other programs gain *absolutely* even if their *relative* sizes shrink? If, for example, an administration follows the military pacification approach, do nonmilitary expenditures rise absolutely in order to cushion the competitive struggle?

Table 10 focuses on programs receiving increments during political crises. Column A represents increases in the total of nonstrategic programs. In four cases—military pacification, bureaucratic recruitment, local interests, and intermediate classes—losers are cushioned by enlarging the total budget. But when executives adopt dominant-class approaches and boost the military budget, their fiscal conservatism forestalls increases in other programs. Column B of Table 10 examines the movements of an indicator of fiscal stress—that is, the ratio of all nonstrategic (or nontarget) programs to the GDP.[36] Except for administrations choosing multiclass strategies, total nontargeted spending expands no faster than resources. Administrations adopting multiclass approaches, however, seem to be under great pressure, so when they spend on their target programs (education and public works), they augment nonfavored programs enough to prevent absolute losses. The military, for example, may see its share of the budget shrink, but actual expenditures will go up. In other words: Multiclass gov-

36. GDP was lagged one year because expenditures themselves affect the GDP and because information about the GDP is not always timely. Executives must use some simple decision rule—for example, the assumption that the rate of change of the GDP will be the same as its rate of change in the previous year. Thus an increase in the budget in year *t* equivalent to the increase in the GDP in year *t* − 1 would be "stressless."

Table 10. *Increases in Adversary Programs During Political Crises*

Strategy	Target Program	Mean Increase in Absolute Expenditures	
		(A) *All* *Nontarget* *Programs (%)*	*(B)* *Ratio of All* *Nontarget Programs to* *Lagged Change in GDP*
Military Pacification	Military	0.091 (0.02)[a]	− 5.46 (0.44)
Recruit Bureaucrats	Salaries	0.047 (0.04)	1.18 (0.55)
Local Interests	Public Works	0.084 (0.003)	− 0.589 (0.86)
Dominant Classes	Military	0.03 (0.33)	5.79 (0.22)
Intermediate Classes	Military	0.213 (0.08)	− 21.44 (0.31)
Multiclass	Education	0.031 (0.26)	1.90 (0.08)
	Public Works	0.031 (0.30)	2.60 (0.10)

[a]The number in parentheses is the probability that the parameter is significantly different from zero.

ernments cannot cut budgets even when faced with economic crises. No wonder they have trouble surviving.

When executives cushion relative losses, which programs do they favor? Table 11 compares the effects of various strategies on key programs in two contexts: while total budgets are rising and while they are stable or declining.[37] When the military pacification strategy is optimal *and* budget totals are rising, education and public works programs cushion their relative loss completely. Because a rising total could allow an even greater relative shift to the military, this cushioning is quite unexpected. In a sense, the finding underscores the curious competitive position of the armed forces: Spending on the military may be politically crucial, but economically it is pure waste. If the total budget cannot grow, military pacification requires relative shifts. When executives can augment the whole budget, popular job-creating programs like education and public works hold their own against the armed forces.

The bureaucratic and local-interest strategies reveal the same tendency for trade-offs to shrink when executives increase the whole budget. Leaders know that losers punish more than winners reward. Hence they reason that it is better to maintain shares and

37. Strategies with insufficient cases have been excluded.

Table 11. *Effects on Key Trade-offs of Rising Budgets During
           Political Crises*

(a) Military Pacification

Expenditure Trade-off Categories	Estimated Parameter	
	Rising Budget	*Stable or Declining Budget*
Military (+) Public Works (−)	− 0.034 (0.40)[a]	+ 0.104 (0.01)
Military (+) Education (−)	+ 0.022 (0.36)	+ 0.055 (0.02)
Military (+) Health (−)	+ 0.050 (0.13)	+ 0.138 (0.0001)
Military (+) Welfare (−)	+ 0.048 (0.21)	+ 0.115 (0.01)
Military (+) Police (−)	+ 0.074 (0.003)	+ 0.060 (0.02)
Military (+) Foreign Relations (−)	+ 0.055 (0.03)	+ 0.127 (0.0001)

(b) Bureaucratic Recruitment

Expenditure Category	Estimated Parameter	
	Rising Budget	*Stable or Declining Budget*
Salaries (+)	+ 0.045 (0.47)	+ 0.226 (0.0007)

(c) Local Interests

Expenditure Trade-off Categories	Estimated Parameter	
	Rising Budget	*Stable or Declining Budget*
Public Works (+) Military (−)	− 0.007 (0.89)	+ 0.159 (0.0003)
Public Works (+) Education (−)	+ 0.060 (0.22)	+ 0.126 (0.008)
Public Works (+) Health (−)	+ 0.014 (0.73)	+ 0.191 (0.0001)
Public Works (+) Foreign Relations (−)	+ 0.052 (0.20)	+ 0.141 (0.0005)
Public Works (+) Welfare (−)	+ 0.085 (0.08)	+ 0.119 (0.05)
Public Works (+) Police (−)	+ 0.050 (0.08)	+ 0.179 (0.0001)

[a]The signed entry is the estimated coefficient from a regression with all dummies included. The entry in parentheses is the associated significance level.

boost everyone, particularly since some budget participants may be more concerned with absolute than relative gains.

Strategies and Inflation

Are budgetary allocations affected by the endemic inflation characteristic of so many Latin American countries? If prices change at a constant rate, executives learn to adjust, and spending should be unaffected. When prices jump suddenly, however, the real incomes of government employees decline. Executives seeking to recruit bureaucrats are forced to increase salaries just to compensate for the unexpected inflation.

When the rate of inflation jumps, the share of the budget going to wages and salaries drops.[38] Since *falling* salaries can hardly cause *increasing* inflation, executives must fail to adjust salaries quickly enough when inflation accelerates. The salary share declines because executives maintain other components of the budget at the expense of wages.

If executives really care about bureaucrats—that is, if the bureaucratic strategy is optimal—the salary share ought to *rise*, not fall, when inflation accelerates. Table 12 confirms the hypothesis: The coefficient of the bureaucratic recruitment variable roughly doubles when inflation is rising. Once again, losers punish more than winners reward. When bureaucrats are the political target, executives prevent losses in wages.[39]

---

38. Consumer price increases are calculated from the IMF's *International Financial Statistics* (line 64). The equation takes the form

Salary share = $A + B$ (military dummy) $+ \cdots + F$ (class dummies) $+ Z$ (inflation)

where Z is the parameter of interest.

39. The conclusion that jumps in inflation cause administrations pursuing bureaucratic recruitment to raise salaries is risky, because salary increases may themselves cause inflation. Note, however, that increases in the rate of change of prices were associated with declines in wages when nonbureaucratic approaches were in effect. Given equal overall spending increases, it would be anomalous if some strategies led to increases in inflation while others led to decreases. It is more reasonable to conclude that gains in the salary share are consequences of bureaucratic strategies. If it is assumed that sudden changes occurring in the first two quarters will be reflected in the salary budget that year, while changes occurring in the last two quarters will affect salaries the next year, then estimates using quarterly price data become even stronger. If the bureaucratic recruitment parameter were not a response to inflation, the estimates would become weaker.

Table 12. *Effects on the Salary Share of Rising Inflation During Political Crises*

	Bureaucratic Recruitment (Estimated Parameter)	
Expenditure Category	*Rising Inflation*	*Stable or Declining Inflation*
Salaries (+)	+0.153 (0.01)[a]	+0.081 (0.20)

[a]The signed entry is the estimated parameter from a regression with all dummies included. The entry in parentheses is the associated significance level.

Conclusion

We learned in Chapter 1 that executives use expenditures as a weapon in their struggle to hold onto their positions. To use the budget efficiently, executives must break it down into specific components targetable for maximum political effect, and they must concentrate changes in these components in periods when they are most vulnerable—that is, in periods of political crisis. The political use of the budget requires a strategy.

Executives gather information about the cleavages of their societies, the resources of each political force, and the state of their economies. They filter that information through their own ideological beliefs and they choose, in the end, one or more of five coalition strategies. Because social and political groups in Latin America consistently demand specific programs, the five strategies can be linked to trade-offs in the components of public expenditure.

We found that survival politics indeed have allocational consequences. Four of the five strategies—military pacification, bureaucratic recruitment, local interests, and social class—yielded essentially the results predicted. One—the transfer strategy—did not, but severe measurement problems hindered evaluation of this approach.

If military pacification is an optimal strategy during political crises, executives boost the armed forces' budget at the expense of programs in health, welfare, and police. Education defends itself fairly well, and public works programs prove invulnerable. When the crises pass, these same leaders alter their military strategy, allowing the armed forces neither gains nor losses.

Salary and public works approaches turn out to be strategic opposites. Bureaucratic recruitment leads to gains in wage and salary shares at the expense of public works (with its substantial physical construction component), while the targeting of local interests reverses that pattern.

The social class strategies are really a group of sharply variant substrategies. Leaders adopting dominant-class approaches stress the military at the expense of education and health. Agriculture, public works, and traditional ministries like foreign relations survive unscathed. Intermediate-class strategies favor education against almost everything, including programs that benefit the poor. When leaders target the subordinate classes, they try to keep the military happy while boosting job-creating programs like public works. Welfare programs enjoy some support, but the central target is the creation of jobs. Executives seeking a multiclass coalition try to do it all: military increases for pacification, public works for job creation, welfare programs for social needs.

Leaders soon discover that losers punish more than winners reward. They respond by attempting to cushion programs whose budget shares decline. But cushioning losers is expensive, because it creates a constant impetus toward budgetary expansion. Multiclass and subordinate-class coalitions fail in part because they cannot reconcile a "no losers" allocation strategy with sufficient economic growth to support that strategy.

For politicians, survival is just one goal among many. Here we asked what governments do to survive. The next step is to determine whether they do anything else.

3. With Time to Breathe: Policy in Postcrisis Administrations

This book has been exploring the struggles of political leaders to hold onto their offices. Though many executives lost their positions, a majority survived to enjoy a time of greater security and autonomy, a time in which they could pursue longer-range goals. This chapter begins the analysis of public spending in such postcrisis periods. It focuses on four questions: Were the allocations of deposed executives different from those managing to complete their terms? Did the allocations of elected leaders succeeded by an administration of the same political party differ from those succeeded by the opposition? Were the budgetary priorities of military governments different from those of civilians? And, finally, were there broadly similar patterns of *overall* postcrisis spending?

These four questions are logical extensions of the analysis of survival strategies. Since leaders rearrange spending priorities because they believe such rearrangements will help them, expenditures ought to increase success in avoiding coups and winning elections. The possibility that military and civilian executives allocate expenditures differently has stimulated a substantial body of comparative research, but the issue remains unresolved. Finally, overall postcrisis spending is important as an illustration of the limits of survival-centered models and as a direction for future investigation.

Victims of Coups: Bad Strategists?

Chapter 2 linked expenditures with the need to pacify the military. In the end, administrations either complete their terms or

Table 13. *Military Coups and Prior Changes in Budget Shares*

| Program | Percentage Change from Previous Administration in Program's Share of Total Expenditures | | Prob[a] |
	Survived	Ousted	
Military	− 0.071	0.033	>0.05
Education	0.068	0.122	>0.26
Agriculture	0.300	0.092	>0.44
Public Works	− 0.034	0.171	>0.03
Health	0.085	0.170	>0.34
Total Budget	0.086	0.051	>0.10

[a]The probability estimated is associated with the percentage of times a difference score of that magnitude could occur by chance. A probability of 0.05, for example, means that 5 times out of 100 a difference in military spending between survivors and victims as large as the difference reported here could occur by chance.

they are overthrown.[1] Will the survivors be the administrations that most increase the military share of the budget, or will the military inevitably remove some administrations—lavish rewards to the officers notwithstanding? For five important programs, Table 13 compares administrations that finished their terms with administrations that failed. Compared to ousted executives, the survivors cut military spending, decreased public works, and expanded total budgets.

This test is too simple, however, and, as a result, too ambiguous. Surviving governments might cut the military budget for a variety of reasons: They might be more secure, or they might believe the military will not respond strongly to budgetary losses. Perhaps ousted administrations lasted as long as they did *because* they paid off the military—that is, the military might have overthrown even more administrations if executives had not granted them substantial budgetary resources.

More precise hypotheses and a more refined measure of spending are required. Table 13, which estimates spending changes between administrations for each of five programs, fails to capture the concept of spending *priorities*. If one executive pays for a mil-

1. Among the countries in our analysis, the only exceptions are Bolivia in 1952 and Nicaragua in 1979, where popular revolutionary groups overthrew the established military.

itary increase at the expense of public works while another finances the same increase at the expense of education, the two administrations are not equivalent. The concept of priorities requires identifying losing as well as winning programs.

Suppose we wish to measure the changes in priority an administration gives to these five programs. First, calculate the percentage change in each program between a given administration and its predecessor. Next, rank these percentage changes from the program gaining the most to the program losing the most. Each rank ordering describes a single administration.[2] An administration favoring the military over education will be distinct from one whose priorities are reversed, even if the actual changes in the military share are the same. Likewise, an administration giving greatest priority to health, with military second and education last, will be distinct from one that ranks health first, education second, and the military last.

Now consider again the differences between the allocations of surviving and failing administrations. Since there is little reason to expect expenditure shifts from executives with no real possibility of being overthrown, only those administrations vulnerable to coups (that is, those for whom military pacification was an optimal strategy) will be included. Among such administrations, twenty-two ranked military spending last or next to last among the five budgetary programs. The armed forces overthrew twelve of those twenty-two, or 55 percent. Sixteen administrations favored military programs, ranking them first or second, and the armed forces overthrew six of these sixteen, or 37.5 percent.[3] Vul-

2. This scaling preserves only ordinal information. Suppose one administration changes three programs $+10$, 0, and -10 percent and another changes the same programs $+5$, 0, and -5 percent. Their rankings would be the same. Since the probability of such large differences in the gain or loss of individual programs depends in part on the absolute size of changes in total expenditures, attention to the latter should minimize distortions caused by the former. For alternative treatments of the measurement problem in budgetary analysis, see Gist (1979) and Peroff and Podolak-Warren (1979).

3. Among administrations ranking the military fourth or fifth and for whom military pacification was optimal, the ousted included Lemus and Sánchez Hernández (El Salvador), Torres (Bolivia), Castillo Armas (Guatemala), López Arellano (Honduras, 1972–1975), Allende (Chile), Vargas (by suicide) and Goulart (Brazil), Perón (Argentina), Bustamente and Belaúnde (Peru), and Velasco Ibarra (Ecuador). Survivors included Arana and Lucas García (Guatemala), Lozano Díaz, Melgar Castro, and López Arellano (1963–1971) (Honduras), Guzmán (Dominican Republic), de la Guardia and Chiari (Panama), Kubitschek (Brazil), and Odría (Peru).

nerable administrations that responded by according the military a high priority were thus more likely to survive, but the differences are not terribly impressive. Consider, however, just those executives who came to office after a competitive election. Since they rarely enjoyed close ties to the officer corps, their administrations should be especially vulnerable. Twelve such executives failed to pay off the military (according them fourth or fifth budget priority); eight were victims of coups. Six elected executives did attend to their military support (according them first or second priority); all but one survived. Thus highly vulnerable administrations found that attention to the military's budgetary needs yielded substantial payoffs.

The military is hardly the only interest group making claims on executives, so leaders threatened by military revolt are seldom able to devote unlimited resources to the armed forces. Twenty-two executives with a military pacification problem stressed spending on education and health programs, ranking neither lower than third.[4] The armed forces removed thirteen, or 59 percent, from office. Of thirty-eight administrations not according the same high priority to education and health, only eleven, or 29 percent, were given the boot.[5] Thus executives who placed a heavy emphasis on

For those who gave the armed forces ranks of first or second, ousted administrations included Chaves (Paraguay), Paz (Bolivia), Onganía and Videla (Argentina), Rojas Pinilla (Colombia), and Pérez Jiménez (Venezuela). Survivors included Romero (El Salvador), Laugerud and Peralta (Guatemala), Román y Reyes (Nicaragua), Torrijos and Robles (Panama), Banzer (Bolivia), Pinochet (Chile), Cruz (Honduras), and Velasco Ibarra (Ecuador, 1952–1956).

4. The criterion of ranking in the top three is admittedly arbitrary. It was chosen to yield enough cases for analysis.

5. Ousted administrations with education and health in priorities 1–3 included Remón and Arias (Panama), Sánchez Hernández and Lemus (El Salvador), Allende (Chile), Vargas (Brazil), Perón and Illía (Argentina), Bustamente (Peru), Torres (Bolivia), López Arellano (1972–1975) and Villeda Morales (Honduras), and Arbenz (Guatemala). Survivors included de la Guardia and Torrijos (Panama), Méndez Montenegro and Peralta (Guatemala), Osorio (El Salvador), Banzer (Bolivia), Lozano Díaz (Honduras), and Betancourt (Venezuela). Of those not giving a high priority to education and health, coup victims included Paz (Bolivia, 1960–1964), Goulart (Brazil), Velasco Ibarra (1968–1971) and Carlos Julio Arosemena (Ecuador), Castillo Armas (Guatemala), Belaúnde (Peru), Frondizi, Onganía, and Videla (Argentina), Rojas Pinilla (Colombia), and Chaves (Paraguay). Survivors included Guzmán (Dominican Republic), Rodríguez Lara and Velasco Ibarra (1956–1960) (Ecuador), Lucas García, Ydígoras Fuentes, Arana, and Laugerud (Guatemala), Cruz, Gálvez, and Melgar Castro (Honduras), Román y Reyes and Tacho (Nicaragua), Arias Espinosa, Alcibiades Arosemena, Chiari, and Robles (Panama), Stroessner (Paraguay), Perón (Argentina, 1951–1955), Siles Zuazo and

social programs were almost twice as likely to be overthrown as executives who did not. Without question, such "reformist" administrations were likely to favor working-class interests in other aspects of economic policy as well, thereby augmenting their vulnerability. According high priority to the military budget was an overwhelmingly safer strategy.

Electoral Success:
Can Spending Buy Votes?

Executives often pursue policies that bring immediate rewards but have costs they can shift to successors. In Latin America the nearly universal prohibition on immediate reelection of the executive reinforces this myopic attitude. If you can't be around when the bills come due, why worry about them? Why even be concerned with the next election?

In fact, executives do care about the election of their successors. Though constitutions may prohibit immediate reelection, many leaders harbor dreams of assuming the presidency again after a term on the sidelines. Even without such hopes, loyalty might stimulate leaders to help their parties' candidates. Victory by the incumbent party in the election of a successor puts the stamp of approval on an administration. If, on the other hand, the election is lost, the president may be a lame duck for many months as his term nears its end.

If executives do care about the election of their successors, particular patterns of spending might increase their chances of victory. Success, unfortunately, occurs pretty rarely, because incumbents nearly always lose. In the entire World War II period, incumbent parties in Brazil, Chile, Colombia, Costa Rica, the Dominican Republic, Ecuador, and Venezuela won only six times in thirty elections. If elections are generally lost, prior expenditure shifts may be irrelevant or even counterproductive. Perhaps the armed forces still need pacification, but group, class, and local strategies become measures of intent and hope rather than predictors of success.

In an important study of Latin American elections, Robert Dix (1984) attributes high executive turnover to both political and eco-

---

Banzer (Bolivia), Kubitschek and Castello Branco (Brazil), Pinochet (Chile), Odría (Peru), Molina and Romero (El Salvador), and Pérez Jiménez (Venezuela).

nomic factors. Constitutional prohibitions on immediate reelection weaken presidential control. Presidents cannot transfer their authority to the candidates of their parties, and these candidates may even choose to attack the president in order to mobilize their own followers. Even without this inevitable weakening of incumbents, executives have a hard time coping with steadily rising levels of social mobilization. As Latin American populations have become more urban, they have become more restive and better organized politically. The result, in Dix's view, is an ever-increasing gap between popular demands and the limited resources of executives.

How can the linkages between expenditures and electoral outcomes be discovered? In some cases the executive's party has no chance at or interest in reelection. When a party exists only to support a certain leader, the victory of an opposing party in the next presidential test is not an instance of electoral turnover. Ecuador's José Maria Velasco Ibarra, a charismatic figure *par excellence,* was constitutionally prohibited from running in 1956. Velasco supported Camilo Ponce, the candidate of another party. Ponce's victory did not make Velasco a winner, but surely he should not be classified as a loser. In the election of 1952, outgoing Ecuadorean President Galo Plaza chose to back no candidate (Martz 1972). Like Velasco, Plaza neither won nor lost.

Personalist parties represent only one of the difficulties in classifying outgoing executives as winners or losers. Democratic Action (AD), the dominant party of Venezuela, split over its attempt to elect a successor to Raúl Leoni in 1968. Together AD's two candidates took a majority of the popular vote, but singly neither could overcome the candidate of the opposition. Since dissatisfaction with Leoni did not cause the split in AD, it is hard to call the electoral result a negative judgment on his administration.

Eliminating such ambiguous cases leaves twenty incumbents clearly interested in the election of their successors. Eight were victorious; that is, the incumbent president or his party captured the presidency for another term.[6]

6. The twelve losers: Frei and Alessandri (Chile), Andrés Pérez and Caldera (Venezuela), Echandi, Ulate, Odúber, Trejos, and Carazo (Costa Rica), Balaguer (Dominican Republic), Kubitschek (Brazil), and Méndez Montenegro (Guatemala). The eight winners: Perón (Argentina, 1951), Figueres (Costa Rica, 1974), Guzmán (Dominican Republic), de la Guardia and Chiari (Panama), López Michelson (Colombia), Betancourt (Venezuela), and Osorio (El Salvador).

Table 14. *Successful Elections and Prior Changes in Budget Shares*

	Percentage Change from Previous Administration in Program's Share of Total Expenditures		
Program	Won Succeeding Election	Lost Succeeding Election	Prob
Military	−0.035	−0.132	>0.23
Education	0.190	0.013	>0.10
Agriculture	0.364	0.123	>0.44
Public Works	0.102	−0.103	>0.32
Health	0.245	−0.058	>0.06
Total Budget	0.046	0.089	>0.20

In part, elections are referenda on the policies of outgoing administrations. Table 14 presents the records of the incumbents in terms of the priorities they gave to each program. Executives who were successful in the subsequent election did not necessarily increase total budgets, nor did they increase the budget share of the armed forces. Only two programs, education and health, grew significantly faster in victorious administrations than in defeated ones.

Consider the interprogram priorities of winning and losing administrations. Of twelve losing executives, seven ranked education and health spending among their three most advantaged programs. Winning executives were only slightly better, with six of eight favoring education and health. None of the eight winners gave military spending a first or second priority, but only two of twelve losers favored the armed forces either.

If executives try to structure program changes to maximize political payoffs, they might cut programs that have done well in the recent past on the grounds that payoffs from such programs are diminishing. In fact, winners do appear to try that strategy. If we compare the absolute size of the budgetary shares these winners inherited, we find that executives cut or granted smaller increases to programs beginning at higher levels. Among losing administrations, there was no relationship between the inherited size of education and health programs and subsequent boosts or cuts. Winners, in other words, acted more strategically. If education and health were already at high levels, additional money would produce smaller payoffs, so leaders gave these programs lesser increments. Losers failed to make such calculations—their increments were unrelated to the budgetary base.

These differences, nonetheless, are small. If changes in spending explain only a small part of electoral success, what factors do contribute to electoral victory or defeat? Remember Dix's social mobilization argument: "Increasing demand [social and political] outruns available resources" (1984:442). If this argument implies that economic downturns lead to electoral defeat, it is incorrect, because losing executives enjoyed an increase in GDP *twice* that of winners. If, on the other hand, Dix is suggesting that voters are more likely to reject incumbents when social mobilization reaches a certain absolute level, then the results are more promising. The eight winning executives generally ranked below the losers on such social mobilization indicators as literacy and newspaper circulation. Of the twelve clear losers, nine were from Costa Rica, Chile, and Venezuela. Of the eight winners, four were Caribbean or Central American (excluding Costa Rica). Thus polities with high levels of social mobilization and politicization make life harder for incumbents.

A further clue comes from examining the countries in Latin America where presidential and legislative elections were not always simultaneous—that is, where presidents faced midterm legislative elections.[7] Table 15 exposes the consequences of midterm elections by comparing changes in the expenditure shares of executives who faced midterms with those who did not. Clearly midterms affected expenditures. The growth rate of overall spending almost doubled when administrations faced midterm pressures. Spending on education—a program with immediate political payoffs—was 40 percent higher. Public works, which grew more than 3 percent in the absence of midterm elections, failed to increase at all in administrations facing midterms. The biggest loser was the military budget, which absorbed a 78 percent larger cut when executives could not avoid midterms.

7. Such elections occurred in Brazil, Chile, Colombia, Ecuador, and El Salvador. Expenditure data were available from the following midterm elections: Brazil, 1954, 1958, 1962; Chile, 1953, 1957, 1961, 1965, 1969, 1973; Colombia, 1960, 1964, 1968; Ecuador, 1950, 1954, 1958, 1962; El Salvador, 1964, 1966, 1968, 1970. Data on Ecuador, however, are incomplete.

Table 15. *Midterm Elections and Changes in Budget Shares*

| | Percentage Change from Previous Administration in Share of Total Expenditures | |
| | *Midterm Legislative Election* | *No Midterm Legislative Election* |
Program		
Military	−0.128	−0.072
Education	0.141	0.101
Agriculture	0.110	0.360
Public Works	0.002	0.034
Health	0.091	0.103
Total Budget	0.102	0.068

Note: This table includes only civilian administrations.

In terms of interprogram priorities, the results are similar. Ten of the twelve executives facing a midterm election ranked military spending fourth or fifth. Only half the no-midterm civilian leaders ranked the military equally low. Health and education programs finished in the top three in nine of twelve midterm-facing administrations but only 40 percent of those free from midterms.

Although the number of cases is small, these results establish the high cost of midterm elections. Executives react to midterms by spending more overall, cutting the military budget, and favoring programs with immediate payoffs. The risks are obvious: Sudden increases in the government budget may stimulate inflation, the military might become dissatisfied and restive, and economic instability could prove damaging to the incumbent party in the next general election. In the long run, moreover, the budgetary shift toward consumption (a consequence of the relative decline of infrastructure programs) diminishes the government's contribution to economic growth. For executives, unfortunately, the pressure of midterm elections is not a pressure they can avoid.

Military Government and Military Spending

Though the link between military government and military spending has become part of the staple fare of specialists in comparative politics, scholars have been able to establish no consistent relationship between the two. Most recent work has argued that military governments spend neither more nor less on the armed forces than civilians, but research on this topic remains curiously tentative and unsatisfying. There are still disputes about the appropriate standards for measuring military spending, and analysts continue to ask whether military budgets grow under military rule rather than asking what factors cause a government to spend more on its armed forces.

In a recent attempt to settle the question, Gary Zuk and William Thompson (1982) measure spending on the armed forces in two ways: military spending as a percentage of the total budget and military expenditures per capita. They find that the military's budget share grows more under military governments than under civilians, but military expenditures per capita are tied mostly to GNP growth, not to the nature of a country's rulers.[8] The authors conclude from these contradictory results that military rulers do not increase the size of military budgets "either in general or in comparison with their civilian counterparts" (p. 71).

The analyses presented earlier in this chapter suggest that Zuk and Thompson's negative conclusion is unjustified. Unless we compare per capita military expenditures to per capita expenditures on education, public works, and other programs, per capita spending cannot measure the priority given to the armed forces. When the GNP rises, the whole budget will rise as well. Military expenditures per capita share in that expansion, but so do expenditures for education, health, and public works. The question, then, is whether the military gets more than other programs. The military spending question, in other words, is one of *relative priorities*. When Zuk and Thompson use an indicator of priorities (the military budget share), they find that military administrations do spend more and that military coups trigger additional increments.

Still, little attention has been given to the *determinants* of spending on the military. Within the framework of interprogram priorities presented here, how can we think about these factors? Philippe Schmitter (1971a) has suggested a useful way to categorize administrations. For each year between 1950 and 1967, Schmitter classified every Latin American country as civilian com-

8. Zuk and Thompson employ a "pooled cross-sectional and time series analysis" for sixty-six countries, including all Latin America except, oddly enough, Chile and Venezuela.

petitive, civilian noncompetitive, or military noncompetitive. Latin Americanists have adopted this typology widely, and it can easily be extended backward to 1945 and forward to 1980. Levels of competitiveness and militarization rarely change during the tenure of individual leaders, so we can aggregate the rankings to whole administrations.

The nature of the regime leads to sharp differences in the gains or losses of budget shares. Sixteen of forty military-noncompetitive administrations (40 percent) gave the armed forces the first or second largest budgetary increase among the five basic programs (military, health, education, public works, and agriculture). Only six of fifty-four civilian-competitive administrations (11 percent) and only five of twenty-seven civilian-noncompetitive administrations (18.5 percent) ranked the military first or second. Overall, military-led administrations were three times more likely than civilian administrations to give a first or second budgetary priority to the armed forces.[9]

Why did military governments spend more? In light of the theoretical arguments elaborated earlier in this book, four sources of changes in spending on the military merit investigation: increases in "illegitimate" political participation before the military took power, a low priority for the military's budget in the preceding administration, the threat of a military coup, and a tight overall budget. Once again, administrations will be labeled military noncompetitive, civilian noncompetitive, and civilian competitive. Expenditure data exist for only 109 administrations, so the analysis will be restricted to simple bivariate relationships.

"Illegitimate" Participation

Certain forms of politics, particularly strikes, demonstrations, and armed attacks, question the government's monopoly on the use of force. These actions threaten governments. Because elites dominate the language of political life, such forms of participation are usually classed as "illegitimate."

9. Moreover, the competitiveness of two of the civilian-competitive administrations that did favor the armed forces is somewhat doubtful. Robles in Panama was impeached by the National Assembly and kept in power by the National Guard. Ydígoras Fuentes in Guatemala was chosen by the Congress in a fraudulent vote.

How does illegitimate participation translate into budgetary rewards for the armed forces? *Overall levels* of military force are a function of past domestic insurgencies and international conflicts. Given the virtual absence of interstate disputes in Latin America in this period, the *change* in priority accorded to the military ought to be a function of change in the level of insurgent threat. Such changes, or "upsurges," of illegitimate activity were defined as a 300 percent increase in any of four indicators: protest demonstrations, riots, armed attacks, and deaths from domestic violence.[10]

Tables 16 and 17 reveal that military administrations are most likely to follow periods of rising illegitimate participation. Civilian-competitive administrations, on the other hand, are least likely to appear after such an upsurge. The expenditure consequences are even more striking: Military administrations are much more likely to respond to upsurges in illegitimate participation by strengthening the armed forces. Civilian-noncompetitive leaders are slightly more likely to spend on the military than their civilian-competitive counterparts, but both are quite distinct from military administrations. If illegitimate participation has been stable or declining, military leaders are still about three times as likely as civilians to favor the military budget, but at such times even military executives seldom respond with expenditures. The central finding, then, is the extraordinary fiscal response of military-led administrations to upsurges in illegitimate participation. Civilian regimes buy carrots; military regimes buy guns.

10. The standard source for counts of semilegal and illegal political activity is the *World Handbook of Political and Social Indicators,* authored by Bruce Russett and others (1964) and by Charles Taylor and Michael Hudson (1983). Covering 1948–1977, its volumes provide annual country-specific information. The data were aggregated to whole administrations. The standard of 300 percent for defining upsurges is obviously arbitrary. These administrations were all coded as *following* such upsurges: Perón (Argentina, 1951–1954, 1955); Paz Estenssoro (1956–1960, 1960–1964) and Barrientos (Bolivia); Castello and Costa e Silva (Brazil); Allende and Pinochet (Chile); Laureano Gómez, Rojas Pinilla, Alberto Lleras Camargo, Carlos Lleras Restrepo, and Turbay Ayala (Colombia); Costa Rica, none; Balaguer (Dominican Republic, 1966–1970, 1971–1977); Velasco Ibarra (Ecuador, 1961); Molina and Romero (El Salvador); Castillo Armas, Peralta, and Méndez Montenegro (Guatemala); Ruíz Cortines, Echeverria, and López Portillo (Mexico); Tacho (Nicaragua); Alcibiades Arosemena, Chiari, Robles, and Torrijos (Panama); Stroessner (Paraguay); Odría, Belaúnde, and Morales Bermúdes (Peru); Pérez Jiménez, Betancourt, and Leoni (Venezuela).

Table 16. *Administration Type and Prior Upsurges in Illegitimate Political Activity*

Administration Type	Activity Rose in Administration of Predecessor	No Change in Activity in Administration of Predecessor
Military Noncompetitive	15	17
Civilian Noncompetitive	10	16
Civilian Competitive	15	36
	40	69

Table 17. *Prior Upsurges, Administration Type, and Current Ranking of Military's Budget Share*

	Activity Rose		Activity Stable or Declining	
Administration Type	*Military 1st or 2nd*	*Military 3rd–5th*	*Military 1st or 2nd*	*Military 3rd–5th*
Military Noncompetitive	9	6	3	14
Civilian Noncompetitive	2	8	3	13
Civilian Competitive	2	13	3	33
	13	27	9	60

Prior Budgetary Cuts

Leaders ignore the corporate interests of the armed forces at their peril. How do different types of administrations respond to cuts made in the military's budget share during *previous* administrations? Table 18 compares administrations following a period of low priority for the armed forces (budgetary rank 4–5) to those following a period of high priority (rank 1–3). Military administrations are actually slightly more likely to succeed an administration that treated the armed forces well, but this is mostly a consequence of the greater likelihood of one military administration following another.

At first glance, Table 19 indicates that military executives react strongly to prior budgetary cuts. Military-led governments are five times more likely than civilians to reverse budgetary neglect. But military governments respond to periods of *high* rewards for the armed forces almost as strongly; that is, military administrations

Table 18. *Administration Type and Prior Budget Cuts*

Administration Type	Previous Administration Ranked Military Share 4th or 5th	Previous Administration Ranked Military Share 1st, 2nd, 3rd
Military Noncompetitive	10	22
Civilian Noncompetitive	10	16
Civilian Competitive	22	29
	42	67

Table 19. *Administration Type, Prior Budget Cuts, and Current Ranking of Military Share*

Administration Type	Previous Administration Ranked Military Share 4th or 5th		Previous Administration Ranked Military Share 1st, 2nd, 3rd	
	Current Share 1–2	*Current Share 3–5*	*Current Share 1–2*	*Current Share 3–5*
Military Noncompetitive	5	5	7	15
Civilian Noncompetitive	1	9	4	12
Civilian Competitive	2	20	3	26
	8	34	14	53

are four times as likely as civilian-competitive administrations to favor the armed forces even if they did well under the prior administration. In other words, prior budgetary neglect is a positive but weak determinant of expenditure response.

Military Pacification

In Chapter 2 we saw that administrations faced with the threat of military overthrow respond by increasing the military's budget share. Here the question is narrower: How do different *types* of administrations respond to that threat?

When the military must be pacified, military-noncompetitive administrations are five times more likely than civilian-competitive administrations to respond by favoring the military budget (see

Table 20.   *Military Pacification, Administration Type, and Expenditure
Response*

Administration Type	Pacification Necessary[a]		Pacification Not Necessary[a]	
	Military Share 1–2	Military Share 3–5	Military Share 1–2	Military Share 3–5
Military Noncompetitive	7	12	5	8
Civilian Noncompetitive	4	6	1	15
Civilian Competitive	2	24	3	22
	13	42	9	45

[a]Administrations were classified in terms of the importance of pacifying the military according to the criteria of Chapter 2—that is, frequency of coups, recency of the last coup, and so forth.

Table 20).[11] In the absence of a pacification problem, military-noncompetitive administrations are still 3.2 times more likely to favor the armed forces. Table 20 also shows that civilian-competitive and noncompetitive administrations behave very differently. Civilian-noncompetitive administrations respond dramatically to the need to pacify the armed forces, while civilian-competitive administrations fail to respond at all. Perhaps noncompetitive administrations are free to reshape budgetary allocations because they do not face hostile legislatures or honest elections. The real split in dealing with potential coups is therefore not between military and civilian administrations; it is between competitive and noncompetitive administrations. Competitive administrations have trouble finding the resources to buy sticks, because the demand for carrots is very high.

The Constraint of Austerity

We saw earlier that per capita levels of military spending are a poor indicator of the military's budgetary priority, because per capita indicators miss the context of budgetary change. Military expansion while other components of the budget are growing implies something quite different from military expansion while the base is steady or shrinking.

11. The military budget is favored by seven of nineteen military-noncompetitive administrations but only two of twenty-six civilian-competitive administrations.

Table 21. *Budgetary Austerity and Administration Type*

	Change in Total Spending	
Administration Type	*Less Than Predecessor*	*More Than Predecessor*
Military Noncompetitive	16	15
Civilian Noncompetitive	9	13
Civilian Competitive	20	22
	45	50

Table 21 shows that administration type is unrelated to changes in the volume of overall expenditures. But in Table 22 we see once again the sharply different proclivities of military administrations. When total spending is rising faster than it rose under the previous administration, military administrations are much more likely to expand the military's budget share. Civilian-competitive administrations rarely use budgetary largesse to benefit the armed forces, and civilian-noncompetitive administrations are even less likely to spend overall expenditure increases on the military.[12]

These findings are far from obvious. One might expect the military to reward its own whatever the overall budgetary constraint. Actually, the possibility of a larger budget liberates military administrations more than civilians. Military regimes do feel the constraint of a tight budget. Conversely, a rising total budget under a military regime trebles the chances of a high priority for the budget share of the armed forces.

Recapitulation

Two problems—insufficient attention to the *measurement* of military spending and insufficient attention to the factors that *motivate* it—led us to question the traditional conclusion that military government and military spending are unrelated. When we measured spending on the armed forces with a multiprogram ranking, it became clear that military-led administrations do favor the armed forces. Military and civilian administrations respond quite differently to upsurges in illegitimate participation, prior budget-

12. It might be objected that the inclusion of military spending itself contaminates the total budget. When the analysis was run using the total minus military expenditures, the results were very close to those given above.

Table 22. *Budgetary Austerity, Administration Type, and Expenditure Response*

	Change in Total Spending			
	Less Than Predecessor		*More Than Predecessor*	
Administration Type	*Military Share 1–2*	*Military Share 3–5*	*Military Share 1–2*	*Military Share 3–5*
Military Noncompetitive	3	13	9	6
Civilian Noncompetitive	2	7	2	11
Civilian Competitive	1	19	3	19
	6	39	14	36

ary neglect, threats of coups, and fiscal austerity. These concepts by no means exhaust the causes of military spending, but they offer important clues about the sources of military behavior.

Overall Patterns of Postcrisis Spending

Our inquiries in this chapter have thus far been related quite directly to the theoretical center of the book—the survival behavior of executives. Leaders, we have assumed, are concerned primarily with keeping their positions. This limiting assumption, that executive preferences can be equated to mere retention of office, is defensible during political crises, but to assume that we can explain *postcrisis* policy with such an extreme simplification would be wrong.

Implicit in the survival model is a broader view of the determinants of policy. In this broader view, public policies are consequences of the interactions of politically relevant actors, each with a set of preferred outcomes and each with a certain degree of power or influence to promote these outcomes. Both dimensions, power and preferences, affect policy. When we speak of the "characteristics of administrations," we mean the institutional arrangements—the structures of power—that magnify or shrink political influence.

The number of characteristics with the potential to affect policy, even if policy is limited to government spending, is very large. Simple typologies like "military versus civilian control of the executive" actually subsume a multiplicity of widely varying regime characteristics, including cohesiveness, degree of control over mass media, coerciveness, nature of societal cleavages, electoral system, level of citizen participation in politics, bureaucratic expertise, and so on. Research based on cross-national statistical estimations typically focuses on a much more restricted set of administration characteristics. Whether constructing new typologies or linking established typologies to outputs, cross-national studies avoid concepts not easily quantified and concentrate instead on three kinds of regime characteristics. In terms of the organization of civil society, one theme is the balance of vertical versus horizontal organization, the strength of challengers to the existing distribution of resources (especially unions), and the degree of "illegitimate" mobilization (especially the level of civil violence). A second theme in cross-national research is the nature of the executive in terms of military involvement or the competitiveness of executive selection. A third theme is the balance of state versus society, especially the dominance of one or the other or the functioning of intermediate institutions such as legislatures or political parties (Remmer 1978).

Implicitly or explicitly, cross-national statistical analyses view regime characteristics as constraints on leaders or, more precisely, as constraints on leaders' preferences. Measuring preferences, unfortunately, is very difficult. Even if we could categorize a regime's public expressions of preferences as either survival or substantive, the collection of comparable information across many countries and periods is a daunting task. Cross-national statistical research usually strives to include large numbers of nations, but for many countries the monographic literature is quite weak. As a result, models analyzing regime characteristics ignore the question of leaders' preferences.

Most social science models leave out significant aspects of reality, so the absence of explicit measures of preferences in policy models is hardly a unique failure. Regrettably, cross-national policy studies almost never offer enough information about specific cases to allow readers to test their own hypotheses. Measures of preferences—surely a major determinant of outputs—are left out, but scholars interested in elaborating and testing such measures get little help.

An extended discussion of preferences is a research project in itself, a project beyond the scope of this chapter. Instead, in this section I identify clusters of administrations exhibiting similar expenditure patterns. Such clusters can guide future investigation by offering clues about executive preferences.

The first cluster is based on the traditional notion of Latin American reformism. Our image of reformist administrations usually includes an expansion of social services coupled with a reduction of military influence (Anderson 1967). Reformist administrations stress education and health spending at the expense of the socially wasteful armed forces. If these "social liberals" are defined as administrations giving highest priority to increases in education and health (in either order) and ranking military spending last or next to last, only eight executives meet the standard:

de la Guardia (1956–1960), Panama

Dutra (1946–1951), Brazil

Lleras Camargo (1958–1962), Colombia

López Mateos (1958–1964), Mexico

Luis Somoza (1956–1963), Nicaragua

Sánchez Hernández (1967–1972), Guatemala

Torres (1970–1971), Bolivia

Trejos (1966–1970), Costa Rica

Administrations of this type are about as likely to be competitive as noncompetitive. Social liberal administrations are almost never military: Bolivia's Juan José Torres is the only military leader in the group, and he lasted less than one year. The social liberals also tend to come either from countries at low levels of social mobilization (Panama, Guatemala, Bolivia, Nicaragua) or from more advanced countries in an earlier period (Brazil in the late 1940s, Mexico and Colombia around 1960). It is striking, indeed, that many come from the early years of the Alliance for Progress.

The scarcity of competitive governments in this group results from the high cost of social liberalism. For *noncompetitive* social liberals the "economic strain" of government expenditures (measured by the ratio of the change in total spending to the change in the gross domestic product) actually declined—that is, their increase in expenditures was less than the increase in GDP. For *competitive* administrations, however, fiscal strain was part of the price of social liberalism—their total expenditures increased 2.4 times faster than the GDP. These governments felt obliged to cushion, by expanding the total budget, the relative loss suffered by the armed forces.

Social liberal governments rarely followed particularly liberal executives. None, for example, succeeded administrations in which education and health were ranked first and second, and in five of the eight cases they followed military leaders who had expanded the military budget and whose nonmilitary expenditures emphasized large-scale public works. As Anderson (1967:289) notes: "The presence of one regime in some ways makes the achievements of its successor possible."

Why are social liberals not found in more advanced countries? Note that these profiles classify administrations according to the *changes* they implemented in spending, not the levels of their budgetary shares. The fastest growth in demand for social services, and thus the fastest growth in spending, should occur during the emergence onto the political scene of middle-class and working-class groups. This period of emergence has occurred more recently in countries like Guatemala and Bolivia, but it is long completed in Chile, Argentina, and Uruguay. In the latter countries other demands, especially those for job creation, have come to the fore. At the same time, the post–World War II decline in military spending that is characteristic of advanced countries like Argentina, Chile, Brazil, and Uruguay was dramatically reversed with the coming to power of authoritarian regimes in the 1960s and 1970s.

Completely reversing the expenditure pattern of the social liberals, one group of administrations gave military spending first or second priority and accorded lowest rank to health and education. Total expenditures increased barely more than the increase in the GDP. These repressive leaders were very confident, and they felt no need to cushion losers by expanding the total budget. Their ranks include some of the most infamous regimes in recent Latin American history:[13]

Banzer (1971–1976), Bolivia
Chaves (1949–1954), Paraguay
Laugerud (1974–1978), Guatemala

13. In the case of Argentina's Onganía, however, military spending was not directed so much at repression as at simple enrichment of the officer corps.

Médici (1969–1973), Brazil
Onganía (1966–1969), Argentina
Paz Estenssoro (1960–1964), Bolivia
Pérez Jiménez (1952–1958), Venezuela
Pinochet (1973–), Chile
Rojas Pinilla (1953–1957), Colombia
Romero (1977–1979), El Salvador
Torrijos (1968–1978), Panama
Videla (1976–1981), Argentina

Military administrations were somewhat more likely to fit this pattern than civilian-noncompetitive administrations, but among fifty-two civilian-competitive administrations, none fell into this category. Only two of the presidents were not actually military officers. Federico Chaves took power in Paraguay during a period of intraparty feuding following the overthrow of dictator Higenio Moriñigo. Chaves was never elected on a contested ballot, and Alfredo Stroessner finally pushed him out. Bolivia's Victor Paz Estenssoro came into office for the first time in 1952 after an insurrection backed by a populist coalition of middle-class and working-class groups. When he was voted back into power in 1960, the economy had collapsed and the U.S. government was supplying 30 to 40 percent of the Bolivian central government budget (Malloy 1970). The price of U.S. aid was a reorientation of Paz's coalition away from the poor. That reorientation could only be consolidated by rebuilding the armed forces to carry out their function as protectors of order (Mitchell 1977).

Leaders in this group often justified their policies as necessary to control armed insurrections, but in fact they were not especially likely to face violent opposition. Laugerud, Romero, Videla, and Rojas Pinilla did come to power in the midst of guerrilla or terrorist activities, but Torrijos and Banzer began their terms with little or no armed opposition, and Onganía hardly faced any at all. Even Médici was very much in control of the weak armed opposition that existed in Brazil.

Perhaps this group's most striking quality is its diversity of economic and social levels. Médici and Videla fall into the more advanced bureaucratic-authoritarian (BA) camp and Onganía represents a BA regime unable to establish itself, but clearly none of the others are at that level. For this group personal substantive preferences (rather than economic or social factors) led to their particular combination of reaction and repression, but those preferences remain unexplained.

A third group of administrations stressed health and education while also according the military a high priority. The group included:

Arbenz (1951–1954), Guatemala
Arias (1949–1951), Panama
Balaguer (1966–1978), Dominican Republic
Betancourt (1958–1963), Venezuela
Díaz Ordaz (1964–1970), Mexico
Illía (1963–1966), Argentina
Leoni (1963–1968), Venezuela
Méndez Montenegro (1966–1970), Guatemala
Osorio (1950–1956), El Salvador
Peralta (1963–1966), Guatemala
Remón (1952–1955), Panama
Roldós (1979–1981), Ecuador
Valencia (1962–1966), Colombia
Villeda Morales (1957–1963), Honduras

These "defensive liberals" were mostly competitive or at least semicompetitive. Only one military ruler rearranged expenditures in this pattern, and competitive administrations were about three times as likely to appear as noncompetitive ones.[14]

With the exceptions of Illía of Argentina and Betancourt and Leoni of Venezuela, defensive liberals came from less-developed countries. Betancourt and Illía were both successors to military governments, and both faced serious military pacification problems. Leoni's army faced the task of coping with an armed rural guerrilla movement.

A striking difference between the social liberals (education and health first, defense last) and these defensive liberals lies in the fiscal strain each accepted. Social liberals spent at a rate three times

14. This group was defined by its ranking of military, education, and health in the top three, in any order.

higher than their GDP gain. Defensive liberals, on the other hand, increased spending little more than the increase in the GDP. Was the support the defensive liberals gave to the military budget simply a way of ensuring that the military maintained its absolute level of expenditure receipts even when economic growth was too low to support an increase in the total budget? Actually, just the opposite is true: During their administrations the defensive liberals enjoyed an average increase in GDP more than double the increase experienced by the social liberals. In other words: Social liberals accepted a much greater inflationary risk when they increased social spending at the expense of the military.

Our final expenditure cohort might be referred to as "builders." These administrations ranked public works spending first or second and military spending fourth or fifth. They included:

Alemán (1946–1952), Mexico
Banzer (1976–1980), Bolivia
Barrientos (1966–1969), Bolivia
Belaúnde (1963–1968), Peru
Bustamente (1945–1948), Peru
Castillo Armas (1954–1957), Guatemala
Figueres (1970–1974), Costa Rica
Frei (1964–1970), Chile
Kubitschek (1956–1960), Brazil
Lanusse (1971–1973), Argentina
Gómez (1950–1951), Colombia
Lleras Restrepo (1966–1970), Colombia
Lucas García (1978–1982), Guatemala
Odría (1950–1956), Peru
Orlich (1962–1966), Costa Rica
Quadros (1961), Brazil
Ulate (1949–1953), Costa Rica
Vargas (1951–1954), Brazil
Velasco Ibarra (1968–1971), Ecuador

Builders were equally likely to be competitive or noncompetitive, civilian or military. Only four of nineteen represented countries as poor as Bolivia or Guatemala. Levels of fiscal strain were moderate, with expenditure increases averaging a little less than twice GDP increases, but the average level of GDP growth was a very high 5.6 percent.

These administrations were as likely to face a military pacification problem as social or defensive liberals, but they adopted policies penalizing the armed forces and favoring projects with payoffs further in the future. For some, the rewards from additional social spending might have begun to diminish. For others, accelerated economic growth required better infrastructure. The fact that GDP was increasing may well have been crucial. Executives expecting substantial resource increases can afford a longer time perspective. Because not every project has to produce an immediate payoff, public works and agriculture can enjoy budgetary largesse. Most important, total expenditures can grow, so losses in the shares of individual programs are not inevitably transformed into losses in absolute spending.

Conclusion

The main argument of this book concerns a set of choices made by executives confronted with a specific problem. Among the many policy areas leaders affect, the book focuses on only one: public expenditures. Among the many problems leaders face, it considers just one: survival. That this perspective opens up important, even critical strategic dilemmas should be evident.

This chapter went beyond the narrowest limitations of the survival perspective to show the usefulness of the approach in a wider but still cross-national framework. The inquiry centered on the consequences of allocations for avoiding coups and winning elections, on the differences in allocations between military and nonmilitary administrations, and on the existence of overall allocation patterns. The answers to these questions have no bearing on the rightness or wrongness of the survival theory itself. Instead, they are guides to using strategic approaches to answer some of the broader questions posed by Latin Americanists and political scientists in general.

The contribution of spending to avoiding coups and winning elections is a logical step in the theoretical argument. Granted that leaders spent the way they were expected to spend, did it help?

Spending on the military did help keep the armed forces at bay, but leaders making it to the next election found the resources they could devote to social and economic programs insufficient to improve their electoral chances by very much. Moreover, the electoral process itself proved costly: Administrations facing midterm elections were forced to increase expenditures just to maintain popularity and legislative strength.

The old question of the policy outputs of military governments was broached precisely because no one has resolved it adequately, although most researchers deny the existence of a military government/military spending relationship. In this chapter, I used a multiprogram ranking of expenditure changes to evaluate leaders' intentions. Using this ranking, the search for the factors determining civilian-military differences revealed that military administrations do spend more on their armed forces. Military governments spend more, it turns out, because they respond differently to domestic violence, budgetary neglect, threats of coups, and fiscal austerity.

Finally, we made a brief search for overall patterns of postcrisis spending. Explanation of these patterns proceeds no further here, because the assembly and codification of systematic information about leaders' policy preferences is a research project in itself. What we have, instead, is a restatement of the puzzle in the shape of a simple typology. The administrations grouped in this typology are important as much for what they fail to explain as for their successes. The repressive-reactionary group cannot be explained either by certain levels of socioeconomic development or by the intensity of popular mobilization, and "builders" could be competitive, noncompetitive, military, or civilian. Our inability to explain these administrations takes us back to the importance of substantive preferences. How did these leaders come to adopt the patterns of spending revealed here? That question is left to future researchers.

Does a dominant theme emerge from this brief excursion into postsurvival policy? If so, it is the fragility of political power. Latin American executives do survive their political crises, but they rarely attain the security and autonomy of their counterparts in industrialized nations. If an executive represents a civilian-competitive regime, the chances of his party electing its successor are slim, and the possibility of implementing a policy package significantly improving those chances is equally poor. When competitively elected leaders face midterm elections, the cost of the political process itself distorts budgets and adds to inflationary pressures. If leaders want to increase spending on social programs, they must boost military spending as well. The only escape from this trap is budgetary expansion, but expansion merely pushes the trade-off into the future. Democratic political leadership in Latin America faces nearly unbeatable odds.

Military regimes differ little from civilians during their initial survival crises, but once crises abate the policies of military-led governments diverge radically. Overall budgets grow more slowly under military leadership, but the increase in spending on the armed forces is marked. Numerous factors trigger spending *by* the military *on* the military, including civil violence, the threat of a coup, and growth in resources. Military regimes seem to replace the politics of compromise and coalition with austerity, corporate self-interest, and repression.

Part II: Two Applications of the Theory

Part II applies strategic coalition theory to Brazil. The two chapters do not test the theory developed in Part I. Rather, Part II *extends* the theory: examining aspects of expenditure policy that cannot be studied cross-nationally, analyzing the strategies of lower-level political actors, and evaluating policy areas unrelated to public spending. The ability of survival coalition theory to guide the detailed studies of Part II is a demonstration of the broad utility of the approach.

Chapter 4, "The Congress Connection," examines the role of the Brazilian Congress in budget making between 1947 and 1964. This period was the high point of pluralism in Brazil, a period in which the Congress exercised real authority over central government expenditures. The chapter focuses on the Congress rather than the president because the Congress was the center of an influence structure involving state and national elections, local and regional elites, and linkages to the presidency and the ministers of the central government. In effect, a particular political structure, a congress full of politicians with their own survival strategies, affected the strategic options of the president. Though elected on a statewide basis, deputies sought to attract funds to their local electoral bailiwicks. To do so they manipulated committees and amendments in the style of classic pork barrel politics. The overall success of states (rather than individual deputies) in attracting central government largesse turns out to depend in part on the efforts of these individual legislators and in part on the organization of the legislative body, on intrastate political conflict, and on the socioeconomic bases of state politics.

Chapter 5, "When Soldiers Need Friends," treats the policy consequences of the transition to democracy of Brazil's post-1964 military regime, a transition that took place during the 1974–1984 administrations of Generals Geisel and Figueiredo. The chapter extends the notion of a "survival strategy" to consider a strategic option not contingent on maintaining office. In this case, the main political actor, the military, sought to build support so that it could remain influential *after* the end of formal military rule. It was not the survival of incumbency, but of influence, that the generals sought, and they wanted to construct a base of support that would make them indispensable to the survival of *future* incumbents.

After suggesting a series of strategies the regime could have followed, I attempt to determine what the Geisel and Figueiredo administrations actually did. Because the expenditures of the central ministries are only a small part of state activity, I consider four policy areas in addition to expenditure trade-offs: agricultural programs in the Northeast, low-cost housing, industrial deconcentration, and wage and salary setting.

In the end, the regime fared poorly. Two factors proved fundamental in impeding its efforts at building support: the acceleration of the economic decline and the fragmentation of the structure of policy making caused by the survival strategies of lesser political actors.

4. The Congress Connection: Politics and Expenditures in Brazil's Competitive Period

Elites are not the only political actors who care about survival. Wherever parliaments have influence independent of executives, legislators pursue their own survival strategies. When legislators represent distinct subnational entities such as states or local communities, they strive to increase pork barrel programs, because such programs allow them to claim credit for the benefits they bring to their constituents.

Executive and legislative survival strategies operate in different ways. Though executives sometimes adopt localist strategies, they use such approaches to reward some localities and penalize others. Legislative localism, by contrast, stresses mutual cooperation and the sharing of rewards among as many legislators as possible. It is no surprise, then, that presidents and legislatures are often at odds. The decline of Chile's Congress in the 1960s, for example, has been indirectly linked to the overthrow of President Salvador Allende (Valenzuela and Wilde 1979), and Ecuador's Congress played a central role in the overthrow of a democratically elected president in that nation (Pyne 1973). Legislatures are also a frequent object of criticism launched by technocratically oriented civilian planners. Their attacks frequently center on the very stuff of legislative politics: bargaining, trading, logrolling—in sum, the politics of pork. But for legislatures, they argue, budgets could be implemented in accordance with national priorities and resources rather than local needs and the reelection strategies of incumbent legislators. Roberto Campos, a civilian architect of Brazil's military regime, made the point succinctly:

> Because of its hypersensitivity to regional pressures capable of destroying the coherence and balance of plans and programs, the Congress

had been transformed into an "inflation machine" multiplying the budget and into a "distortion factor" vis-à-vis investments (Mendes 1975:36).

Is Campos right? Do legislatures inevitably increase and redistribute spending to suit electoral needs? Many scholars agree. James Scott, for example, suggests that elections in Southeast Asia shift the balance of exchange in the direction of clients. Regimes under pressure to engage in distribution "resort to budget deficits, especially in election years, to finance their networks of adherents" (Scott 1972:113). Raymond Hopkins (1979) reports that in Kenya and Tanzania congressmen used central government funding to boost their electoral chances. On the other side, Arturo Valenzuela and Alexander Wilde (1979) agree that Chilean legislators logrolled on behalf of local interests, but they argue that legislative politics had the beneficial effect of reducing conflict and that only a small percentage of the budget was diverted to truly wasteful projects.

For which legislators is the pursuit of pork—of geographically separable public spending—a survival strategy? Under what conditions?[1] In developing countries we still have very few answers to these questions. The biggest obstacle to understanding legislative survival strategies is the absence of data. Rarely is information about both legislative budgets and final expenditures available over a period of years, and even more rarely can final expenditures be linked to specific constituencies.

This chapter explores legislative strategies affecting the distribution of central government expenditures to Brazilian states between 1947 and 1964. In these years the Brazilian Congress was an active participant in the budgetary process.[2] The chapter treats

1. A promising start in answering these questions has been made in research on South Korea. Kim and Woo (1975) found that constituency service in the Korean assembly was related to a variety of factors. Certain parties were more constituency-oriented than others; rural assemblymen were more active than their urban counterparts; veterans were less active than junior members; and members from single-member districts were more active than those elected at large. Although Kim and Woo's concept of constituency service excluded budgetary appropriations (which the legislature could not modify), their findings could extend to a broader notion of legislative pork barrel.

2. Brazilianists have not systematically treated this topic, but there has been considerable writing about other aspects of the Congress. For essays on such topics as party alignments, voting mechanisms, social backgrounds of deputies, budgetary incrementalism, recruitment, and styles of representation, see Santos (1979), Car-

the Congress as the focal point—though in no sense the sole determinant—of an influence process involving state and national elections, local and regional elites, and linkages to the presidency and the ministries of the central government. The strategic activities of congressmen turn out to be consequences of the decision-making structure of the legislative body, intrastate political conflict, the socioeconomic bases of state politics, and the individual motivations of legislators to seek geographically targetable public goods.

The discussion is divided into four parts. The first section begins with a brief introduction to the formal and informal structure of pre-1964 Brazilian politics. I then examine movements of selected expenditures in order to demonstrate that considerable change occurred over the course of the pluralist epoch. The next section develops a model of legislative survival strategies affecting the expenditure process. The following section evaluates the hypotheses generated by the model and explores a number of deviant cases. The chapter concludes with a brief comparison of the pluralist years to the authoritarian period that began in 1964. Appendix B at the end of the book discusses some problems in evaluating the model developed here.

The Development of Competitive Politics

Political Background

Getúlio Vargas assumed the presidency of Brazil in 1930, victor in a revolution that marked the beginning of the modern Brazilian state (Fausto 1970). That revolution had ended the Old Republic, a regime dominated by coffee planters and the governors of economically powerful São Paulo, Minas Gerais, and Rio Grande do Sul. The origins of the revolution of 1930 remain historically controversial, but the struggle clearly led to a more centralized and interventionist government, a government that could break the hold of the planters and admit the military and middle class into political life.

---

valho (1973), Fleischer (1976, 1977, 1981), Lima Junior (1977), Nunes (1978), and Packenham (1971).

Vargas gradually consolidated presidential authority until, in 1937, he created the Estado Nôvo, the New State: centralized, antiparty, repressive, and nationalistic. Free from the restraints of liberal constitutionalism, the government began to innovate, expanding welfare policies, fostering and controlling unions through its new Ministry of Labor, and investing directly in steel, iron ore, and river valley development. Although the tentative industrialization that followed was partly a consequence of the collapse of Brazil's import capacity in the world depression and World War II, the government's self-transformation had enabled it to become an active participant in economic management.

Centralization during the Estado Nôvo also affected the *political* process (Souza 1976). Vargas closed the Congress and replaced most governors with powerful federal appointees. The new Administrative Department of the Public Service (DASP) acted as a superministry at the federal level, and little DASPs served the same function in the states. To circumvent the traditional bureaucracy, Vargas and his advisers created new autarchic agencies and public enterprises. Increases in the power of the armed forces (at the expense of the once largely autonomous state militias) expanded the military's role in national policy making to include such issues as industrial development.

At the conclusion of World War II, pressure to liberalize the regime became irresistible. In a bloodless coup, the military removed Vargas. A constituent assembly soon produced a new constitution, a document that established the formal structure governing Brazilian political competition until the military coup of 1964.

The Constitution of 1946 created a presidential system with a bicameral legislature. Three senators, elected to staggered eight-year terms in majority elections, represented each state. In the Chamber of Deputies each state was entitled to seats in proportion to its population except for two deviations: No state had fewer than seven seats, and above twenty seats each new seat required 250,000 electors rather than 150,000. The rules thus penalized large industrial states, especially São Paulo, in favor of small, rural, and poor states.[3] Deputies were elected to concurrent four-

3. Conservative representatives to the constituent assembly from industrial states accepted this arrangement, because limiting the influence of the urban work-

year terms through a system of proportional representation. Whole states constituted districts, and electors (literate adults) selected one candidate from a party list. After the balloting, votes for all candidates on each party's list were added together, and the fraction of the total vote represented by each party's share determined the number of seats allocated to that party. The number of votes each candidate had received determined the actual holders of the seats.

Getúlio Vargas's influence over Brazilian politics did not disappear with his ouster in 1945. At the close of the Estado Nôvo, Vargas and his followers organized two political parties. The Social Democratic Party (PSD) rooted itself in the state political machines Vargas had fostered. Though influential everywhere, the PSD was particularly strong in rural areas and poorer states. The Brazilian Labor Party (PTB), by contrast, was organized by Varguistas in the Labor Ministry and the unions. The PTB's strength was concentrated in big cities (though not in São Paulo) and in Vargas's home state of Rio Grande do Sul. As time passed, the PTB also became home to a diverse collection of dissidents from other parties.

The major opposition to the Varguistas came from the National Democratic Union (UDN). The UDN combined losers in the intra-oligarchic power struggles of the Estado Nôvo, constitutionalists who opposed the dictatorship on principle, and upper-middle-class city dwellers repelled as much by the populism of the PTB as the conservatism of the PSD (Benevides 1981). Though laissez-faire constituted the most important current of UDN economic thinking, its raison d'être was opposition to Vargas.

The UDN's hopes that the dictator's fall would lead to its own ascension to power were dashed at the end of 1945, when the joint candidate of the PSD and PTB, General Eurico Dutra, was elected president. The PSD received 42 percent of the congressional vote and took 52 percent of the seats in the Chamber of Deputies. The UDN came in second, with 29 percent of the seats, and the PTB finished a distant third with less than 8 percent.

The Dutra administration was cautious in its economic policy. By 1947 Brazil's hard currency reserves from World War II had

ing class was more important than the interests of their own states. (See Souza 1976, Soares 1973, and Kinzo 1980.)

disappeared, and huge deficits appeared on the current account. Rather than devalue the currency, the government adopted rigid import controls. Import substitution in consumer durables began, but the government's share of national income stagnated and blockages in infrastructure became evident.

The election of 1950 returned Getúlio Vargas to office. The PSD had refused to go along with the PTB's nomination of Vargas, but many PSD supporters backed the former dictator anyway, and Vargas won an absolute majority of the popular vote. In the Chamber of Deputies the PSD lost its majority, never again surpassing 37 percent. The PTB doubled its seat share (to about 17 percent), and small parties became a major force.

Vargas's administration was both activist and limited. Public investment in energy and transportation increased, the National Economic Development Bank (BNDE) became a major source of investment capital, and the government controlled exchange rates to help ration imports. The government was unable, however, to increase taxes, and it met inflationary pressures in 1954 and 1955 with another try at contraction. But contraction and austerity were difficult to accept in the middle 1950s, because the vigorous industrial sector was quite import-dependent and Brazilian nationalism (encouraged by the government and fueled by Vargas's suicide in 1954) had grown enormously.[4]

In 1955 the PSD and PTB rebuilt its former alliance, electing Juscelino Kubitschek to the presidency. Kubitschek's "Target Program" was Brazil's first thoroughly developmentalist strategy (Lessa 1975). Emphasizing transport, energy, basic industry, and the construction of the city of Brasília, Kubitschek paid less attention to price stability, the balance of payments, agriculture, and income distribution. Though the resources for the program had to come from the government and foreign capital, domestic industrialists were supportive, because the government was creating new areas of growth and leaving intact the prerogatives of domestic capital.

Initially Kubitschek's strategy worked. Between 1957 and 1961 domestic production climbed 7.0 percent annually, and key sectors

4. At his death, Vargas left a letter attacking foreign enterprises for making exorbitant profits and for blocking the government's efforts to aid workers and take a bigger role in the economy. The letter unleashed a wave of public sympathy for Vargas and strengthened nationalist feeling. See Skidmore (1967).

like transportation advanced even faster. Brazil began the sixties with a more mature economy, but the financing of the development program inevitably encouraged a hyperinflation. Agricultural production per person had barely increased, regional disparities had worsened, and employment had grown less than the increase in the work force.

A political crisis paralleled the developing economic crisis. Rapid industrialization and urbanization had broken the dominance of the conservative parties, especially the PSD, but malapportionment and electoral instability prevented the emergence of a stable legislative realignment. Increasingly, deputies were elected by multiparty coalitions whose composition varied from state to state. These coalitions, moreover, were rarely based on enduring ideological differences, so they changed from election to election. The electoral rules also encouraged small parties to ally with larger ones as a way of guaranteeing themselves at least one legislative seat. Along with the overrepresentation of traditional regions like the Northeast, this combination of electoral instability and the diminished weight of the three major parties made the Congress consistently more conservative than the president and produced a legislative deadlock.[5] While President João Goulart (first elected vice president in 1960) was drifting leftward in the face of pressure from populist groups and challenges from conservative economic and military interests, Congress was in a state of disorder and paralysis. The legislative process came to a halt as both the number of bills introduced and the number passed shrank. The result was political and administrative chaos—a chaos that contributed, in no small measure, to the overthrow of the competitive regime at the end of March 1964.

Central Government Expenditures

The Brazilian Congress had constitutional authority over the national budget, but legal control over a budget does not translate automatically into effective control. Deputies might not see budgets as part of their survival strategies, and informal patterns of influence outside the Congress could negate their efforts. But public expenditures were strategically important for Brazilian congressmen, and though some important political actors bypassed

5. See Soares (1964, 1971, 1973), Schwartzman (1970), and Souza (1976).

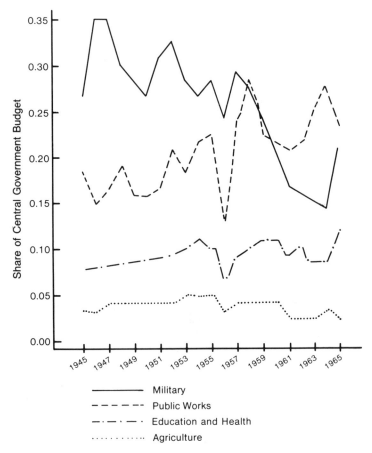

Figure 7. Program Shares: 1945–1965

the legislative branch to deal directly with the executive, most budget-related political activity did involve the Congress.

We begin our examination of congressional behavior with some simple expenditure patterns. Figure 7 shows the shares of final expenditures devoted to key programs between 1945 and 1965. The military was the chief loser, falling from 35 percent of expenditures in 1947 to just 14 percent in 1964.[6] Public works pro-

6. The military share is defined as the sum of all the military ministries and other military programs divided by the total of all central government spending.

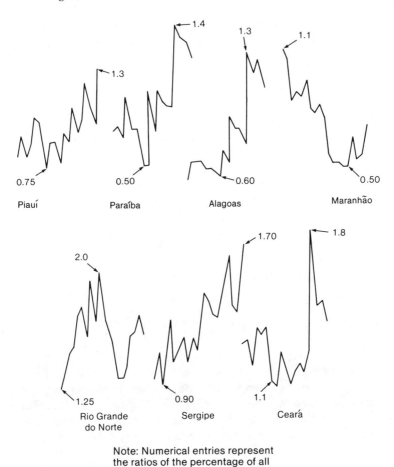

Note: Numerical entries represent the ratios of the percentage of all spending received by the state to its percentage of Brazil's population.

Figure 8. Central Government Spending on Northeastern States: 1948–1966

grams stagnated during Dutra's administration but prospered during the terms of Vargas and Kubitschek. Education and health programs, which aided increasingly powerful middle-class and working-class voters, grew steadily until the military takeover.

The programs enjoying the strongest growth are those often

called "pork barrel"—that is, programs targetable to specific regions or localities. Since the severe malapportionment of the Chamber of Deputies favored less-populated regions, small Northeastern states should have received more than their share of such programs. Overall, the small states of the Northeast did indeed improve their position. But if we examine these states separately, as in Figure 8, their budgetary record seems quite mixed. Four states clearly gained, two showed no trend, and one actually declined.

Figure 8 presents a puzzle. What explains the diverse movements of expenditures into states and programs? We know, of course, that pork barrel politics is legislative politics *par excellence*.[7] Did the legislative process produce the patterns in Figure 8? And if so, how?

Congressional Influence in the Expenditure Process

Why Legislators Want Pork

Legislators care about reelection. In the hope that voters will reward them, deputies support projects aiding their electoral bases. To ensure that their pet projects will pass the legislature, deputies seek allies who will join coalitions backing their projects. This search for allies leads to the time-honored practice of logrolling, each member supporting the projects of others in return for their support on his. The division of the total budget shifts to favor programs with more pork potential. Funds for hospitals, schools, and roads expand. Programs that cannot easily be subdivided or that barely affect individual districts (such as foreign relations or military wages) suffer.[8]

Unless legislators can claim credit for new government projects placed in their districts, they have no incentive to seek such projects. As a result, legislative survival strategies are affected by

7. See Lowi (1964). The geographically separable component of military spending does not seem to be as important for the military in Latin America as it is in the United States, probably because there is much less local procurement in Latin America.

8. The best theoretical statement of this position is found in Shepsle and Weingast (1981).

electoral laws. If each legislative district elects one representative, credit is unambiguous, but representation in Brazil was proportional, with whole states serving as multimember electoral districts. Did incentives for the pursuit of pork exist nonetheless? They did, for two reasons. Voters cast ballots for individual candidates, not for party lists, so voters could reward individual legislators. Moreover, many states developed a system of *informal* districts akin to the "bailiwicks" of Ireland.[9] Candidates concentrated their campaign efforts in these districts and drew most of their votes from them. So even though Brazil used a system of proportional representation, legislators seeking reelection should have attempted to influence the programmatic and geographic distribution of public expenditures.

Deputies seeking more central government spending in their states had a variety of options.[10] They could amend budget proposals with projects benefiting their bailiwicks, they could seek membership on committees dealing with budgets, and they could try to join the leadership of the Chambers or the party directorates. If all deputies' survival motivations were equally intense, no matter which states they represented, the malapportionment of the Brazilian Congress would benefit the poor, rural states of the Northeast. This was not the case. Not all Northeastern states were winners, and some states gained much more than others. What else counted, then? What conditions made some members of Congress more eager and more successful in the pursuit of targetable budgetary goods?

Insecurity. If deputies expect to seek future terms in office, the insecurity of their current seats stimulates their search for district-specific benefits. In Brazil's system of proportional representation, deputies' electoral fortunes were determined by their party list ranking after the balloting. Deputies with low ranks or bare mar-

9. On Ireland see Sacks (1976). For evidence of bailiwicks in Brazil see Fleischer (1976, 1977).

10. After proposed budgets were submitted by the president in the second quarter of each year, hearings were held by program-specific subcommittees of the Budget Committees of the Chamber and Senate. Presidential budgets could be amended in committee and on the floors of both chambers. Budgets were originally under the control of the Finance Committee, but in the early 1950s a Budget Committee was created. I shall usually refer to the Budget Committee, but in budgets made before its creation this is the Finance Committee.

gins of victory were uncertain of seats in future legislative sessions. Visible central government projects could help them rise in the party list at the next election. As deputies accumulated more seniority, however, their security increased, so the longer legislators held office, the lower were their motivations to seek pork.

Party Ethos. The National Democratic Union (UDN) was a partial exception to the undisciplined, clientelistic, and decentralized nature of Brazilian political parties. As Benevides (1981:172) points out, the raisons d'être of the UDN included fighting President Vargas, denouncing administrative corruption, and opposing government intervention in the economy. Udenistas emphasized order, austerity, and the importance of a national rather than a local vision. Udenista-held ministries tended to be in Foreign Relations, Justice, and the Treasury—the classic "collective goods" ministries. Many UDN deputies ignored the pieties of party leaders, of course, but to the extent that UDN legislators shared the party ethos, they would decrease their use of budget-increasing activities as survival strategies and increase their visibility as "Guardians of the Treasury" (Fenno 1966).

Bailiwicks. Though deputies in each state were elected at large, they often limited their campaigns to clearly delimited zones of political influence and electoral support (Fleischer 1976). The effects of such *redutos* ("strongholds") on legislative behavior depended on two considerations: the number of candidates from each deputy's own party who entered his electoral zone and the number of candidates from other parties who entered. If no opponents at all entered, the deputy obviously had a safe seat and no survival problems. If a few candidates from the deputy's own party entered, their votes would push the deputy down in the party list, reducing his chances of election, but these votes would add to the party's total, thereby increasing the deputy's chances. As the number of competitors from the deputy's own party grew, they would take votes from each other, and the likelihood of changes in rank would decrease. The deputy would benefit, and his budgetary incentives would decrease.

Candidates from other parties posed a greater threat. Votes going to these candidates pushed the candidate down in his own party list, so the deputy would be less likely to be a winner. But candidates from other parties also cut into the votes going to any candidate of the deputy's own party, so fewer total seats would be allotted to members of his party. We can expect competition from other parties, therefore, to stimulate deputies to seek projects for which they can claim credit.

Why States Get More Pork

Insecurity, party ethos, and bailiwicks all affected the budgetary strategies of *individual* deputies. The consequences of these individual survival strategies for allocations to states *in toto* are the subject of our second model. This model includes five delegation-wide characteristics: committee representation, stability, leadership, ministerial linkages, and occupational skills.

Committee Representation. How was committee membership determined? Seats on committees were distributed proportionately, first by party and then by state. There were too few members to enable each party and each state to have just the right number of members on each committee. Since *party* proportionality was the dominant criterion, *states* might be over- or underrepresented by as many as nine or ten members on a large committee. Indeed, the median misrepresentation per state over the whole competitive period was such that a typical state might have 15 percent too many or 15 percent too few members on a committee. "Extra" seats were important to the deputies, because seats increased state influence over a committee's substantive business.

In both the Senate and the Chamber, the Budget Committees were the key committees affecting expenditure legislation. After the executive sent a budget proposal to the Congress, the leadership of the Budget Committee divided the proposal into programs and picked individual committee members to be *relators*, that is, "narrators," for each program. *Relators* conducted hearings, gave opinions on amendments, wrote substitutes subsuming the individual amendments, and defended the committee bill on the floor. A negative committee opinion usually killed an amendment, and a favorable opinion almost always guaranteed passage.[11] Since extra members on a key committee would help states

11. Vocal opposition to the dominance of the Budget Committee was common, especially during its "Guardian of the Treasury" phase in the Dutra administration. See, for example, the speeches and motions of Deputy Jurandir Pires, *Diário do*

in the business of that committee, we can expect overrepresentation on the Budget Committee to increase spending in a state.

Delegation Turnover. Though the legislature began in 1947 as a
totally new body, seniority soon became a prerequisite for influence. States with unstable internal politics suffered higher turnover
and thus had fewer senior members. Such delegations were less
likely to produce leaders of the Chambers or party directorates
and less likely to hold seats on key committees.

At the same time, delegations with high turnover were more
likely to include electorally insecure members, and insecurity, as
we have seen, *increases* the motivations of individual deputies to
pursue survival strategies. Thus delegations with high turnover
were simultaneously more eager and less able to attract funds to
their states. As a result, we cannot predict the effects of delegation
stability.

Congressional Leadership. Each branch of Brazil's legislature
had two kinds of leaders: party leaders and Chamber leaders
(*mesa*).[12] Party leaders organized positions on issues, arranged
quorums on votes, and so on. Because the party directorates tried
to apportion leadership slots regionally, rather junior deputies
could aspire to them. These party directorates, however, were
somewhat less prestigious than the Chamber leaderships, because
the latter controlled committee assignments and the legislative calendar. Leaders were well positioned to garner bigger shares of
government programs, so we can expect states whose members
participated in these two leadership groups to receive more federal
largesse.

Vertical Linkages. Though the legislature was the pivot of budget
making, it operated in a rich context of ministries, state governors,
and presidents. Linkages worked in both directions: Parties and
states made claims on ministries, and the president involved him-

---

Congresso Nacional, September 24, 1948. The guardian role is much stronger in
a system like that of the United States. See Fenno (1966) and Pressman (1980) for
parallel treatments.

12. Party leaders included, for each party, a "leader" and a group of "vice
leaders." Chamber leaders included a president, two vice presidents, and four secretaries. The Chamber leadership was always headed by a deputy from the PSD.

self in the selection of Senate and Chamber leaders.[13] Ties between governors and presidents increased state bargaining power, and a successful electoral campaign in a state might encourage a president to look with favor upon its requests. Executive survival coalitions often included ministers from politically important states. These states gave support to the executive and gained influence over programs. A state's lobbying would be facilitated if its residents filled ministerial positions.

Skills. In any legislature, state delegations lobby for the interests of their states. Because good lobbyists need to be familiar with the details of programs, Brazilian congressmen usually gravitated to legislative activities related to the skills and expertise they brought into the Chambers. Military officers involved themselves in military programs; engineers worked on big construction projects; doctors dealt with health problems. A congressman should benefit when the fit between his skills and the committee's business was close.

Overall, governmental activities encompass many areas of expertise. The more limited the range of occupations in a state's delegation, the less often will its members find a committee matching their own specialties. If a delegation included members with a variety of professions, the overall match between programs and skills would be closer, and the delegation could place an expert near more programs. Thus delegations with more varied professional backgrounds were better positioned to attract government spending.

Analysis

In this section the hypotheses developed above are tested empirically. The analysis begins by considering the budget strategies of individual deputies. Next, I assess the budgetary success of whole states. The analysis then shifts from a cross-sectional to a dynamic mode, comparing congressional to presidential survival strategies over the whole pluralist period. Finally, I consider a select group of states individually, facilitating the examination of such factors as intrastate political conflict.[14]

13. See Café Filho (1966), Benevides (1976), and Cintra (1979).
14. A brief discussion of problems in operationalizing the hypotheses developed in this section is presented in Appendix C at the end of the book.

Individual Strategies

Budget Committee Membership. Without exception, deputies agreed which committees in the Chamber were the most sought after.[15] Constitution and Justice was crucial because it had the power to obstruct key legislation. Finance—later divided into two committees (one on finance and a second specifically on the budget)—was important because it handled central government expenditures.

An individual deputy's chances of getting a seat on a choice committee would improve if he had done well in the previous election. State party lists were often headed by some popular vote-getter who might well garner 50 percent of the total received by all the party's candidates. Because the votes of such deputies increased the party total and facilitated the election of less popular deputies, they were powerful legislators. In 1948, for example, the twenty-one members of the Chamber Finance Committee included six who had finished first on their lists. Since the average number of members elected per party was about nine, the twenty-one-person committee had more than double the number of first-place finishers it would have received on a random basis.[16] In 1952 the committee boasted twelve first-place finishers, once again double the number expected.

The success of first-place finishers in getting on the Finance Committee does not prove that electoral success always dominated insecurity and need in predicting committee membership. In only one session (1951–1955) did the budget-making committee's *over-all* composition—rather than merely its top vote-getters—reflect electoral success. In that session twenty-seven of the thirty-eight members of the Finance Committee finished in the top half of their lists.

The reason why top vote-getters—the state heavyweights—chose budget-making committees in the 1951–1955 legislature lies in the change of presidential administrations. During the fiscally conservative administration of General Dutra, the Finance Committee functioned as a budgetary watchdog *preventing* additions

15. Interviews conducted in 1983.
16. If rank in list had no effect on committee placement, 11 percent of the committee would have been composed of first place finishers, 11 percent of second place finishers, and so on, down to 11 percent of ninth place finishers. Instead, 28.6 percent of the committee finished first.

to the president's budget. During the populist-developmentalist administration of Dutra's successor Getúlio Vargas, the Finance Committee loosened its purse strings. With budgetary opportunities too good to pass up, the electorally powerful exercised their prerogatives and took seats on key committees.

Vargas's suicide in 1954 was succeeded by two years of austerity budgets submitted by provisional presidents.[17] Opportunities for pork were paltry, and the Budget Committee's new members came as often from the bottom half of their party lists as the top half. The Kubitschek and Goulart presidencies brought a renewed budgetary expansion, and after the congressional election of 1958 new members once again came from the upper half of party lists.

Why did deputies want these Budget Committee seats? For top vote-getters electoral anxiety was hardly a strong incentive. Instead, they treated the Budget Committee as a source of long-term political capital. Passing out budgetary largesse to colleagues was an important way of amassing influence, both in their own states and nationally. Lesser vote-getters, by contrast, needed to assure their own reelection. They sought Budget seats because a position on the committee would increase their political resources and improve their immediate chances for survival.

Deputies sought or avoided seats on the Budget Committee for three reasons: party ethos, vote concentration, and competitive pressure. As we saw in the first section, the National Democratic Union (UDN) had a streak of antipopulism and fiscal conservatism. This orientation inclined Udenistas away from the budget committees. When deputies were asked (in the mail survey) which of their committees was most important to them, Udenistas were half as likely as members of other parties to name the Budget Committee, and they were much more likely to seek seats on the Constitution and Justice Committee. When asked to rate the importance of "helping local areas" in committee selection, UDN members were slightly more likely to *downgrade* local benefits.

Nonetheless, Udenistas did serve on the Budget Committee, because party shares of committee seats corresponded closely with party shares of total Chamber seats. Why, with their aversion to pork, did UDN members accept Budget Committee spots? When

17. Local leaders in Rio Grande do Norte testified that President Café Filho particularly disappointed his followers, who expected lots of money.

Table 23. *Campaign Concentration and Key Committee*

	Area of Campaign		
Key Committee	*No Regional Concentration*	*Concentration in Contiguous Municipalities*	*Concentration in Group of Scattered Municipalities*
Budget	11.1%	20.6%	20.0%
Finance	11.1%	15.6%	26.7%
Other	77.8%	63.8%	53.3%
	100% (27)	100% (34)	100% (30)

Note: This table is a result of two questions: "When you ran for a seat in the Chamber, where did you concentrate your campaign?" and "These areas where you concentrated the greater part of your campaign were. . . ." The numbers in parentheses are the number of respondents.

asked which committee members were particularly associated with the role of "Defenders of Order" (a Brazilian euphemism for fiscal conservatism), a long-time Budget Committee staffer responded with six names: Adauto Cardoso, Pedro Aleixo, Aliomar Baleeiro, Herbert Levy, Gustavo Capanema, and Wagner Estelita. All were distinguished deputies, but four of the six represented the UDN. Thus a party that averaged less than one-quarter of all Chamber seats from 1947 until 1964 generated two-thirds of the leading budgetary conservatives. UDN members got on the Budget Committee in order to *resist* pressures to spend, not to get a piece of the action. Ideology—in this case the ethos of the party—prevented adoption of a strategy that might have broadened the political appeal of some UDN deputies.

Deputies representing discrete electoral zones could claim they were responsible for attracting government programs to those zones. Survey respondents were asked whether they concentrated their campaigns or spread their efforts all around their states. As Table 23 shows, concentration led members to rely on the Budget and Finance Committees. Asked what percentages of their votes came from their areas of greatest support, deputies who believed that a single key area delivered more than 60 percent of their votes were twice as likely to regard the Budget Committee as most important as those whose key areas delivered less than 40 percent.

Respondents were then asked why certain committees were most important to them. Their responses were coded into fifteen

Table 24. *Campaign Concentration and Committee Efforts*

Helping Base or Region	Campaigned in Whole State	Campaigned in Some Areas More Than Others
Most Important	7.0%	30.1%
2nd Most Important	18.5%	23.8%
3rd Most Important	7.4%	6.3%
	27%	63%

Note: Columns do not add to 100% because respondents may give a criterion no rank.

categories. Two are especially localistic: "because of my region" and "because of my voters." Deputies with concentrated campaigns were twice as likely to give these constituency-oriented responses. Moreover, as Table 24 demonstrates, these deputies were three times as likely as those with no campaign concentration to believe that helping their base or region was the most important criterion in committee selection. In sum, deputies sought places on the Budget Committee because they campaigned in and drew support from political subregions in their states.[18] They understood that rewarding these subregions was a matter of political survival.

Amending Behavior. Deputies unable to attain seats on the Budget Committees were far from helpless. They could sponsor and promote amendments to budget bills in committee hearings and on the floor of the Chamber of Deputies or the Senate. Among those programs subject to frequent amendments, the grant-in-aid budget of the Education and Culture Ministry was typical. Its grants, ranging from a few hundred to thousands of dollars, went to a variety of social services, including shelters, asylums, and clubs. Though only a small part of the total Education and Culture budget, these funds were important to deputies, because their recipients would become loyal supporters. In 1957, some 23 percent

18. Richard Winters has suggested in a personal communication that deputies with uncertain electoral prospects may have been forced to concentrate their campaign activity and subsequent vote getting. I lack the data to pursue this interesting hypothesis, although in many cases bailiwicks predated the deputy; that is, they were creations of family and heritage.

Table 25. *One-Term Deputies and Amending*

Proposed Amendments	Term	
	One Term Only	*All Other Deputies*
Yes	15%	26%
No	85%	74%
	(93)	(287)

Source: Brazil, Congresso Nacional, *DCN,* October 4, 1952, pp. 5–107. The numbers in parentheses are the number of respondents.

of the total Chamber membership made amendments to the 1958 education grant-in-aid budget.[19]

What factors explain amending behavior? Party affiliation mattered: UDN members continued to keep their distance from budgetary politics, making only about two-thirds as many amendments as members of any other party. The number of terms a deputy had served did not affect amending. But, as Table 25 shows, deputies in their initial term who did not serve again—exiting defeated or choosing not to run—were considerably less likely to be active on the budget.[20]

Perhaps the number of terms a deputy had served was less important than the time remaining until the next electoral test. In this regard it is helpful to examine amending in the Senate, because senators served staggered terms. Some of the senators serving in 1957 would be up for reelection in 1958, while others faced no challenge until 1962. Senators facing a 1962 electoral test made about twice as many amendments as those facing an immediate test in 1958. When an electoral challenge was only months away, it was too late to spend money. Because elections four years distant afforded sufficient lead time, deputies were able to use expenditures as part of their survival strategies.[21]

19. This calculation excludes members of the Budget Committee, because their needs could be attended without amendments.

20. If appropriate data were available, one might ask whether these deputies reduced their activity because they knew they intended to withdraw or whether their inactivity led to defeat or withdrawal.

21. Mayhew (1974) argues that in the United States claiming credit for future performance (that is, promises) may be more important than seeking credit for projects already completed. In Brazil, however, political communication is too weak for the electorate to hear and believe such promises.

The Issue of Permeability. How did the existence of electoral strongholds affect budgetary behavior? The survey data discussed earlier tied deputies' *perceptions* of electoral zones to their committee choices. Rather than relying on perceptions, can we calculate individual bailiwicks' actual permeability (or penetrability) to the campaigns of other deputies? Such a calculation requires county-level election returns, but these returns rarely exist. Suppose, instead, we could identify localities benefiting from the individual amendments each deputy made. Assuming that no deputy would waste political capital seeking benefits from places that contribute no votes, localities getting aid constitute deputies' bailiwicks.[22] If *no* other deputy from the same state made amendments for any of the places aided by a particular deputy's amendments, then the latter had a completely impermeable bailiwick. If *all* the other deputies in a state made amendments for every site aided by the deputy, the bailiwick was completely penetrated—that is, it was no bailiwick at all. The key, then, is the bailiwick's permeability, defined as the ratio of actual to potential entrants in one's zone:

$$P_x = \frac{a_x}{(n-1)s_x}$$

where P_x = permeability of deputy x, ranging from 0 to 1
a_x = number of sites mentioned in amendments by deputy x that are also mentioned by each other deputy in the state
n = total number of deputies in the state
s_x = number of places for which deputy x makes amendments

Permeability can also be defined in a second, more limited way, in terms of bailiwick incursions made only by members of *other* parties. This alternative version, in other words, ignores entries by members of the deputy's own party because they are less threatening.

Focusing on members of three important committees, I used the 1953 grants-in-aid budget of the Ministry of Education and Health

22. In a few states all the deputies joined together to sponsor a single amendment. Joint sponsorship indicates cooperation, but it does not mean that all the deputies received votes everywhere in the state.

Table 26. *Average Permeability Ratings and Committee Membership*

Committee	All-Party Permeability	Other-Party Permeability
Budget ($n = 22$)	0.343	0.364
Constitution and Justice ($n = 14$)	0.154	0.142
Diplomacy ($n = 5$)	0.187	0.210

Source: Brazil, Congresso Nacional, *DCN*, October 4, 1952, pp. 5–107.

to calculate these two experimental versions of bailiwick permeability. On both measures Minas Gerais matched its reputation in Brazilian political folklore as the state with the most impermeable districts. Experts on São Paulo and Bahía confirmed that these locality-defined bailiwicks corresponded to the electoral districts they knew. Finally, county-level electoral data for the state of Rio de Janeiro were available for the year 1962, and although the overlap between the experimental bailiwicks and the election results was imperfect (due to turnover among the deputies), it was quite high.

Did the existence of electoral bailiwicks affect survival strategies? Table 26 demonstrates that, with both measures, representatives of more permeable (that is, less secure) districts were more likely to hold seats on the Budget Committee.

Suppose the actual monetary size of amendments is affected by bailiwick permeability. Do deputies from more permeable districts make *larger* amendments? Table 27 answers that question in the affirmative. In other words: Deputies whose electoral bases were easily invaded sought committees that could reward their districts and made larger amendments to budget proposals.[23]

Determinants of Success at the State Level

We now turn to the budgetary success of whole states. More precisely, what determined average per capita spending on each

---

23. One other set of amendments, those modifying the 1959 building budget of the Postal and Telegraphy Department of the Ministry of Transportation and Public Works, was reported in detail sufficient for the calculation of the indices. An index calculated for this program yielded results similar to those reported here.

Table 27. *Permeability and Amendment Size*

State[a]	Correlation Between Deputy's Nonparty Entry Ratio and Size of Average Amendment		
	Correlation	n[†]	F[‡]
Minas Gerais	0.39	32	5.48
São Paulo	0.52	23	7.99
Bahía	0.44	15	3.12
Ceará	0.63	10	5.51

Source: Brazil, Congresso Nacional, *DCN*, October 4, 1952, pp. 5–107.

[a]These states were selected because they have the largest numbers of deputies making individual amendments.

[†]Here n is the number of deputies making amendments.

[‡]All F's are significant at the 0.05 level except that of Bahía, which reaches the 0.10 level.

state over the entire 1947–1964 period?[24] Pursuant to the model developed in the second section, the effects of five factors were estimated with multiple regression techniques.[25] The five variables and their indicators are as follows:

Budget Committee Representation: the total of the annual over- or underrepresentation on the Budget Committee of each state as compared to its percentage of all Chamber seats

Party Leadership: the average annual ratio of a state's percentage of positions in the party leaderships to its percentage of total Chamber seats

Chamber Leadership: the average annual ratio of a state's per-

24. For each year, the percentage of total central government spending going into each state was divided by the state's percentage of Brazil's population. A state receiving a share of central government spending equal to its population share would receive a score of 1, states proportionately better off would receive a score greater than 1, and so on.

25. The ambiguity of the "turnover" hypothesis was noted above. High delegate turnover seemed likely to increase motivation to seek pork but reduce the possibility of success. In preliminary estimations of the multiple regression, the zero-order correlation of this variable with spending was low and its partial regression coefficient was insignificant. Since it was both theoretically and statistically weak, it was dropped from the analysis. In addition, a control such as "economic development" might be expected. Initially, the percentage of the work force participating in industry was included as such a control. It is not reported here because its partial was essentially zero, with a 0.99 significance level. Note also that the Federal District was removed from the analysis since so much federal spending technically originates there.

Table 28.   *Average Spending by Central Government on States in Relation to Population: 1947–1964*

Variable	Estimate[a]	T	Prob > |T|
Intercept	1.04	4.71	0.0003
Budget Committee Representation	0.041	3.63	0.0027
Party Leadership	− 0.126	− 1.03	0.320
Chamber Leadership	0.250	3.32	0.005
Vertical Linkages (Ministerial Positions)	0.018	2.27	0.039
Skills (Liberal Professions in Delegation)	− 0.008	− 1.48	0.162

Note: R^2 = 0.62; F = 4.51; Prob > F = 0.012.
[a]These coefficients are unstandardized. They cannot be directly compared with each other to measure the relative importance of the factors.

centage of positions in the Chamber leadership to its percentage of total Chamber seats

Vertical Linkages: the total number of years in which someone born in a state directed any of the following ministries: Agriculture, Justice, Public Works, Education and Culture, Health, and Labor

Skills: the average annual percentage of the Chamber delegation whose principal occupation was medical doctor or lawyer[26]

The results of the multiple regression are shown in Table 28. Three factors produced strong effects in the directions expected. States with "excessive" representation on the Budget Committee (in comparison to their share of all Chamber seats) pulled in a bigger share of central government spending. Ceará, for example, which placed ten extra members on the Budget Committee over the whole 1947–1964 period, received a 41 percent boost in its receipts because of this overrepresentation. States active in the Chamber leadership also did well. Minas Gerais had only half the number of leadership positions its seat share merited, and this

26. Occupations were coded as medicine, law, public functionary, journalism, commerce or banking, industry or entrepreneur, military, engineering, teaching, agriculture, clergy, low-level banking, and others. The medical and legal professions are regarded generally as the traditional "liberal professions" in Brazil. See also Greenfield (1977).

factor lowered the state's receipts by 10 percent. States that placed many of their residents in ministerial positions also profited. Residents of Bahía, for example, occupied ministerial positions twenty times, and the state's gain in spending reached 36 percent.

Two factors (in addition to the "turnover" factor rejected earlier) proved less important. States with delegations dominated by doctors and lawyers—that is, states with deputies whose skills were too narrow for effective lobbying—received, as expected, less spending, but the effect was small. The party directorates in the Chamber, expected to be less important than Chamber leadership, in fact mattered little.

Since most of the Chamber's folk wisdom attributes more influence to the leadership than to the committees, the central finding is surely the importance of the Budget Committee. States that managed to get their deputies on the Budget Committee were rewarded with significant boosts in central government spending.

Congressional vs. Presidential Survival Strategies

Earlier chapters uncovered an electoral-expenditure cycle in Latin America. Spending in response to elections was not designed—as it might be in the United States—to influence macroeconomic conditions. It was meant, instead, to provide jobs and projects for supporters and allies. In a case such as Brazil, where the legislature obviously plays a central role in the spending process, it is important to seek the source of the electoral-expenditure cycle. Is it the Congress, the president, or both?

The notion of an electoral–expenditure cycle implies that expenditures have deviated from some norm—that is, from the distribution that would have occurred without elections. In Brazil normal receipts were determined by each state's economic needs, often defined in terms of per capita income, and its capacity to absorb spending, frequently measured by the size of the total population and urban population. Suppose annual central government spending on a state is a function of these three factors. The proportion of the total fluctuation in spending explained by these three determinants is a rough baseline, an "apolitical" norm, from which to evaluate short-term "political" deviations. In Figure 9 the percentage of the total fluctuation in spending explained by these yearly equations (R^2) is plotted over the course of the plu-

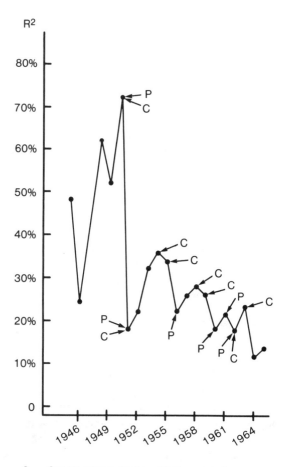

C = Congressional election effect expected
P = Presidential election effect expected

NOTE: The data for income, total population, and urban
population come from the decennial figures of the Anuário
Estatístico do Brasil. They were interpolated to yield annual
estimates. In the years covered by these data, presidential
elections were held on October 3, 1950; October 3, 1955;
and October 3, 1960. Elections for the Chamber of Deputies
were held on October 3, 1950; October 3, 1954; October 3,
1958; and October 7, 1962. Because a caretaker government was in office in 1955, no preelection effect is expected.
The year 1962 has also been identified with a "P" because it
was the first year of the administration of João Goulart, who
took office after the resignation of Jánio Quadros.

Figure 9. Explained Variance of the Baseline Regression of Total
Central Government Spending on States

ralist years. The higher the percentage of total fluctuation explained, the less important are "political" factors.

The dramatic decline after 1950 in the explanatory value of the baseline equation reflects the increasing politicization of expenditure politics that resulted from the end of PSD dominance. Within that decline, elections played a significant short-term role. In 1950, the first election year, the baseline regression actually improved its performance (R^2 rising from 52 to 76 percent). The increased weight of income, total population, and urban population in explaining state shares resulted from the apolitical quality of the outgoing Dutra administration and the conservative role taken by the Finance Committee. In 1951, however, President Vargas and the new Congress had their own ideas about state shares. Political coalition building became much more important, and the percentage of the interstate distribution explained by the equation declined from 72 to 17 percent. The congressional election of 1954 did not affect the distribution, but in the aftermath of the 1955 election—held by a caretaker government after Vargas's death— the baseline regression fell back to 21 percent. The congressional election of 1958, like its predecessor, left distribution unchanged, but another low in the baseline model was reached in the presidential election of 1960. Two years later, when a new president took power and congressional elections were held, the predictive power of the equation declined again.

Deviations from the baseline regression represent an increase in the use of the budget as a survival weapon. Electoral deviations attributable to the executive were much stronger than those attributable to the legislature. Indeed, the midterm congressional elections of 1954 and 1958, which did not coincide with presidential elections, affected the distribution of spending very little.

Why did the distribution of expenditures change so little around midterm congressional elections? In Chapter 3 we saw that *total* spending rose during midterms, because the executive's survival chances were improved by spending more. For individual deputies this one-time largesse would be beneficial, but it would not cause them to rearrange their own distribution pattern. Each deputy could bring in a little more spending without incurring the political cost of pursuing a major budgetary redistribution. In other words, the willingness of the executive to spend more enabled incumbent legislators to engage in their own form of shock-cushioning. The fact that the interstate distribution of expenditures changed during presidential elections may be a sign of the president's *weakness* relative to the legislature—for only at presidential elections could the president modify an interstate division basically determined by the Congress.

Some Individual Cases

The study of individual cases is a way of enriching our understanding of the underlying processes generating statistical estimates. Six states were selected for intensive analysis on the basis of the cross-sectional regression's residuals (that is, the differences between the model's predictions and the actual federal spending the states received).

Rio Grande do Sul, Paraná, and Santa Catarina.   These relatively wealthy states are all in Brazil's prosperous South. In budgetary terms they differ sharply: Rio Grande do Sul received extraordinary amounts of central government expenditures; Santa Catarina did quite well; and Paraná received far less than its population merited—and far less than our model predicted.

Rio Grande do Sul has long been politically blessed. Because it borders on once-hostile foreign countries, it hosts large contingents of Brazilian soldiers and receives a substantial chunk of the military budget. It also receives "excessive" shares of almost every other program. To the student of Brazilian political history, this success is no accident. The revolution of 1930 was made by gaucho (citizen of Rio Grande do Sul) Getúlio Vargas, and his government was always dominated by gauchos. Before Vargas's coup, Rio Grande do Sul was already receiving twice the share of expenditures its population merited, and by 1933 it was collecting three times its per capita share.

Post-1945 administrations were equally kind to the gauchos. The sole exception was General Dutra—during his government the state's share of all federal spending declined 20 percent. With Vargas's return in 1951, Rio Grande do Sul resumed its privileged position. Vargas's successor, Juscelino Kubitschek, needed the strong support of the state's PTB for his election, so he gave the vice president, gaucho João Goulart, control over patronage in agriculture, labor, and social security. The last administrations of the competitive period, the ill-fated Quadros and Goulart presidencies, maintained Rio Grande do Sul's budgetary preeminence, and even in the supposedly apolitical military regime the state did well. Four of the five military presidents were gauchos, and the state's share of federal largesse never declined.[27]

Rio Grande do Sul's neighbor, Paraná, was a budgetary loser. In the competitive years Paraná was predominantly a coffee producer. After 1947, when the United States removed its wartime price ceilings, coffee became extraordinarily lucrative. The coffee elite in Paraná wanted coffee's profits, but they also wanted a share in the direction of the Brazilian Coffee Institute, the government autarchy that set domestic coffee prices and controlled marketing. It was difficult for any state to plead poverty—an important argument for pork—while simultaneously claiming that its economic importance entitled it to a share in policy making.[28]

Not all political leaders in Paraná were linked to coffee. Why were those outside the coffee sector equally poor at attracting pork? The extreme fragmentation of state politics was one major hindrance. In the elections of 1954, 1958, and 1962, five different parties elected deputies. The local UDN split into two antagonistic wings, one centered in the capital (Curitiba) and the other, comprised mostly of natives of the state of Minas Gerais, located in Londrina. The PSD and PTB were also fragmented and contentious, and as a result Paraná had the highest turnover of all congressional delegations. With such conflict, relationships between presidents and the state's governors were often strained. Kubitschek actually finished third in Paraná's balloting (even behind Plínio Salgado, the candidate of the neofascist Integralist party), and the president got along quite poorly with the state's governor.

Neighboring Santa Catarina, on the other hand, was highly successful in obtaining federal funds. Santa Catarina's internal political struggles were much milder than those of Paraná. Only the three main parties ever elected deputies, and the state supported the winning ticket in all four presidential contests. Whereas Paraná's leaders were predominantly from the liberal professions, in-

27. João Figueiredo counts as a gaucho because even though he was born in Rio de Janeiro his family was all gaucho and many of his formative experiences were in Rio Grande do Sul.

28. Information based on interviews in July 1983 with Paraná deputies from the UDN and the PSD.

dustrial and commercial groups (groups who could profit from federally supplied infrastructure) dominated the important parties in Santa Catarina. Santa Catarina's UDN, for example, was very different from the moralistic and austere UDN of Paraná. The UDN leadership in Santa Catarina came from two dynamic families, the Konders and the Bornhausens. When members of these two families married, the union joined a bank and a family of traditional politicians.

Though elections in Santa Catarina were vigorously contested, cooperation on budgetary issues never broke down. During the presidential administration of Getúlio Vargas, the UDN governor of Santa Catarina (Irineu Bornhausen) persuaded Vargas to approve funds for the "Wheat Highway," a road running across the state to connect São Miguel d'Oeste with Itajaí. As the price of Vargas's cooperation, the first stretch linked the towns of Campos Novos and Lajes. Lajes, it happens, was the political seat of Nereu Ramos, PSD boss and Vargas ally in Santa Catarina. The Ramos and Bornhausen families competed fiercely, but their competition brought rewards to Santa Catarina.[29]

Ceará, Maranhão, and Rio Grande do Norte. These Northeastern states are not equally poor or backward, but they are all poorer than Rio Grande do Sul, Paraná, or Santa Catarina. In relation to its population, Ceará was Brazil's champion in attracting central government expenditures. It was also the champion in Budget Committee members and Chamber leaders. Why did Ceará do so well?

Located in the center of a region subject to severe droughts, Ceará is a state whose leaders have learned to profit from adversity (Cuniff 1975). With a vulnerable economy based on cattle and cotton, Ceará's elites discovered even before Brazil became a republic that federal largesse was no threat. In the major drought of 1877–1880, representatives of Ceará led the lobbying effort in Rio de Janeiro. Overcoming the usual bitterness of local politics, they achieved a scrupulous bipartisanship. The results were heartening: The Liberal government taking over in 1878 spent

---

29. Interviews with Santa Catarina deputies in July 1983. It is worth noting that after 1964 the Bornhausen and Ramos families finally did unite in the government party, ARENA. For a similar struggle between the Andrada and Bias Fortes families in Barbacena, Minas Gerais, see Carvalho (1966).

almost thirty times what its predecessor had spent just one year earlier. In the early 1950s Ceará persuaded the directors of the new Northeast Development Bank to locate the bank in Fortaleza, their capital, over the opposition of both the Vargas administration and most bankers.[30] While other Northeastern delegations split over the issue, every Ceará deputy supported the coming of the bank. By 1958 one Pernambucan newspaper, comparing Pernambuco with Ceará, put it nicely: "The Cearenses unite; we split. The Cearenses work; we fight. The Cearenses take care of life; we take care of politics."[31]

One factor behind Ceará's success was the unimportance of ideology in state elections. Party was just a label. Candidates frequently jumped from the UDN and PSD to the PSP (Social Progress party) or PTB, and the smaller parties could tip the electoral balance either way. The price of their adhesion was not principle but patronage. The absence of working-class mobilization made ideological flexibility easier; indeed, the PTB (nominally a working-class party) was basically conservative and rural in Ceará, getting less than 20 percent of its vote in the capital (Montenegro 1960).

Deputies from other states joined Budget Committee staff members in seeing Ceará's deputies as the most pork-oriented delegation in the Congress.[32] Ceará's lobbying centered on the Budget Committee. At one time the president of the committee was Paulo Sarasate, a Ceará representative from the usually conservative UDN. No defender of economic order, Sarasate was widely known as a spender. When a Ceará committee member left the Chamber, he was immediately replaced by another Ceará deputy from the same party.[33] In 1962 the PSD and UDN in Ceará united, the state was able to achieve its highest degree of overrepresentation on the Budget Committee, and expenditures grew.

30. See *Revista Bancária Brasileira,* no. 228, December 12, 1951, p. 1, which ranked Recife first, Campina Grande second, and Fortaleza third.

31. See *Diário de Pernambuco,* December 18, 1958, p. 4. See also Banco do Nordeste (1958) and *Jornal do Comércio,* May 13, 1951, p. 12.

32. This observation is based on interviews with former deputies and current staffers. Ceará deputy José Colombo de Souza, when asked if he had ever tried to limit spending, could only remember one incident: He had once offered an amendment to prohibit government offices from buying smoking supplies for their employees.

33. For example, Colombo de Souza was replaced by Alvaro Lins, then by Paes de Andrade, all from the PSP.

Rio Grande do Norte, which resembled Ceará politically, was another substantial recipient of federal funds. The leading politicians in both the UDN and the PSD were associated with commerce and cotton.[34] The parties downplayed ideological differences, and cross-party transfers were common. Even UDN candidates sometimes ran as populists, and the two main cities, Natal and Mossoró, dominated political life by virtue of their weight in the total state electorate.

Maranhão was the poorest of these three Northeastern states, but its poverty did not lead its congressional delegation to pursue central government programs. Indeed, per capita federal expenditures in Maranhão were vastly inferior to almost all other states. Why did its delegation do so little?

The passivity of politicians from Maranhão stands in stark contrast to the aggressiveness of politicians from Ceará and Rio Grande do Norte. Free from the periodic shock of drought, the oligarchy of Maranhão merely desired solitude, and the political machine it developed was well attuned to its goal.[35] Throughout the competitive period the last federally appointed governor of the Estado Nôvo, Vitorino Freire, controlled politics in Maranhão. His political machine functioned with extraordinary smoothness, drawing its energy not from projects but from nominations, particularly judgeships.

Freire's extremely conservative PSD was totally dominant. In the federal elections of 1954, 1958, and 1962, the PSD always controlled a majority of Maranhão's deputies, and a majority of the electorate always supported PSD presidential candidates. The second largest party, the PSP, picked up votes primarily in rural areas, and it was as conservative as the PSD. The PTB and UDN were also conservative, but they were so weak that often they failed even to compete in federal elections.

34. In the PSD, the powers were Georgino Avellino, who lived in Rio; Theodorico Bezerra, with interests in cotton and hotels; João Câmara, cotton; and Jessé Pinto Freire, linked to commercial groups. The UDN's leaders included Dinarte Mariz, a cotton marketer; José Augusto Bezerra de Medeiros, background unknown; Aluísio Alves, cotton; and Djalma Marinho, also cotton. Thanks to Jardelino de Lucena Filho for advice on *potiguar* politics.

35. In the words of sociologist José de Ribamar Caldeira, Maranhão was "little touched by the processes of transformation to which the national society had been subjected in the period 1956–1976 ... a society isolated, marked profoundly by the action of a long political domination that had been capable of imprinting upon it a political, social, economic and cultural stagnation" (Caldeira 1978:57).

Where, in the midst of this malaise and apathy, was a new generation to catalyze the process of change? Potentially, one such leader was Renato Archer, son of a former governor and scion of a traditional PSD family. Archer was the prototype of the modern, progressive leader Maranhão lacked. Linked to the left-nationalist wing of the national PSD, his position on the Chamber's Budget Committee was just the place from which to start something in Maranhão. But Renato Archer had distanced himself from the state. Living in Rio and spending little time in Maranhão, Archer developed a "national vision"; indeed, he was known in Brazil as a nuclear power expert.[36] On the Budget Committee, Archer took charge of the navy budget (he was a former naval officer), a branch of the military that could hardly transform Maranhão. In a sense, the tragedy of Maranhão was that it skipped the pork stage. Its leaders reflected either the iron bands of tradition or a modernity alien to the needs of their state.[37]

Recapitulation. This inquiry into individual states highlights the importance of political climate, of context, both in determining the intensity with which deputies pursue budgetary allocations as a survival strategy and in determining the success of whole states in attracting expenditures. Any notion that the poorest states are always the most eager to feed at the central government trough is dispelled by the case of Maranhão. Elites in that state actually feared federal programs, because they might eventually lead to a more diverse society and a political competition that could escape from elite control. Immediate survival meant *avoiding* federal intervention. Only when a state's elite learned to profit from central government spending, or when its economic interests depended on government support, would efforts to attract such spending become part of its survival strategy.

Political climate was important even where individual politi-

36. Archer became minister of science and technology in the postmilitary administration of José Sarney.
37. Goiás, in the West, and Paraíba, in the Northeast, appear similar to Maranhão. Wagner Estelita, a politician from Goiás who at one time headed the Budget Committee, also took a "national" position. Paraíba, too, seems full of politicians caring little about local interests. Ernani Sátiro, for many years a member of the Budget Committee and still in the Chamber, boasted to me that he had never gotten anything for his electoral zone except one stretch of road, and even that had never been finished.

cians saw the advantages of expenditures. Paraná's intense interparty conflicts reduced the political influence of the state as a
whole. Each deputy might actively pursue his own pork-oriented
survival strategy, but interparty hostility kept Paraná's deputies
from cooperating and high turnover kept the delegation from at-
taining much seniority. In this case the structure of political competition damaged the interests of the whole state.

Pork Barrel Politics
Under Military Rule

When the military came to power in 1964, the role of the Congress in the distribution of federal expenditures changed dramatically. The hostility of the generals and their civilian advisers toward the Congress was not merely rhetorical. Within a few days
of the coup the junta issued a decree granting the president the
exclusive right to initiate all financial bills and preventing the Congress from voting any additions to expenditures. The junta soon
wrote a new constitution strengthening these restrictions. The
Constitution of 1967, in the words of Ronning and Keith
(1976:231), "curbs the ability of any congressman to build up his
own clientele via 'pork barrel' legislation."[38]

As an institution independently able to modify expenditures,
Congress ceased to exist, but the junta went even further, mounting an intense attack, particularly during the Costa e Silva and
Médici administrations, against national and state-level "professional politicians." These attacks notwithstanding, clientelistic politics survived. The regime had made the conventional trappings of
parliamentary democracy, including parties and elections, part of
its own survival strategy. As a result, it had to rely on municipal
authorities to deliver the vote in its highly controlled elections. As
Paul Cammack (1982) points out, once central authorities concentrated resources in their own hands, and once civilian politicians could make no credible claim to effective roles in representation or policy formation, municipal authorities were in a strong
position to manipulate resources to benefit the government party.
For Congress as a body and for most individual politicians, however, budgetary politics disappeared.

Some of the deputies responding to our mail survey continued

---

38. For a comprehensive description of these reforms see Baaklini (1977).

to serve after the fall of the pluralist regime. Without exception, they agreed that the Congress had lost its ability to participate in budget making. Only those individual congressmen who were favored by the junta were able to make requests that might elicit a positive response.

Systematic comparison of the distribution of expenditures before and after 1964 is not yet possible. Little information was published during the early, repressive phase of military rule, and statistical research on the post-1974 period has been hampered by the economic crisis of the 1980s. The fragments of information that do exist suggest that during the early years of military rule rapidly growing states like São Paulo improved their relative position in expenditures. Between 1964 and 1966, for example, São Paulo's per capita share of all central government spending climbed from 80 to 101 percent of the national average. Between 1970 and 1975 São Paulo's share of total spending continued to grow, and most individual programs benefited from the overall gain. Moreover, the per capita distribution across states, which congressional logrolling had tended to even out, now became *less* even. Not only did the differences between the states in total central government spending increase, but in almost every specific program there was more variation among the states.[39]

After 1974 the influence of the technocrats declined. With its shocking defeat in the 1974 election, with civilian pressure for liberalization mounting, and with the increase in oil prices threatening the "economic miracle," the regime embarked on a gradual political opening. Since formal withdrawal from power was never intended to end military influence in policy making, the military began to cultivate its regional and social bases much more systematically. Clientelistic practices increased sharply. But this is the story of our next chapter.

Conclusion

This chapter has focused on the budgetary survival strategies of the Brazilian legislator, a political actor below the level of the executive. What has been learned?

39. Variance increased in spending in general government, agriculture, energy, transport, industry and commerce, labor and welfare, and defense. It decreased in housing and remained the same in roads, education and culture, and health. See Fundação Getúlio Vargas (1978, 1980).

Deputies or senators seeking central government spending for their electoral bases could use two strategies. They could get on the Budget Committee or the Chamber leaderships, and they could propose amendments. Congressmen adopting these strategies were less likely to be members of the UDN, more likely to plan another run for office, and more likely to concentrate their campaigns and votes locally.

The nature of *presidential* strategies also affected strategic legislative behavior. During Dutra's austere administration, the Budget Committee became a watchdog of the Treasury. Vargas's and Kubitschek's populist developmentalism increased opportunities for pork enormously, and the Budget Committee became a dispenser of largesse and a locus of congressional power. The availability of more resources, however, did not necessarily ease the survival crises of insecure deputies, because during these periods more powerful deputies monopolized Budget Committee seats. When more meat was available, in other words, the older lions chased the cubs away.

The budgetary success of whole states (rather than individual deputies) depended on a number of factors. Not surprisingly, states were likely to do well if a large number of their representatives sought expenditures. Moreover, the structure of legislative organization affected states. Because the rules of the legislature ensured each *party* a proportional share of seats on each committee, *states* could be overrepresented in key decision-making sites like the Budget Committee, and overrepresentation contributed to expenditure success. Overrepresentation on the Chamber leadership helped as well, and politicians from one's state who occupied ministerial positions were able to bring home more pork. Congressional delegations with mixed occupational backgrounds, rather than simply the traditional liberal professions, could lobby a bit more effectively.

Political climate also mattered. Some state delegations were so contentious and unstable that deputies rarely had the seniority to attain positions of influence in the legislature. Others were so backward that survival depended on avoiding federal programs, because such programs might increase political competition.

Finally, the disappearance of the Congress as a political force in the post-1964 military era did not eliminate budgetary politics. Instead, it elevated other political figures, especially state governors and municipal authorities, who delivered votes in exchange for allocations. This new political structure did change the overall distribution of public expenditures. The pre-1964 Congress had brought together hundreds of deputies into a structure that made them all political equals. As a result, the structure of policy making they created emphasized stability, logrolling, and compromise. Although some states received more spending than others, almost everyone got a piece of the action. When the military eliminated the Congress, the executive branch became much stronger and some states did much better than others. The executive was able to pursue its own survival strategy at much lower cost and with much greater success when the Congress was no longer a factor.

5. When Soldiers Need Friends: The Search for Influence by an Authoritarian Regime in Retreat

Although Chapter 4 shifted the locus of strategic choice from executives to legislators, it retained the short-term nature of survival strategies. Presidents sought to stay in office; legislators sought reelection. For both kinds of actors, influence required formal position. Suppose we relax the assumptions of immediacy and position. Might a political actor strive to preserve influence even while yielding the formal position which originally guaranteed that influence?

In 1973 and 1974, Brazil's military regime experienced two shocks. The first blow was the dramatic increase in oil prices following the Arab–Israeli conflict. The oil crisis exposed the vulnerability of the "economic miracle" that had legitimized the military junta and made Brazil the toast of the developing world. The second blow was the stunning electoral defeat suffered by the military government at the end of 1974. That defeat signified a growing rejection by Brazilians of the military regime itself. The newly installed administration of General Geisel had already committed itself to a gradual democratization, but after these twin shocks it was plain the military would need a new claim to legitimacy if it wanted a significant role in a pluralist political future.

This chapter broadens the notion of survival strategies by examining the social and economic programs General Geisel and his successor, General João Figueiredo, adopted as part of their efforts to ensure long-range influence for the military. The first section briefly discusses the background of the *abertura* ("opening"). I argue that even though the dialogue between the regime and civil society revolved primarily around the *political* aspects of the opening, the intent to infuse it with social and economic content was soon evident in the public pronouncements of key leaders. Because other scholars have documented the political dimensions of the *abertura,* I give more attention to the *causes* of the opening than to specific aspects of liberalization. The next section explores various strategies available to the regime and links alternative group and regional targets to appropriate policy instruments. The third section discusses five broad policy areas: rural development in the Northeast, housing for the poor, the programmatic division of central government expenditures, industrial deconcentration, and wage setting. This is followed by a comparison of policy evolution in the five areas. Focusing on the deterioration of the economy and the collapse of administrative coherence and credibility, this section asks why the regime could implement certain policies more successfully than others. Throughout the chapter the approach is inductive and comparative, inferring policymakers' motivations from the evolution and implementation of the various policies themselves.[1]

The "Why" and "What" of *Abertura*

The military conspirators who overthrew João Goulart in 1964 divide into four groups: the Castelistas (after President Castello Branco), the hard line, the right-wing nationalists, and the military professionals. Leadership of the first military administration fell to Castello Branco and his followers, a group of officers trained in Brazil's Higher War College and linked to the conservative National Democratic Union party. Although Castello Branco had an ample range of arbitrary powers at his disposal, there were indications he was committed to returning the nation to democracy. His ruling coalition, however, also included hard-liners and right-wing nationalists. Expecting a prolonged spell of military rule, the hard-liners wanted a more extensive purge of political opposition. The right-wing nationalists were equally authoritarian, but they

1. Because policy making cannot be directly observed—Brazil was, after all, a dictatorship—not much can be learned about the goals and tactics of individual decision makers. The chapter gives little attention, therefore, to the "black box" of decision making. Brazilians have carried out a number of interesting studies of the formal structure of certain policy-making organs, but none approach the kind of depth achieved, for example, in Allison's (1971) study of the Cuban missile crisis. See, however, Guimarães (1979).

opposed the Castelistas' efforts to open the Brazilian economy to foreign investment.[2]

Castello Branco resisted efforts to intensify the political repression. Though in the first year after the coup the hard-liners demanded five thousand purges, only four hundred people lost their political rights (Velasco e Cruz and Martins 1983). The government set expiration dates for its arbitrary powers, and most observers expected the restoration of a liberal-democratic regime.

In 1965 Castello Branco and his coalition held the previously scheduled gubernatorial elections. The outcome was generally favorable for the new government. Of the eleven governorships contested, candidates committed to the revolution won nine.

Even though the regime lost only two governorships (and even in those cases the victors were not antimilitary), the election put the president on the defensive and strengthened the hard-liners. They forced Castello Branco to accept new arbitrary powers through the Second Institutional Act (AI-2), a decree that set off another wave of political purges and suspensions of civil rights. Castello Branco watched his war minister, Artur da Costa e Silva, accumulate power as a mediator between the Castelistas and the hard-liners.

Costa e Silva replaced Castello Branco in 1967. In retrospect, Costa e Silva's assumption of the presidency signaled the prolongation of the revolution. As opposition (now including armed insurrections) grew, repression intensified. In early 1968, student grievances escalated into riots, and major strikes broke out in the industrial centers of Osasco in São Paulo and Contagem in Minas Gerais. The Congress had begun to reassert itself, and it now found itself totally at odds with the military rulers. When civilian supporters of the regime (such as presidential hopeful Carlos Lacerda) saw that their own ambitions had no more future than those of leftist politicians, they broke away from the regime's support coalition and joined the opposition.

Costa e Silva's response, the Fifth Institutional Act (AI-5), turned the regime into a more repressive dictatorship. This act could be used to close the Congress, replace the administrations of states and municipalities, and deprive any citizen of political rights. These abrogations of democratic liberties were not merely

2. For the best introduction to the period, see Skidmore (1967).

abstract possibilities—they were applied with a vengeance. The Congress was temporarily shut, and the loss of political rights affected 40 percent of the members of the already docile official opposition party plus some five hundred distinguished people in the universities, the media, and the civil service. Political opponents of the regime disappeared, and torture became commonplace. Censorship was everywhere. In the end, center-left opposition was crushed.

The regime's only remaining challenge came from the rightwing nationalists. Led by General Albuquerque Lima, they opposed the internationalism of the Castelistas' economic strategy. When a stroke immobilized Costa e Silva in 1969, Lima went to the barracks to campaign for the presidency on a platform of nationalist authoritarianism. The top generals closed ranks against him, forced the competing factions to compromise, and imposed Garrastazú Médici as an "apolitical" candidate. In the words of Velasco e Cruz and Estevam Martins:

> The compromise excluded no one: it went from the latifundio to the multinationals, covering all the possibilities of exploitation of man by man, from the most modern to the most retrograde, even including those contrary to the interests of production. The cost would be paid through the wage squeeze, and it would be guaranteed by corporativist unionism, inflation, and internal and external indebtedness (1983:40–41).

The Costa e Silva and Médici administrations implemented a brutal repression, but they presided as well over the beginnings of Brazil's economic miracle. Regime propagandists had no difficulty linking rapid economic growth with social peace. With the gross national product increasing more than 10 percent annually, the government appeared to enjoy considerable popularity, particularly among the rapidly growing middle and upper middle classes constituting its primary clientele.

The Beginnings of Abertura

Because they benefited disproportionately from Brazil's prosperity, elites ought to have supplied the regime's strongest support. Did they respond? The only systematic study of elite opinion during these years is Peter McDonough's *Power and Ideology in Brazil* (1981). In 1972 and 1973 McDonough and a Brazilian research team carried out an elaborate program of interviews focusing on the leaders of six groups: the opposition party (the Brazilian Democratic Movement or MDB), the church, business, labor, high-level civil servants, and the government party (ARENA). When McDonough's team asked these leaders who should receive *less* attention from the government, most believed technocrats, the military, and transnational corporations all deserved less attention. Moreover, the elite respondents supported agrarian reform, reduced military influence in government, redistribution of income, greater political participation by students, and a relaxation of censorship. McDonough's conclusion is unequivocal: "The very legitimacy of the reigning coalition seems problematic" (p. 125).

As McDonough shows, opposition to the regime was based not just on the absence of civil liberties but also on the consequences of the economic model. By the early seventies most observers believed Brazil's already poor distribution of income had worsened during military rule (Tolipan and Tinelli 1975). The regime's economic czars were unmoved: There was no point, they insisted, in a redistribution of poverty. Brazil had to wait "until the cake grew." Still, by 1972 the GNP had been growing rapidly for five years. Had not the time for redistribution arrived?

Civil society also began to stir. The Catholic church and the National Association of Lawyers became especially active. Protesting against arbitrary arrests, disappearances, and tortures, the bishops and lawyers were symbols of the unwillingness of Brazil's elites to accept what McDonough calls "sustained intrusions into their own spheres of privilege and influence" (p. 125).

The choice of General Ernesto Geisel to succeed Médici marked the reascension of the Castelista group, but only a minority of the higher officers supported the liberal attitudes of the Castelistas. The generals who picked Geisel probably had little idea of the depth of his commitment to *abertura* (or *distensão,* "relaxation," as it was then called), and his selection as president may owe much to the fact that his brother, Orlando, was Médici's minister of defense (Lamounier and Faria 1981).

Geisel's early proclamations about relaxation were nothing new. His predecessors had talked of a return to democracy, but their rhetoric had always given way to repression. Under Geisel the rhetoric became, haltingly and unevenly, a reality. The opening endured.

The *abertura* managed to survive for three quite different reasons. Authoritarianism, as we have seen, was only one strand in the ideology of the 1964 coup, and it was a strand that had never been fully institutionalized. If Geisel, as representative of the anti-authoritarian element, wanted to strengthen the Castelistas against the hard-liners and the right-wing nationalists, he would need the support of elites outside the military. For business and professional leaders, political liberalization was the minimum requirement for support. *Abertura* survived as well because Geisel and his chief strategist, General Golbery Couto e Silva, were enormously clever in controlling its pace in such a way that neither left nor right ever felt its situation was hopeless. Finally, given that liberalization fit Geisel's beliefs and his need for allies, it made sense to start the process at the beginning of his term. The liberal opposition was disorganized and quiet, and the militant left had been decimated. The time was right. Why not liberalize?[3]

If Geisel's conception of *abertura* indeed extended beyond political liberalization, his early statements reveal few such intentions. His remarks at the occasion of the first meeting of his cabinet were typical:

> Facile distributivism, which tries to reduce individual inequalities by generosity in the readjustment of nominal wages, is destined to fail, because it generates inflationary tensions and weakens the potential of saving and development. Improvement in the personal distribution of income will have to come from ... education, job creation, and from perfecting fiscal policy, creating savings funds for workers, and improving health and social assistance (Geisel 1974:52).

The minister of planning, João Paulo dos Reis Velloso, echoed the president. Responding in 1973 to studies critical of Brazil's income distribution, Velloso attacked the methodologies of these studies and insisted that growth deserved continued emphasis. For Velloso, the government's drive for higher median incomes would eventually raise the real income of every group.[4]

3. This is not to imply that the *abertura* proceeded smoothly. At least until 1977, when Geisel managed to remove the heads of the "security" operations, periods of intense repression (including torture and imprisonment) were common. See Kucinski (1982).

4. Reis Velloso, speech published in *Ultima Hora*, March 29, 1973.

The Abertura *Broadens*

Liberalization was to begin with the election of 1974. If the election could take place in an atmosphere free from coercion, and if the government received a resounding vote of confidence, the president would have the support his gradualist strategy required. Until a few weeks before the election, the government expected an easy victory.[5] Instead, the opposition scored a smashing success, taking 16 of 22 Senate seats and 160 of 364 Chamber seats.[6]

Why did the regime fare so poorly when four years earlier it had achieved a great electoral success? Admittedly, the election of 1970 had been held in an atmosphere of intimidation, but even so the opposition was clearly in disarray. Moreover, McDonough's public opinion survey, implemented in 1972–1973 at the height of the "miracle," found high levels of support for the regime in all social classes, with only a small falloff among workers (Cohen 1982). Why, then, was the regime so badly defeated in 1974? Why did the same *paulista* industrial workers who had supported the regime in 1972 vote 8–1 for the opposition candidate in the 1974 São Paulo Senate race (Cardoso and Lamounier 1975)?

Economic collapse did not cause the reversal of opinion. True, GNP growth between 1973 and 1974 declined from 14 to 9.8 percent, and inflation grew from 12.8 to 27.6 percent. Still, employment was high and real wages were improving. Older workers knew their real incomes had declined since 1964, but their memories of the chaos of the Quadros and Goulart years made them distrustful of open politics. Younger workers saw themselves as beneficiaries of an orderly economic growth directed by a moralistic military.

Mass opinion during the heyday of growth was supportive, but that support was fragile. The government bombarded the population with news of its achievements, and opposing views faced an impenetrable wall of censorship. The 1974 electoral campaign was the first time the opposition was able to make its case about the gap between rich and poor, the deterioration of urban health conditions, the rights of workers, and other issues. The military's

5. See, for example, the statements of one of the civilian leaders of the administration, Petrônio Portella, in *Veja,* October 30, 1974.
6. Prior to the election the MDB had 7 of 66 senators and 87 of 310 deputies.

version of history could not prevail, especially in an atmosphere of economic uncertainty.[7]

By March 1975, Geisel began talking about social policy. Pointing to the recently created Social Development Council (which brought together ministers involved with education, health, housing, and the like), Geisel emphasized the new importance he would give to social programs. Massive infusions of funds would go to education and health, and a new wage policy would provide the working class with gains above the rate of inflation.[8] In a televised speech in August 1975, the president went much further, leaving little doubt of his intentions:

> "Relaxation" should not be only political, nor even predominantly political. What we seek for the nation is an integrated and humanistic development, capable of joining all sectors of the national community—political, social, and economic.[9]

The president went on to link socioeconomic liberalization to the post–oil crisis economic difficulties, and he boasted of his success in avoiding recession and unemployment and even continuing to innovate in social policy. A few years later, Geisel made the point again, arguing that his goal had been to slow the economy gradually in lieu of a recession. The same theme was elaborated by Reis Velloso: "The maintenance of growth itself, though at rates below those of the earlier phase, would be a factor in the preservation of internal and external confidence."[10] For Geisel, expansion of social programs had become a necessity. He knew the political opening "could not endure a social crisis of serious proportions."[11]

Policy was inseparable from partisan activity. In a speech to

7. On the subject of working-class support for the military, see Stepan (1971:47–49).

8. Speech of December 30, 1974, on television.

9. Speech of August 1, 1975. Geisel also noted that "relaxation" is "often presented with an exclusively political connotation. . . . One feels in these propositions a conspicuous nostalgia for the not too distant past, a past in which formal liberties were emphasized. This assuaged the consciences of many, but because these liberties weren't really practiced, they had the opposite effect, serving the appetites and greed of a few to the detriment of the real national interest."

10. Speech of May 18, 1978. In a speech on September 24, 1975, Velloso stressed the wage increases that government policy was stimulating and expressed the hope that real wages could soon return to their level of 1960!

11. Speech of December 20, 1978, to the Economic Development Council.

the leadership of the government party in October 1975, the president emphasized his desire for an electoral victory by the party. Three elements, according to Geisel, were crucial for an ARENA triumph: the program of the party, its leadership, and the deeds of the government. In a juxtaposition that was hardly coincidental, Geisel went on to stress the real wage increases workers had been receiving in 1975.

Geisel's hand-picked successor, João Figueiredo, had been head of the National Information Service, the Brazilian secret police. That affiliation was an unlikely background for a president expected to continue a political liberalization, but Geisel had confidence in Figueiredo and took pains to help the new president soften his image. Indeed, Figueiredo's achievements in granting a general political amnesty and conducting the 1982 elections were extremely significant. The president's commitment to the social *abertura* was also widely accepted. Even more than Geisel, Figueiredo's speeches stressed wage increases, expansion of education programs to reach the poor (especially in rural areas), and the central role of agriculture.[12]

In sum, at least after 1974 and perhaps earlier, *abertura* included a social component. At bottom, *abertura* had to mean more than just political liberalization, because none of the competing factions expected the military to divorce itself from political life.[13] The Castelistas knew they wanted to avoid military intervention in future governments, and they knew social unrest encouraged intervention. Unless liberalization had a social component, no political relaxation could be secure.

The desire to prevent social unrest implies little more than a short-term modification of economic and social policy while the

12. See, for example, his message at the opening of the Congress in 1981.
13. Walder de Góes, perhaps the closest observer of the Geisel administration and the military elite in general, writes that:

It is taken as a given, in the vital centers of the regime, that the political-economic model has not become totally obsolete and that the current crisis is only a crisis of the system of alliances of the regime. A new scheme of participation—through new relations between the state and elites—and a reform of decision mechanisms would further the reconstruction of the political pact and the restoration of normality, which is understood as the peaceful acceptance of military-bureaucratic domination and of the elites linked to it. It is only a question of making state corporatism more flexible and more inclusive (1978:129).

withdrawal proceeded. Why might the military want *long-term* influence? As we have seen, the military was never ideologically monolithic, and the inevitable fragmentation accompanying the long years of military rule further reduced the unity of military thinking. Still, most officers were strongly anticommunist, pro-Western, procapitalism, and antipopulist.[14] Military officers were intent that a new civilian regime should not reverse the gains of the post-1964 period. They did not want to see the politicians they had overthrown return to power. They definitely did not want too much probing into the Brazilian version of the "dirty war" against subversion. The officers rarely knew specifically what they wanted, but they feared a civilian regime could undo all they had achieved. To the degree they could induce the population to support conservative politicians, and to the degree the military commanded respect, civilian rule held less danger.

Strategies of Social *Abertura*

We come now to the four survival strategies available to the regime. Each hypothetical alternative implies a strategic coalition, and each coalition requires a distinct pattern of policy outputs. The goal of all these survival strategies was "popularity" for the military; the strategies themselves answer the question: "Popularity with *whom?*"

Hypothesis 1: Return to the Barracks

The Castelista faction controlling the regime after 1974 sought to ensure its influence in policy making after political liberalization. But influence over what? If military leaders simply wanted veto power over decisions affecting their professional interests, they would hardly need broad popularity. No one could forget the coup of 1964.

A military with no long-term political interests would still face one problem. Political liberalization, it was said, could not withstand an economic crisis. A recession would hinder the political opening and prevent the military from carrying out its withdrawal. Social turmoil would compel a military presence, weakening the Castelistas and strengthening the hard-liners. Still, if the armed

14. These comments are based on conversations with high-level officers and observers of the military.

forces merely wanted a clean withdrawal, their objective could be minimal: Avoid economic collapse. This hypothesis, in essence, says the *abertura* really had no social content.

Hypothesis 2: Appeal to Elites

Legitimacy, we sometimes assume, is only attained when everyone in society regards the regime positively. Emmanuel Wallerstein suggests, however, that the masses actually matter very little:

> It is doubtful if very many governments in human history have been considered "legitimate" by the majority of those exploited, oppressed, and mistreated by their governments. The masses may be resigned to their fate, or sullenly restive, or amazed at their temporary good fortune, or actively insubordinate. But governments tend to be endured, not appreciated or admired or loved or even supported (1974:143–144).

If legitimacy required only the support of economic elites and regional politicians, the regime had a number of options. Most industrialists sought a decentralization of decision making and a reduction in government intervention in the economy (*de-estatização*). Nongovernmental elites of all types, according to McDonough (1981), wanted the government to pay less attention to transnational corporations. Right-wing nationalists in the military backed any program favoring Brazilian over foreign firms.

The government could also shape traditional social programs to attract upper-status groups. The regime had already shown, in its post-1968 expansion of the university system, a willingness to accommodate the demands of the upper middle classes (Ames 1973), and since most of the central government's allocation for education already went to universities, elites would appreciate a general expansion of educational funding.

In spite of the seeming attractiveness of these policy options, an elite-centered strategy would be difficult to implement. Public health programs could not be made attractive to elites, because elites rarely used public health services. Housing projects in the National Housing Bank were already overwhelmingly skewed toward upper-income groups. "Elite interests," moreover, were actually quite diverse. Manufacturers would oppose higher wages for workers, but commercial interests would welcome them. Firms dependent on government purchases would protest against any reductions in the government's role in the economy. Nationalist programs might aid domestic producers, but goods purchased by elites would become more expensive.

Hypothesis 3: Seek Mass Support

If, on the other hand, the regime were to seek the support of the urban working and middle classes, it would have many policy options. It could spend more on health, welfare, and primary education. The National Housing Bank could build low-cost dwellings, and social security programs could broaden their coverage. In terms of macroeconomic management, the regime could pursue income redistribution through wage policy reforms.

Strategically, however, the programmatic approach (targeting specific government programs) was of dubious value. The regime could shift any number of expenditure programs to benefit low-income groups, but it is questionable how much support such redirections would produce. In 1965, in its first postcoup budget, the military regime had tried to win over the poor with increased spending on primary education. That effort failed—in part because the Ministry of Education possessed an extraordinary capacity to waste money (Ames 1973) and in part because the regime's leaders feared education might increase popular mobilization. Ten years later, when the hostility of the working class was much deeper, could the regime spend enough to buy support?

Significant income redistribution, on the other hand, would certainly elicit a positive response. The problem with redistribution was macroeconomic: Would redistribution inevitably lead to higher inflation and unemployment?[15] If the regime tried to go halfway, seeking merely to prevent further declines in real wages, workers might not respond positively at all. Was a change in policy worth the risk?

Hypothesis 4: Strengthen
Regional Support

The regime always drew its strongest support from the conservative, predominantly agricultural states of the Northeast. These

---

15. This is not to argue that inflation or unemployment were regarded by most economists as inevitable consequences of higher wages. Inside the regime, however, that linkage had been at the root of post-1964 wage policy.

states, especially Bahía, Ceará, Maranhão, Paraíba, Piauí, and Rio
Grande do Norte, were far less populous than those of the industrialized Southeast, but the malapportionment of Brazil's electoral system exaggerated their influence.[16] Three senators represented each state, and the apportionment rules of the Chamber of
Deputies produced a similar (though less pronounced) result. In
the election of 1982, for example, the nine states of the Northeast
plus four small states (Rondónia, Acre, Mato Grosso, and Mato
Grosso do Sul) had only 26 percent of the voters, but they claimed
38 percent of all Chamber seats and 49 percent of PDS deputies.

A regional survival strategy could target rural areas in all parts
of the country, or it could target both urban and rural areas in a
selected region. If the strategy were purely rural, policies setting
crop prices or agricultural credit terms would be central.[17] If the
targets included both rural and urban areas in a certain region,
then programs such as road building or housing could easily be
manipulated for political objectives.

Suppose President Geisel had analyzed the results of the 1974
congressional election with the notion of using current budgetary
trade-offs to maximize future electoral gains. One group of states
could be written off. Rio de Janeiro, where the opposition MDB
won sixty-five of ninety-four seats, and São Paulo, where the MDB
took forty-five of seventy seats, were hopeless. More money in
those states would yield few benefits. A second group of states
was politically important but electorally uncertain. Rio Grande do
Sul had supported the opposition in 1974, giving the MDB thirty-
three of fifty-six seats, but Rio Grande do Sul was the home base
of many active political figures, both in the opposition and in the

16. Their influence was also increased by the willingness of the government to
engage in blatant rigging of electoral and legislative rules. Fearful of losing control
of the Senate, for example, the government in 1977 packed that chamber, adding
a group of "bionic" members whose indirect election it could control. The regime
fused two generally antigovernment states, Guanabara and Rio de Janeiro, into
one, thereby reducing their legislative representation, and Mato Grosso, a supportive state, was split into two, thus increasing progovernment strength. These
practices became so well known in Brazil that *casuismo* ("casuistry") became an
everyday word.

17. Price setting provides a powerful means of buying support. In 1980, Delfim
Neto, the minister of planning and at that time the leading civilian candidate for
the presidency, increased the price the government paid for sugar. Coincidentally,
Delfim Neto used the occasion to ask the growers to join the government party.
See *Jornal do Brasil,* June 3, 1980, p. 19.

military regime, so it could never be written off. Economically important Minas Gerais gave the government thirty-seven of sixty-one seats, but Minas was surely no government bailiwick. Minas boasted an extremely active political elite, one that would respond quickly to signs of neglect (Fleischer 1973). A third group of states offered better long-term prospects. Northeastern states had smaller concentrations of blue-collar workers and lower levels of class-based opposition. Moreover, clientelistic relationships between landowners and their dependent tenants guaranteed a heavily pro-regime vote in rural areas. These factors point to the Northeast as the key to a regional strategy. But one caveat remained: Why invest resources where the lead is already secure? If ARENA elects thirty-seven out of fifty deputies in Bahía, thirty of forty in Ceará, and nineteen of twenty-four in Piauí, these states are safe. Why not put resources in politically important but electorally marginal areas?

A strategy that favors marginal cases, ignoring both unyielding opposition and unwavering support, runs into one major obstacle. For local elites, survival depends on securing government largesse for their regions. The greatest pressure on the regime came from states with the largest progovernment delegations. Because Bahía strongly supported the regime, its leaders expected rewards commensurate with that support. The regime, on the other hand, should treat Bahía as a "safe" region and devote its efforts elsewhere. Thus the regime's political interests were directly opposed to the claims upon it.[18]

Recapitulation

Four distinct strategies of long-range survival were available to Geisel and Figueiredo. It would be surprising, however, if they had implemented only one strategy, because few administrations can act as single-mindedly as the preceding hypotheses demand. If pressure from loyalist states was too strong to ignore, the regime might have opted for a region-wide approach, putting money everywhere in the Northeast. It might have adopted multiple strat-

18. In an interesting piece on Mexican presidents, Coleman and Wanat (1973) discovered that one president appeared to be putting resources where the PRI was weakest, while his successor rewarded those states that were strongly pro-PRI. Such tactical choices would have been somewhat easier in Mexico, with its more institutionalized authoritarianism.

egies or even inherently contradictory combinations. Combining a Northeast regional approach with social spending, for example, would have been counterproductive. Since most of the beneficiaries of social programs were located in industrial areas, higher social spending would have inevitably reduced the share of the budget going to the Northeast.

Strategies are truly contradictory only in the long run. In the short run, the irreconcilable can be reconciled through expansion—that is, by doing everything simultaneously and letting successors pay the cost. By 1983, as we shall see, the economic decline was so steep that the consequences of such expansion were felt almost immediately, and the military regime had so degenerated that it could no longer make choices. It could only "push with its stomach" (*empurrar com a barriga*)—that is, postpone without deciding.

Five Policies

The five policies discussed here are not a random sample of the universe of policy areas, nor do they include every important issue. They were chosen because together they affect the vital interests of all potential regime targets. Put another way, each regional or class target cared intensely about at least one of these policies.

Agriculture

The Northeast supported the military regime, but its support was not the response of a conservatism based on wealth, for the Northeast, especially its interior, is actually Brazil's poorest region. Concentration of landownership is extreme, agricultural productivity is very low, and per capita incomes are less than one-fifth those of the prosperous South and Southeast. As a result, migration is very high from the interior to cities in the Northeast and to other regions.

The close relationship between the military regime and Northeastern elites was like the relationship between right-wing regimes and backward regions in many parts of the world, but in Brazil a dominant ecological factor, the periodic drought suffered by the arid *sertão* region, conditioned the linkage as well. Occurring about every seven years, these droughts led to a long history of dam construction and river-valley development. In the late 1950s, under the leadership of Northeastern economist Celso Furtado, regional planning took on a more comprehensive tone with the creation of the Superintendency for the Development of the Northeast (SUDENE).

SUDENE's goals included greater agricultural productivity, crop diversification, and even colonization, but its main objective was industrialization. By the middle sixties, it was obvious that SUDENE had failed. Its resources were insufficient, its management was too influenced by the region's conservative oligarchy, it was unable to enforce compliance with its plans, and its industrialization strategy was technically deficient. The industrial park of the Northeast had grown, but industry created small numbers of jobs, developed few links to agriculture, and magnified intraregional disparities by locating new plants in the large cities.

While successive Brazilian governments tried various schemes to integrate the Northeast into the nation, the structure of the national economy was changing. In the fifties and early sixties, Brazil's civilian administrations emphasized import-substitution industrialization at the expense of agriculture. The military government dismantled many industry-promoting controls as part of a general economic liberalization, but agriculture still needed compensation for the distortions of food price controls, overvalued exchange rates, and export taxes.

Agricultural policy after 1964 responded to two factors. One was poverty and the cyclical problem of drought. The other— more a national than a regional problem—was the need to create an environment conducive to the expansion of capitalism in the countryside. The regime's attempts to promote agricultural exports had led to the creation of firms producing inputs for modern agriculture. Unless farmers had access to credit to invest in new technologies, the new firms would have no customers (Muller 1982).

The regime made many efforts to deal with the twin problems of rural poverty and agricultural modernization.[19] This section evaluates three such programs: a nationwide system of rural credit; a land reform scheme begun after the drought of 1970; and a program of integrated rural development projects.

19. A thorough discussion of the regime's agricultural policy, including the massive alcohol project, is found in Nunberg (1986).

Rural Credit.   The National System of Rural Credit was created in 1965. Composed of the Central Bank, the Bank of Brazil and other official financial institutions, and the private commercial banks, the system was based on subsidized interest rates. Until 1979, *nominal* interest rates were fixed at 13 to 21 percent with no monetary correction—that is, without adjustment for inflation. Since inflation never descended to that level, *real* interest rates were always negative. Commercial banks were naturally unenthusiastic about lending to rural borrowers at such rates, so the Central Bank required the banks to reserve 10 percent of their passbook deposits for rural credit.

Demand for rural credit was intense because real interest rates were quite favorable. From a level of −46 percent in 1965, real rates moved as high (that is, became less favorable) as −1 percent in 1973. But in 1974, the first full year of the oil shock, real interest rates declined to −14.5 percent, reaching −27 percent in 1977 and −69 percent in 1980. The result was a substantial transfer of real income to agriculture. Before 1974 such transfers were never more than 3 percent of agricultural income, but in 1974–1975 they averaged 9 percent and between 1976 and 1980 the average was 16.6 percent (Da Mata 1982).[20]

By the late 1970s the credit system was coming under considerable attack.[21] The World Bank (1981:23) offered proof that credit was skewed toward larger loans and, by implication, toward larger farmers. In 1976, according to the World Bank, 72 percent of all loans were below fifty minimum salaries in size. Even though these loans accounted for nearly three-fourths of all individual contracts, they absorbed only 11 percent of all credit. The largest loans, those over five hundred minimum salaries, accounted for only 4 percent of all loan contracts, but they absorbed 52 percent of all credit.

The trend over the course of the "miracle" toward lending to

20. Agricultural credit declined sharply in 1977 as a result of the efforts of Treasury Minister Simonsen to restrict the money supply as inflation accelerated. The real volume of rural credit declined continuously in subsequent years, although by quite variable amounts.

21. One criticism, noting that land prices rose fastest when real interest rates were negative, suggested that subsidized credit tended to drive up the price of land (Contador 1975). But Rezende (1982b) rebutted this critique by showing that land prices rose during general economic downturns regardless of interest subsidization because land was regarded as a hedge against economic decline.

big farmers was even more striking. In 1969, the largest loans had represented only about 20 percent of total credit and about 1 percent of loan contracts. By 1976 such loans had grown fourfold in number and more than doubled in volume. Brazilian officials also faced strong criticisms of the regional distribution of loans. According to the Bank of Brazil, the Northeast contributed 22 percent of the value of total 1977 crop output but received only 12 percent of crop credits.

By 1979, however, the situation had changed considerably. In documents (Sampaio and others 1980) and in interviews conducted as part of this study, Brazilians reported that the World Bank had pressured them to redirect their efforts toward smaller farmers and toward the Northeast. Loans to "mini" and small producers, loans that had accounted for 39 percent of contracts and 14 percent of credit in 1977, now accounted for 71 percent of contracts and 26 percent of credit volume. In its 1981 report on Brazilian agricultural policies, the World Bank noted approvingly that the share of total crop credit going to the Northeast had risen from 12 to 14 percent between 1977 and 1979.

Table 29 allows a more detailed examination of the regionalization of credit. In both the Northeast and North, more farmers received loans. It happens, however, that the redistribution of credit began *before* the World Bank applied pressure. For Amazonas, Pará, and Maranhão, 1975 was the first year of uninterrupted gain in their shares of credit. For Piauí and Rio Grande do Norte, the improvement began in 1974. Paraíba, Alagoas, and Bahía began their climb in 1973, while Ceará started to receive more in 1976. The loser in this redistribution was São Paulo, whose share of total credit declined from 27 to 19 percent between 1974 and 1981.

Did the redistribution of total credit put money in the hands of more farmers, or did big farmers simply get bigger loans? Smaller farmers did benefit, but their rewards came later. Of the ten states in the North and Northeast showing gains in *total* credit, the lag before a higher percentage of farmers began to benefit averaged almost four years. In other words: The regime began shifting credit to the Northeast around the beginning of the Geisel administration, but until Figueiredo's presidency credit failed to reach more small farmers.

Can we conclude that Geisel sought to recruit larger land-

Table 29. *Loans Granted to Producers and Cooperatives by the Rural Credit System: 1970–1981*

State[a]	1970	1971	1972	1973	1974	1975	1976	1977	1978	1979	1980	1981
Amazonas												
Value	0.31	0.28	0.27	0.21	{0.15}	0.17	0.28	0.35	0.45	0.62	1.03	0.64
Number	0.28	0.30	0.40	0.22	{0.16}	0.19	0.28	0.37	0.45	0.71	0.99	0.64
Pará												
Value	0.62	0.70	1.03	0.96	{0.67}	0.88	1.02	1.10	1.26	1.40	1.33	1.12
Number	0.28	0.48	0.75	0.79	0.72	{0.72}	0.76	0.83	0.90	1.17	1.44	1.42
Maranhão												
Value	0.38	0.54	0.54	0.57	{0.40}	0.61	0.59	0.67	0.71	0.93	1.55	1.39
Number	0.62	0.80	0.97	0.85	0.88	0.95	{0.86}	1.25	1.28	1.89	3.35	3.65
Piauí												
Value	0.30	0.49	0.39	{0.28}	0.35	0.49	0.48	0.40	0.52	0.73	0.57	1.10
Number	0.98	1.49	1.43	1.02	1.08	1.20	1.22	{1.11}	1.41	1.83	2.61	3.94
Ceará												
Value	1.04	1.48	1.55	1.43	1.49	{1.30}	1.76	1.78	1.85	2.09	2.39	2.45
Number	1.68	3.14	2.83	2.42	2.65	2.52	2.54	2.76	{2.34}	2.94	2.97	4.73
Rio Grande do Norte												
Value	0.35	0.62	0.60	{0.57}	0.59	0.68	0.76	0.87	0.93	0.85	1.02	1.19
Number	0.57	1.14	1.03	0.78	0.98	0.93	0.98	1.01	{0.98}	1.09	1.29	1.86
Paraíba												
Value	0.74	1.19	{0.81}	0.86	0.93	0.92	1.05	1.08	1.01	1.01	1.11	1.15
Number	1.15	1.77	1.68	1.66	1.96	1.66	1.85	1.84	{1.65}	1.75	1.83	2.49
Pernambuco												
Value	2.93	3.72	3.48	3.03	2.35	2.45	2.48	2.31	2.23	2.28	2.76	2.93
Number	2.27	3.46	3.53	2.74	2.35	2.02	2.15	{2.07}	2.18	2.55	2.93	4.15

Alagoas												
Value	1.23	1.02	{1.07}	1.08	1.29	1.53	1.49	1.64	1.46	1.41	1.68	2.06
Number	0.70	0.85	0.80	0.50	0.92	0.83	0.93	0.91	{0.90}	0.95	1.16	1.47
Sergipe												
Value	0.51	0.53	0.87	0.65	0.70	0.61	0.57	0.52	0.63	0.63	0.58	0.65
Number	0.79	1.03	1.11	0.97	0.95	0.85	0.25	0.83	0.88	0.89	1.05	1.77
Bahia												
Value	3.29	3.34	{2.78}	2.98	3.49	4.07	4.39	3.47	3.73	4.03	4.61	5.99
Number	2.41	2.83	2.58	2.74	2.86	2.74	3.85	{3.41}	3.68	4.42	5.85	7.88

Source: IBGE (1970–1982).
Note: Braces indicate year beginning unbroken increase in value or number of loans received.
[a]State percentage of national total by monetary value and number of loans.

owners while Figueiredo appealed to the rural middle class and the poor? Regardless of his political objectives, Geisel knew that if the South was to become the source of Brazil's export agriculture, the Northeast would have to play a bigger role in domestic food production. Small farmers, however, are difficult to reach with loans. Frequently they lack clear land titles, and their economic viability may be limited. Moreover, until the Bank of Brazil built its "advanced posts" in the back country, credit could not be physically put in the hands of small and medium farmers.[22] Furthermore, the World Bank—an institution with considerable leverage—undoubtedly had an impact on policymakers. In the end, rural credit flows responded more to technical and external constraints than to political strategy.

Finally, is there any evidence that credit flows reflected the disproportionate political power of small states? Figure 10 traces the interstate distributions of credit volume and individual contracts. Both distributions became more equal, but the number of contracts per state evened out much more. States with small numbers of farmers must therefore have received more credit per farmer. In this case the political importance of small, rural states helped them attract a greater subsidy for their farm populations.

Land Reform. Though elite fears of a radical agrarian reform contributed to the 1964 coup, the concept of land reform remained attractive to the military government, at least symbolically, as a tool for rural modernization. Certainly a well-designed agrarian reform could increase both production capacity and rural incomes. Even so, the regime did practically nothing during its first six years in power. But in 1970 a drought hit the Northeast, and after a trip to inspect the affected region, President Médici created the Program for Redistribution of Land and Support for Agroindustry in the Northeast (PROTERRA).

PROTERRA's objectives included "the promotion of better access to land, the creation of better opportunities for employment

22. Moreover, special loan programs were set up for the purchase of inputs, but they increased credit concentration in crops such as sugar, a heavy user of fertilizer but a crop increasingly grown in larger units. Similarly, when attempts were made in the early 1970s to orient credit toward employment-generating activities (as a result of the drought of 1970), credit shifted toward livestock, eventually causing greater land concentration. See Nunberg (1986).

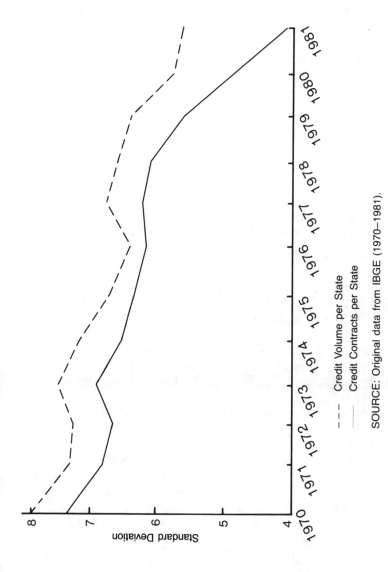

Figure 10. Interstate Distribution of Loans to Producers and Cooperatives (State Percentage of All Loans)

- - - Credit Volume per State

——— Credit Contracts per State

SOURCE: Original data from IBGE (1970–1981).

of unskilled labor, and the development of agro-industry in the Northeast." Specifically, PROTERRA could:

Acquire or expropriate (with indemnification) land required for the public good. This land could be sold to small and medium rural producers to achieve better distribution of cultivable land.

Make loans to small and medium rural producers for the acquisition of farmable land and the expansion of holdings to a profitable size.

Finance projects destined for the expansion of agro-industry, including sugar and the production of inputs for agriculture.

Provide financial assistance to organize and modernize rural properties and to organize and broaden agricultural research, warehousing, transport, electric energy, and so forth.

Provide subsidies for the use of modern inputs and guarantee minimum prices for exports.

The accomplishments of PROTERRA in land reform are best exhibited by disaggregating its budgets. FUNTERRA, the subprogram responsible for land acquisition, was budgeted in 1972 at 2.6 percent of the PROTERRA budget. In 1973 FUNTERRA's budget climbed to 18.7 percent of the total, and in 1974 it received 15.8 percent. In 1975, however, land acquisition programs absorbed only 7.9 percent of the total, and they dropped to 3.5 percent and 3.0 percent in 1976 and 1977. By 1978 FUNTERRA had almost disappeared, attracting only 0.8 percent of the PROTERRA total. Funding for agro-industrial projects, by contrast, grew to almost three-fourths of PROTERRA's total budget.[23]

The failure of land acquisition programs was also reflected in PROTERRA's system of implementation. Land acquisition and expropriation were placed under the command of the National Institute of Agrarian Reform (INCRA). INCRA's initial regulations

23. The credit lines of the Bank of the Northeast provide a parallel test of the implementation of land reform. Land acquisitions received 3 percent of all PRO-TERRA credit in 1972 and 5.4 percent in 1973 but only 0.35 percent of all PRO-TERRA credit in 1974. In later years no loans were made for land acquisitions at all. The lending of the Bank of Brazil also illustrates the powerful concentration of PROTERRA capital behind agro-industry. Between 1971 and 1978, more than 97 percent of the bank's loans went for land acquisition, but more than 62 percent of the loaned *funds* went to agro-industry.

exempted farms of less than a thousand hectares from expropriation. Larger landowners who submitted "letters of adherence" to the program became responsible for its implementation. The landowners themselves would determine which portions of their land would be bought by INCRA and which tenants would receive land. Moreover, adhering landowners received extremely favorable compensation for the expenses of relocation and resettlement.

In August 1974, when it was clear that nothing was happening, INCRA assumed sole control of the project, giving the landowners thirty days to accept INCRA's proposals or face immediate expropriation. INCRA's proposals, however, were simply grants of credit to the recipients of individual parcels, and INCRA compensated landowners generously for quite marginal pieces of land. Very little redistribution ever took place. By 1975 PROTERRA credit had been used to purchase only about 1.5 percent of the total farm area in the "priority zone" of Pernambuco. No expropriations had occurred. Only 840 families had settled on acquired land, and after 1975 the number of new owners declined steadily (Carvalho 1982).

Why was PROTERRA so unsuccessful? PROTERRA's land acquisition policy was barely an improvement over mere credit. Land recipients had to pay for their land at market prices, former landowners were well compensated, and the parcels of land were too large.[24] PROTERRA was also administratively weak. At the inception of the program INCRA relied on the landowners themselves. When that failed, it lacked the personnel to do the work itself.

Most important, however, was the absence of political will. President Médici may have believed in PROTERRA, but economic czars Delfim Neto, Reis Velloso, and Simonsen did not. According to informants, Delfim Neto had told the World Bank, which supported agrarian reform in the Northeast, that he had nothing against land reform. Since the World Bank had the money, the World Bank could pay for redistribution. But acquiescence was not support. PROTERRA needed active backing, because the land-

---

24. INCRA wanted to avoid the creation of a *minifundista* class, so it mandated minimum sizes for land parcels. These parcels had to average 150 hectares in Ceará and 60 hectares in Pernambuco. People living on such parcels who were not land recipients naturally were unhappy with the new owners and with INCRA, and their relocation became a source of tension.

owners, for whom redistribution embodied the specter of radical change, were the mainstay of the state oligarchies.

Rural Development. By the middle 1970s, the context of rural policy had changed. Rural development specialists had acquired much greater technical expertise, and the World Bank had begun pursuing Robert McNamara's "Basic Needs" strategy. With PRO-TERRA an acknowledged failure, it was time for a new beginning.

In late 1973 the central government created an interministerial commission to develop a program of "integrated rural development" for the Northeast. Integrated projects would combine infrastructure, extension, marketing, land title assistance, and social projects. After McNamara's famous Nairobi speech stressing basic needs, and after a number of World Bank rural development missions had visited Brazil, the World Bank began to receive funding requests. One of the earliest, coming from the Brazilian state of Rio Grande do Norte, invited the bank to evaluate an ongoing project called Serra de Mel. The bank eventually rejected Serra de Mel but offered to consider new requests. Projects initiated by other states followed, first in Ceará and then elsewhere in the Northeast. At the end of October 1974, these incipient projects were brought under the control of the central government by the creation of POLONORDESTE. Officially, POLONORDESTE sought to promote the "development and modernization of agricultural and livestock activities in priority areas of the Northeast." POLONORDESTE would include feeder roads, rural electrification, crop storage, agricultural research and extension, and rural credit. These activities were to be concentrated in specific areas called Integrated Rural Development Projects (PDRIs). Ultimately there were forty-three projects, nine supported by the World Bank. Every Northeastern state had at least one, and between 8 and 9 million people were included as project beneficiaries.

Funding for POLONORDESTE projects never reached the levels originally expected. After peaking at almost US $2 billion, Brazilian funding declined 8.7 percent (in real terms) in 1979–1980 and another 12 percent in 1980–1981. According to World Bank informants, funding levels would have declined even more after the credit crunch of 1977, but the bank threatened to suspend its own disbursements unless the Brazilians maintained their contributions.

Did funding decline because of the change in presidents? Informants from the World Bank admitted they worried when Figueiredo replaced Geisel, but they attributed the slide in POLO-NORDESTE's funding to the growing economic crisis rather than a deliberate attempt to sidetrack the program. At lower levels of policy making, support for the program had actually increased because many state-level agricultural experts who were enthusiastic about POLONORDESTE had moved up to federal jobs when Figueiredo assumed the presidency.

Recapitulation. Clearly redistribution had little support. PRO-TERRA's only serious backing came from the World Bank, but even the bank realized that significant agrarian reform was a dream. An agrarian reform would be financially practical in Brazil only if it deferred compensation or simply confiscated land. Since the landed elite would never accept deferred compensation, no consensual agrarian reform was possible. A confrontational policy was simply inconceivable—a regime backed for ten years by the upper strata was hardly likely to change horses in mid-flood.

In the end, agricultural credit replaced the zero-sum politics of PROTERRA with an expanding-sum game. Conscious of the need to increase production of food crops, both post-1974 administrations shifted credit to the Northeast. Geisel backed bigger farmers, while a slight shift toward smaller farmers was evident under Figueiredo. Whether this shift came from a deliberate search for allies is uncertain, because the technical and external constraints affecting lending were at least as important as political motivations.

If the regime had a *long-range* survival strategy targeting the poor in the rural Northeast, the best evidence might be POLO-NORDESTE. In the economic crisis POLONORDESTE suffered but endured. But without the money and encouragement of the World Bank, and without the enthusiasm and technical skill of agricultural experts in the states, POLONORDESTE would have died, because the political support of high-level policymakers was quite weak.[25] POLONORDESTE might produce support for the

25. The bureaucratic infighting that hampered implementation of POLO-NORDESTE was a sign of the absence of support in Brasília. Formal responsibility for POLONORDESTE was located at the federal level, in a coordinating council consisting of representatives from the Planning Ministry (SEPLAN), the Ministries

regime in the future, but its development was apparently not the consequence of a deliberate search for a rural base.

Housing

At the time of the 1964 coup, the Brazilian housing industry was near collapse. Fixed interest rates combined with rapidly climbing inflation to produce negative real rates of return on capital applied in housing. The social security pension funds were almost the only source of finance available to the middle class and the upper working class, but they built few dwellings, and the high degree of subsidization implicit in the system made it subject to political favoritism.

The deterioration of the housing industry could not continue. Housing was too important—not just to construction companies and their employees but to the regime's middle-class supporters and to the leadership itself. Brazil's extraordinary urbanization in the fifties and early sixties had left the country short millions of units of housing, and some key figures in the regime believed the mushrooming squatter settlements were potential hotbeds of social upheaval and political radicalism (Ames 1973:16–26). If the government wanted to eradicate squatter settlements, it would have to house their residents.

The regime also sought to increase its support among the urban middle and working classes. In a letter to President Castello

---

of Agriculture and Interior, and the Central Bank. At the regional level POLO-NORDESTE projects were controlled by SUDENE. It was originally expected that SUDENE would be a monitoring and coordinating agency between the states and the government in Brasília. The latter, however, would not yield its financial control to SUDENE. Rather than transferring a block of money to SUDENE for the whole of POLONORDESTE, the government in Brasília parceled out the money state by state. The World Bank followed suit, refusing to give SUDENE control of its block grant. As the states developed more expertise, they began to bypass SUDENE and deal directly with the central government. Unable to provide logistical support to the states and unwilling to relinquish control over their activities, SUDENE became a bottleneck in the program. In the early 1980s, a debate took place over the relative emphasis on social versus infrastructural components in individual POLONORDESTE projects. According to World Bank informants, this debate was mainly carried on inside the bank and among the state agricultural experts rather than at the level of the central administration. Brasília may have linked POLONORDESTE to potential political supporters in the northeast, but its concern did not reach the point where the relative importance of the program's components became a political issue.

Branco, Sandra Cavalcanti, the first president of the new National Housing Bank, wrote that:

> The masses are destitute and hurt, and we will have to make an effort to give them some pleasure. I think that a solution to the problems of shelter . . . will have a mollifying and soothing effect on these civic wounds (Azevedo and Gama de Andrade 1981:108).

In a similar vein, Roberto Campos, perhaps the leading civilian in the early post-1964 leadership, argued that:

> Ownership of housing contributes much more than rental property to social stability. The owner of a private dwelling thinks twice before getting involved in street brawls or pillaging other people's property and becomes an ally of order (Azevedo and Gama de Andrade 1981:109).

If a restored housing industry was a necessity for the regime, its challenge was the reconstruction of the sector on a footing congruent with its overall economic program. Housing construction would have to offer positive rates of return without large subsidies. The regime's solution was the creation of the National Housing Bank (BNH) and the Housing Finance System. All transactions in this system were subject to quarterly monetary correction, assuring positive rates of return.[26]

The activities of the BNH encompassed a broad range of urban projects, including finance for dwellings, sanitation, site improvements, and transportation. Programs directly aiding the urban poor were organized under the bank's Social Operations Portfolio. Under this program the bank built some residences directly, while others were built by the bank-financed housing companies '(CO-HABs) organized at the state and local level.

The Social Operations Portfolio was designed to construct housing for families earning from one to three minimum salaries,

26. When the first budgetary allocation of the BNH proved inadequate, it was given the use of the Seniority Security Fund, or FGTS (Fundo de Garantia do Tempo de Serviço). This fund, financed by deposits of 8 percent of each employee's wages, had been created to provide employers the freedom to fire workers by giving the latter the right to lump-sum payments upon retirement, dismissal, or illness. The FGTS funds grew rapidly—so rapidly, in fact, that by 1972 their net increase amounted to 1 percent of the GDP (Carpenter and Reynolds 1975). BNH funds also came from voluntary savings through the passbook accounts of thrift institutions. By 1972 these outstripped the FGTS and became the largest source of BNH income.

or US $65 to $195 per month in 1980 dollars. With twenty-year financing (rather than the usual ten or fifteen) and interest of 4 to 6 percent plus monetary correction, the borrowing conditions were much better than those governing middle and upper-middle-class units. By 1970 the COHABs had financed over 170,000 dwellings, more than 40 percent of all units developed by the Housing Finance System (Azevedo and Gama de Andrade 1981).

The National Housing Bank's low-income programs started promisingly, but they soon entered a period of decay. While the GNP soared and middle-income housing boomed, low-income programs collapsed. Between 1970 and 1974 the government constructed fewer than 77,000 "popular" sector units, a decline of 57 percent from the total reached between 1964 and 1969. As a percentage of all BNH programs, low-income housing declined from 40 to 12 percent.

With *abertura,* however, came revitalization. From a low in 1974 of 7,831 units, low-income housing grew rapidly, peaking in 1980 at almost 200,000. The rise, as Figure 11 illustrates, was steady and almost unbroken.

Over the whole period, then, low-income housing followed a cycle: expansion under the relatively liberal Castello Branco government, near-total decline during the repression-cum-growth of Médici, restoration during the gradual democratization of Geisel and Figueiredo. Why did these programs wane so quickly in 1970–1974 and recover so dramatically afterward?

Officially, popular housing collapsed because an extremely high percentage of its residents fell behind in their payments. By December 1973 more than 36 percent were at least three months behind, and the percentage of vacant units reached 6.7 percent (BNH 1979). Médici apologists blamed poor tenant selection, bad building sites, and low-quality materials. These are valid reasons, but the underlying problem was simpler: The wages of poor Brazilians were rising more slowly than their house payments.[27] The BNH was having difficulty recouping its costs, and since it was not in business to subsidize the poor, low-income programs had to be reduced.

The post-1974 resuscitation of low-income housing followed a series of technical improvements in the program. Payments were

27. It has been estimated that between December 1970 and December 1974 the number of hours of labor required to earn the minimum food ration rose from 103 to 158. See DIEESE (1975).

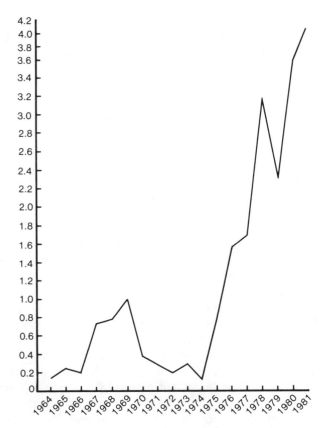

SOURCE: BNH (1981). 1969 = 1. Author's estimate for 1981.

Figure 11. Index of Loans Approved by Social Operations Portfolio: 1964–1981

lowered by extending the mortgage term from twenty to twenty-five years and by reducing the interest rate three percentage points. COHABs were also given the right to construct and finance housing for a wealthier section of the lower middle class, those earning three to five minimums.[28] With these changes the vacancy rate—

28. Because speculation had driven up housing prices, such buyers became much more interested in low-income dwellings. In a comparison of projects com-

6.7 percent at the end of 1973—dropped to 0.3 percent in September 1978, and the percentage of residents at least three months behind in payments—36.3 percent in 1973—dropped to 12.6 percent.

Did these changes in housing programs reflect a class strategy or a regional strategy? If the regime was appealing directly to actual or potential housing recipients, the interstate distribution of government housing *per urban dweller* should have become more equal.[29] If the regime's strategists were assuming that each state had equal importance as a target, then the distribution between states, regardless of the states' urban populations, should have become more equal. In Brazil such a regional strategy would inordinately favor the Northeast, because its states are mostly smaller and more rural.

Figure 12 plots the distribution of COHAB units per state, both in absolute terms and in relation to the percentage of Brazil's urban population residing in the state.[30] Both distributions become more even. Because the distribution prior to Geisel's administration was heavily skewed toward São Paulo and Rio, putting money in Northeastern cities resulted in a distribution that was more even both in regional and in class terms.

Figure 13 traces the distribution of all BNH investments (sewage, water, electrification, and the like). Here the picture changes. The distribution per state evens out dramatically during the *abertura,* but the distribution per urban dweller does not. In the provision of infrastructure, therefore, the regime appealed to states as states rather than to urban dwellers as individuals. In effect, the regime was appealing to political elites and commercial interests in conservative regions.

---

pleted in Minas Gerais in 1968 and 1978, Azevedo and Gama de Andrade (1981:124) found that 94 percent of 1968 borrowers earned one to three minimum salaries; only 40 percent of 1978 borrowers were in this category. Those earning three to five minimums rose from 4 to 51 percent. Richer borrowers were less likely to be in arrears on their payments, of course, so the bank would recoup its loans.

29. This strategy assumes that regardless of the state of residence, urban dwellers respond equally to equal amounts of housing, so the units provided ought to be equal in relation to local population.

30. A perfectly even distribution (zero standard deviation) means that each state had 1/21 of the total number of units built. In terms of urban dwellers, each state should have $X \times T$, where T is the total units built and X is the percentage of all Brazilian urban dwellers residing in the state.

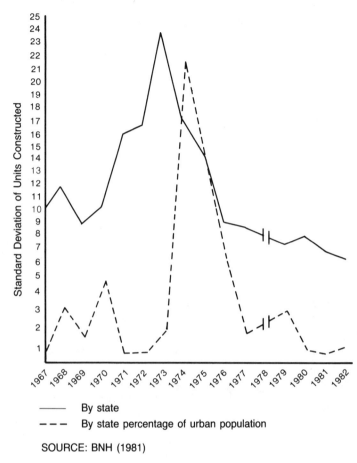

Figure 12. Distribution of COHAB Housing per State and
per Urban Dweller: 1967–1982

While the Geisel and Figueiredo administrations sought to ensure the influence of the military in the coming pluralist regime, some of their lower-level officials had much more personal survival strategies. Mário Andreazza sought the presidential nomination of the government party (the Democratic Social party, or PDS) from the time he became minister of the interior in 1979 until he finally lost the nomination in September 1984. In an attempt to garner

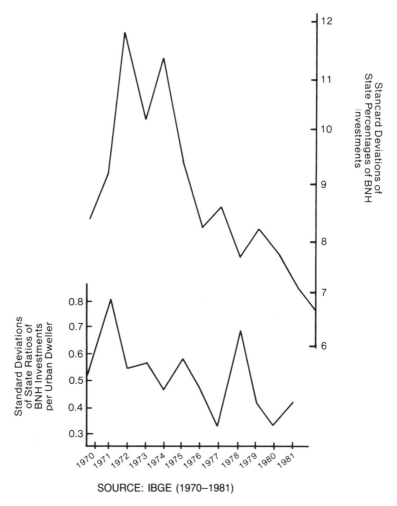

SOURCE: IBGE (1970–1981)

Figure 13. Distribution of BNH Investments: 1970–1981

support from the governors of the Northeast, Andreazza tried to put a BNH project in every Northeastern municipality. He knew that the Northeastern governors would command small but unified delegations at the PDS nominating convention, and because the PDS itself was disproportionately Northeastern, these delegations would heavily influence the convention. Andreazza lost the PDS nomination, but without this strategy he would not have been a viable candidate. His ambitions also produced, without question, an increase in housing for the poor.

Trade-offs Among the Ministries

If indeed Generals Geisel and Figueiredo were attempting to ensure the long-term survival of military influence, we would certainly expect changes in allocations to the central government ministries.[31] Our first step is to examine actual expenditures. Table 30 presents the share of the budget spent by each ministry during each administration. Election years are separated in order to assess short-term electoral effects.[32] Both presidents reduced the budget share of the three military ministries and the Ministry of Transport.[33] Both presidents increased the shares going to agriculture, education, and welfare. Health programs grew under Geisel, while housing programs (in the Interior Ministry) expanded under Figueiredo.[34]

The "deviation" columns in Table 30 measure the changes in expenditures during the election year from each administration's

31. In order to uncover policymakers' perceptions of the linkage between expenditures and beneficiaries, I carried out a series of interviews in the Planning Secretariat, the civilian policy staff of the president (the Casa Civil), and in nine ministries. These interviews were conducted in the summer of 1982 and between March and August 1983. Whether respondents were technocratic or political in orientation, or high or low in rank, they thought certain programs aid specific classes. Health and sanitation benefit the urban poor. Agricultural programs aid farmers, naturally, especially prosperous farmers. Welfare helps the urban middle and working classes. The effects of educational programs depend on their level: The higher the grade, the higher the social class of the beneficiary. Public works projects provide construction jobs, but most policymakers saw these programs as responses to infrastructural needs and to the clout of local business and political leaders.

32. Note that the 1982 election was gubernatorial as well as legislative.

33. The decline in spending on transportation had been called for by the Second National Development Plan, issued in 1974 after the oil shock. Transport was still the largest single ministry.

34. A complete evaluation of regional and class expenditure strategies would require an analysis of expenditures for each program in each state. Official government reports have begun to cross-tabulate programs with states, but these reports vastly overestimate the amount of spending in the federal capital. The program totals are thus accurate, but the state totals are not. The Getúlio Vargas Foundation, a semipublic Brazilian research institution, is currently engaged in an accurate regionalization of expenditures by program at five-year intervals, but only the years 1970 and 1975 have been completed. The limited data that are available, however, are sufficient to provide a sense of the regime's strategy.

Table 30. *Final Expenditures of Central Government Ministries in Médici, Geisel, and Figueiredo Administrations (Percentage of Ministerial Total)*

Ministry	Médici			Geisel			Figueiredo	
	1971–1973	1974	1975–1977	1978	1978 "Deviation"[a]	1979–1981	1982	1982 "Deviation"[a]
Presidency	1.74	2.37	3.64	3.97	−0.30	4.51	4.41	−0.39
Aeronautics	10.65	9.35	9.34	8.24	−0.67	7.17	6.98	+0.53
Agriculture	2.35	3.56	3.97	5.19	+0.69	5.27	6.06	+0.36
Communications	2.13	2.11	1.95	1.23	−0.63	0.59	2.55	+2.41
Education and Culture	10.13	11.68	15.46	17.12	−0.10	17.38	16.81	−1.20
Army	19.72	14.61	14.66	12.70	−0.29	10.86	9.52	−0.09
Treasury	3.28	3.02	4.73	5.25	+0.04	4.47	3.41	−0.97
Industry and Commerce	0.20	0.20	0.55	0.65	−0.02	2.01	5.61	−3.12
Interior	3.96	4.36	4.37	3.93	−0.58	7.89	6.83	−2.22
Justice	0.98	1.18	1.35	1.22	−0.25	1.07	0.92	−0.06
Navy	9.56	8.40	9.17	8.58	−0.46	7.08	6.40	+0.01
Mines and Energy	5.29	6.57	1.89	1.66	+0.89	2.94	4.42	+1.13
Foreign Relations	1.33	1.39	1.50	1.54	−0.02	1.38	1.43	+0.09
Health	2.21	2.25	3.97	4.67	+0.12	3.79	3.09	−0.64
Labor and Welfare	1.55	1.62	7.25	10.46	+1.33	8.83	4.21	−5.14
Transportation	24.23	27.31	16.13	13.27	−0.19	14.78	17.33	+3.00
	100	100	100	100		100	100	

Source: Ministério da Fazenda, *Balanço Geral da União* (1971–1982).
[a]Positive entries mean spending was greater than the prediction based on the extrapolated trend.

trend.[35] Figueiredo's election year deviations were much greater than those of Geisel; indeed, the average difference between predicted and actual shares in 1982 is more than three times the same difference in 1978.[36] Different programs also deviated in each administration. Geisel boosted agriculture and welfare in the election year and made extra cuts in the already declining military ministries.[37] These shifts fit a strategy centered on agricultural aid to Northeastern farmers and welfare for the urban middle and working classes. By contrast, Figueiredo's election year deviations seem confused. His administration had emphasized social programs, but in 1982 he switched toward infrastructure (transport and communications) and away from education, housing, health, and welfare. Well before the election, however, the economy had begun to deteriorate, and economic conditions were the paramount issue of the election. Public works spending creates private sector jobs that can be targeted and controlled by local elites. Social programs disproportionately benefit urban groups unlikely to vote for the government party in any event.

Figueiredo's election year expenditures reflect more than just a short-term survival strategy. The Army Ministry, profiting from the insecurity of an administration faced with restive officers and strident opposition politicians, managed to reverse the fall of its budget share. The army's gain, along with the increased volatility in ministerial spending in 1982 (as compared to 1978), is our first indication of Figueiredo's loss of control of his administration.

The programmatic shifts of the Geisel and Figueiredo years represent a broadening of the regime's social base, but *regional* shifts are less clear. Table 31 shows that central government expendi-

35. Rates of change were calculated for each program—first between 1971–1973 and 1975–1977 and then between 1975–1977 and 1979–1981. The first rate of change was extrapolated to 1978 and the second rate of change was extrapolated to 1982. The differences between these predictions and the actual shares for each program during the election years were then calculated. The election of 1974 was not included because Geisel had little control over spending during his first year in office.

36. The means of the absolute values of the differences equal 0.41 for Geisel and 1.34 for Figueiredo.

37. Geisel's confidence in his military support must have increased after 1977, when he removed General Frota, a dissident member of the high command. See Góes (1978). Why the expenditures of the Interior Ministry suffered is uncertain. Housing programs are one component of Interior, but since the National Housing Bank itself grew in 1978, it may be that the nonhousing components of the Interior Ministry bore most of the short-term reduction.

tures going to the Northeast declined during the administrations of both Geisel and Figueiredo. These reductions, however, might simply have been by-products of the increases in social programs, because social programs weigh more heavily in expenditures into the industrialized Southeast.[38]

If a regional strategy was pursued, it might show up in the movements of *direct transfers* to state governments. Although some transfer payments are subject to long-term arrangements and thus cannot easily be manipulated from year to year, transfers also have a "controllable" component that includes grants in such areas as management of health care facilities, support of universities, and provision of agricultural services.[39] Overall, large increases in transfers benefited the Northeast during the Figueiredo government, and in 1982 (an election year) the steady upward trend culminated in the delivery to the Northeast of almost half of all transfers to states (Rezende 1982a).

In sum, then, in the industrial Southeast Figueiredo chose to stress direct programs like education and health, but in the Northeast the real objects of political recruitment were state and local elites. In that clientelistic realm, state and local elites were *patrons* to program beneficiaries but *clients* of the central administration.[40]

Proposed vs. Actual Budgets. After 1981 the "decomposition" of the Figueiredo administration became a common theme in the

38. Whether the regional shifts were totally an artifact of program changes cannot be definitively answered until the completion of the 1980 regionalization project. Using the regionalizations available for 1970 and 1975, there was no evidence of a bias either toward programs or regions. This was determined by first calculating, for each program in each state, the share of total central government spending received in 1970. The percentage change in that share between 1970 and 1975 was then calculated. If the changes across programs for individual states varied less than the changes across states for individual programs, then program shifts dominated regional shifts and vice versa. Calculating the standard deviations of each program across states and each state across programs, then taking the means of the standard deviations for programs and for states, one finds that the means are almost identical. Thus neither programs nor states dominated the shifts that occurred.

39. Published reports of transfers do not allow a separation of their components, but year-to-year changes inevitably reflect changes in the controllable component. According to Rezende (1982a), local and state elites were deeply involved in determining the size and distribution of controllable transfers.

40. A excellent discussion of clientelistic practices during the Médici years is found in Cammack (1982).

Table 31. Regional Distribution of Central Ministry Expenditures by Administration (Percent)

| Region | Médici | | Geisel | | | Figueiredo | |
	1971–1973	1974	1975–1977	1978	1979–1981	1982
North	8.93	9.78	9.78	8.92	9.87	9.23
Northeast	33.30	32.60	30.35	29.41	27.43	26.00
Southeast	30.10	34.40	31.03	31.21	30.83	26.50
South	23.10	18.90	22.80	24.02	24.53	30.50
Center-West	4.61	4.29	5.55	5.82	6.33	7.69
	100%	100%	100%	100%	100%	100%

Source: Ministério da Fazenda, Anuário Econômico-Fiscal (1971–1982).

Brazilian media and in intellectual circles.[41] The regime, it was claimed, had become directionless. Its plans were made not for years ahead but for months or even weeks. Ministers like Mário Andreazza saw their programs as springboards to the presidency; other officials lined their own pockets or those of their friends.

Figueiredo's decline is reflected in the way ministerial allocations changed from original budget proposals to actual spending. Suppose we compare the proposed-to-actual changes that occurred in the election year to changes in other years of the same administration.[42] Of all Geisel years, the proposed–actual change was the *smallest* for fifteen of sixteen ministries in the election year of 1978. Of all Figueiredo years, however, proposed–actual differences were smallest in the election year of 1982 for only two ministries. For seven ministries, in fact, the 1982 change was the *largest* of any Figueiredo year. These midcourse deviations reflect Figueiredo's intense electoral effort, an effort greater in vigor than Geisel made either in 1974 or in 1978.

A comparison of the differences between the proposed budgets of the election year and the year just prior to the election supports this interpretation. The average change between Geisel's 1977 and 1978 budget proposals was 42 percent. Figueiredo's proposals averaged only a 23 percent shift from 1981 to 1982. In other words, Figueiredo's *plans,* illustrated by the proposal-to-proposal jumps, changed little in election years, but his actual expenditures changed greatly as the election itself unfolded.[43]

Did Figueiredo modify budget proposals simply because he changed his mind, deciding to restructure spending once the year was under way? Probably not; the president rarely exercised leadership. Rather, the pulling and pushing of ambitious ministers led to the sharply changing allocations of 1982.

41. See *Veja* and *Isto é* during these years; see also Assis (1983) and Lessa (1980).

42. Proposed budgets, published in December of the preceding calendar year, represent a statement of intent. Everyone knows that they change, and in general the changes occur in the direction of the underlying trend of each program. Between 1970 and 1982 the greatest differences between proposed and actual expenditure shares occurred in the Geisel administration. Ministerial shares themselves were changing rapidly, and each proposed budget represented a partial movement along Geisel's trend.

43. Note also that the mean difference between proposed budgets for 1978 and actual budgets for 1977 was 22.9 percent, while 1982's proposal differed from the 1981 actual by 78.3 percent.

Expenditures in Education. Figure 14 disaggregates the expenditures of the Ministry of Education and Culture by level of education.[44] Under Geisel higher education did very well, even surpassing the peak attained by Médici.[45] Figueiredo, on the other hand, sought to redistribute education spending.[46] His planners viewed university allocations as subsidies to the upper middle class, and as the economy declined the number of university graduates seemed excessive. Literacy rates, moreover, had been growing very slowly in the 1970s. Many of the regime's more conservative economists, especially those with backgrounds in "human capital" theories, began urging cuts in higher education spending. Figueiredo's political strategists, hoping for a substantial popular response to spending on primary schools, agreed.

Primary schooling's share of education spending began to grow under Figueiredo, and by 1981 its growth had become significant.[47] Still, the spending of the Ministry of Education and Culture needs to be put in perspective. The ministry represented less than 40 percent of total education expenditures, and the president had much less control over the foundations and autarchies dominating educational finance than over the ministry itself. Figueiredo managed to increase primary expenditures even outside the ministry, but the increase was smaller. Moreover, secondary schooling, not the universities, paid for the gain in primary education.

Once again we see the "decomposition" of the Figueiredo administration, at least in relation to the centralized decision making of Geisel. Under Geisel, the losers and winners in education were the same both in the ministry and in the decentralized educational institutions. Figueiredo had less control, so programs

44. Figure 14 shows only those expenditures of the ministry that can be divided into higher, secondary, and primary levels. Such expenditures amounted to about 80 percent of all the ministry's expenditures.

45. Apologists for the Geisel administration frequently mention the overall increase in education spending realized during his presidency. Rarely do they give equal prominence to the shifts in spending between the various levels of education. See Albuquerque (n.d.) and Reis Velloso (1978).

46. In Brazil's federal system, public higher education is the responsibility of the central government, and about 50 percent of all federal spending on education goes to the universities. Primary and secondary education are basically state and local. The federal share in all levels has grown rapidly in recent years as the central government has increasingly preempted the tax powers of states and municipalities.

47. It is worth noting that in 1984 universities all over the country went on a prolonged strike to protest inadequate funding. The strike was partly a result of these shifts in budget shares.

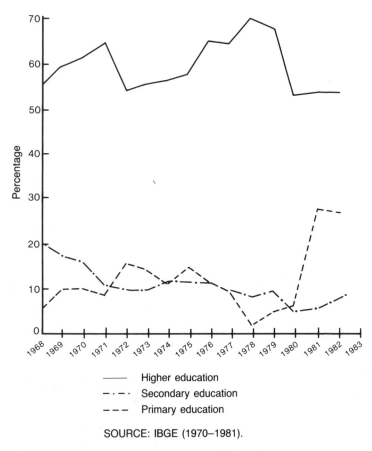

Higher education
Secondary education
Primary education

SOURCE: IBGE (1970–1981).

Figure 14. Percentage Division of Actual Expenditures
in Ministry of Education and Culture

moved in opposite directions. To a certain extent, then, Figueiredo's political weakness negated his social strategy.

Recapitulation.   Geisel's and Figueiredo's expenditure policies reveal similarities and differences. They both cut the shares of the
military and transportation ministries, and they both increased
spending on agriculture, education, and welfare. Figueiredo also

aided housing, a program nicely attuned to the presidential ambitions of Interior Minister Mário Andreazza.

The elections of 1978 and 1982 illustrate the difference between the two presidents. Expenditure shifts in Geisel's last year (1978) reflected a continuation of the strategies that had motivated his administration earlier. Figueiredo, on the other hand, had the bad luck to preside over a deteriorating economic and political situation. His expenditures in 1982 represent a midcourse correction just before a crucial election: more spending to pacify the military and more spending on public works to cut unemployment and reward state and local elites.

The regional distribution of expenditures initially seemed confused. The Northeast lost from changes in the distribution of ministerial expenditures but gained from changes in the payment of transfers. Regional political differences, however, explain the apparent contradiction. In the clientelistic Northeast, transfers increased the political clout of powerful elites. In the industrialized Southeast, direct programs were appeals to the middle and working classes.

The priorities of the two administrations are also reflected in the changing distribution of education spending. Geisel reached out to all segments of civil society, but his prime target was the upper middle class, a group for whom access to higher education was paramount. Figueiredo sought to widen the regime's base by increasing spending on primary education at the expense of universities. The effort met with only partial success: Figueiredo controlled the Ministry of Education and Culture, but less than half of all educational expenditures were under its control, and the bureaucracy outside the ministry resisted his efforts and reduced the overall shift away from higher education.

The Politics of Industrial Deconcentration

Industry locates near markets, cheap transportation, and raw materials. The primary "growth pole" in Brazil is the Rio de Janeiro–Belo Horizonte–São Paulo triangle, especially the city and state of São Paulo. In 1980 São Paulo state contained 21 percent of Brazil's population, produced 54 percent of its industrial product, and consumed 39 percent of all energy. With its surrounding area, the city of São Paulo represents one of the largest industrial concentrations in the world. Because the pace of industrialization has been so rapid and the influx of newcomers so large, the delivery of urban services has never caught up with demand. Transportation is woefully inadequate; infant mortality extremely high; environmental damage already substantial. São Paulo, it may be said, is *over*-industrialized.

Official recognition of the problem came in the basic planning document of the Geisel administration, the Second National Development Plan (PNDII). PNDII called for a reduction in the interregional inequalities created by industrialization:

> To avoid continuing the tendency for industrial activity to concentrate in a single metropolitan area, stimulus will be given to a better balance in the São Paulo–Rio–Belo Horizonte triangle. The objective will be a decentralization compatible with the preservation of economies of scale (Brazil, PNDII:40).

Industrial deconcentration was by no means the sole concern of PNDII. It primarily emphasized the dilemma of expensive oil, a dilemma it sought to resolve through a quantum leap in Brazil's level of development. Central to this leap would be the development of basic industry, including capital goods, electronics, and such industrial inputs as metals, petrochemicals, fertilizers, paper and cellulose, raw materials for pharmaceuticals, and construction materials. PNDII stressed exports of manufactured goods and efforts to reduce the cost of technology and increase the production of foodstuffs.

Whether central to PNDII or not, industrial deconcentration was now on the regime's policy agenda. What were its strategic implications? Deconcentration would strengthen the regime in states benefiting from new industry. Though it would diminish the political weight of São Paulo, in the long run it would help the *paulista* working class, because social services could catch up with demand. But if the regime wanted the *paulista* industrialists to move to the hinterlands, it would have to tilt toward domestic industry and away from transnational corporations seeking investment opportunities. PNDII made promises to domestic entrepreneurs, but its promises were vague: creation of strong entrepreneurial structures, use of the development banks to aid domestic firms, formation of national conglomerates, and help for small and medium-sized companies.

Table 32. Projects Approved by Industrial Development Council: Fixed Investment as a Percentage of Value of National Total

Region	1975	1976	1977	1978	1979	1980	1981	1982
North	0.3	—	—	—	—	—	—	1.2
Northeast	8.4	7.2	3.81	9.63	12.33	24.85	45.53	36.4
Southeast	79.2	86.1	67.16	64.14	57.66	69.66	34.07	12.1
(São Paulo)	(51.4)	(24.3)	(40.04)	(21.24)	(17.63)	(36.74)	(20.63)	(9.8)
South	11.2	6.7	28.29	19.75	25.45	2.69	20.37	49.9
Center-West	0.4	—	0.74	6.48	4.56	2.80	0.03	0.3

Source: CDI, Relatórios (1975–1982).

Table 33. Projects Approved by Industrial Development Council: Fixed Investment as a Percentage of Number of National Total

Region	1975	1976	1977	1978	1979	1980	1981	1982
North	0.3	0.3	—	—	—	—	NA[a]	2.2
Northeast	2.6	7.8	5.4	7.54	10.8	11.5	NA	20.0
Southeast	81.4	76.8	77.3	73.0	66.2	70.8	NA	54.4
(São Paulo)	(64.5)	(54.2)	(57.1)	(51.3)	(46.9)	(44.8)	(NA)	(30.0)
South	15.4	15.1	15.8	18.6	17.7	13.6	NA	21.1
Center-West	0.3	—	1.5	1.01	5.4	4.1	NA	2.2

Source: CDI, Relatórios (1975–1982).
[a]NA = not available.

One of the most important tools for implementing deconcentration was the fiscal incentive program.[48] Fiscal incentives were exemptions from taxes on income and on imported equipment. They were granted by the Industrial Development Council (CDI), an organ of the Ministry of Industry and Commerce. An industrialist desiring a tax exemption would present a project to the CDI. If the project met the council's criteria, it would grant a tax exemption.

The annual distribution of projects approved for fiscal incentives, by value and absolute number, is shown in Tables 32 and 33. The Northeast, expected to be the major beneficiary of industrial deconcentration, did increase its percentage of incentives, and the Southeast and São Paulo received smaller shares. But the changes were rather small, and until 1981–1982 (when a few enormous projects absorbed a huge share of incentives), São Paulo still attracted a substantial portion.

However we judge the interregional shifts in incentives, their magnitude pales before the huge decline in the *total value* of the incentives granted. After peaking at 53 percent of all direct federal receipts in 1976, incentives declined to 10 percent of taxes in 1978 and only 2 percent in 1980. The Northeast, in other words, may have gained in the battle for incentive shares, but the virtual disappearance of the incentive program itself makes the victory rather hollow.

Deconcentration was also implemented through the lending of the two major official development banks, the Bank of Brazil and the National Economic Development Bank (BNDE). As Tables 34 and 35 demonstrate, their lending pattern differed from the fiscal incentives of the CDI. The distribution of loans from the Bank of Brazil (basically a commercial bank) shifted toward the Northeast after 1974, although the region had actually been gaining since 1969. São Paulo's share, along with the shares of the Federal District, Rio Grande do Sul, and Paraná, declined after 1974. The geographic distribution of BNDE loans is harder to characterize, because its emphasis on a small number of very large projects produced a volatile loan distribution. The Northeast's share of BNDE loans did not grow until the beginning of the Figueiredo

48. Two other programs of deconcentration are ignored here: the regional division of locally collected taxes and the Fund for the Development of Integrated Programs.

Table 34. *Interstate Distribution of Loans of the Bank of Brazil: 1970–1980*

Region	1970	1971	1972	1973	1974	1975	1976	1977	1978	1979	1980
North	0.83	0.95	1.28	1.30	1.13	1.12	1.37	1.54	1.77	2.06	2.20
Acre	0.04	0.07	0.19	0.14	0.03	0.02	0.04	0.05	0.07	0.09	0.10
Amazonas	0.25	0.36	0.42	0.44	0.54	0.43	0.40	0.49	0.51	0.65	0.69
Pará	0.54	0.52	0.67	0.72	0.56	0.67	0.93	1.01	1.19	1.32	1.41
Northeast	9.49	11.42	12.53	14.04	13.72	16.93	18.32	17.95	18.95	17.77	17.37
Maranhão	0.47	0.56	0.57	0.62	0.49	0.71	0.72	0.68	0.74	0.88	1.11
Piauí	0.46	0.54	0.54	0.47	0.40	0.51	0.54	0.51	0.60	0.70	0.79
Ceará	1.33	1.63	1.85	2.17	1.98	2.06	2.29	2.27	2.41	2.53	2.79
Rio Grande do Norte	0.57	0.71	0.80	0.85	0.77	0.89	0.91	1.05	1.13	1.06	1.14
Paraíba	0.91	1.15	1.23	1.21	1.06	1.12	1.26	1.24	1.34	1.26	1.13
Pernambuco	2.16	2.49	2.71	3.26	3.32	4.06	4.47	4.12	4.33	3.83	3.21
Alagoas	0.76	0.87	1.01	1.48	1.71	2.32	2.75	2.99	3.16	2.57	2.06
Sergipe	0.38	0.46	0.62	0.69	0.61	0.69	0.66	0.64	0.67	0.62	0.56
Bahia	2.45	3.01	3.20	3.29	3.38	4.57	4.72	4.45	4.57	4.32	4.58
Southeast	37.80	39.3	41.7	42.3	44.4	43.6	43.1	46.4	46.3	46.2	47.3
Minas Gerais	7.11	6.88	7.29	8.18	8.32	8.66	7.96	8.02	8.11	9.96	10.6
Espírito Santo	0.88	0.88	1.00	1.07	1.12	1.29	1.16	1.20	1.04	1.29	1.45
Rio de Janeiro	1.68	1.80	2.07	2.31	2.42	9.83	12.10	15.8	16.7	14.6	14.7
Guanabara	8.99	9.22	9.19	9.37	8.31	—	—	—	—	—	—
São Paulo	19.12	21.05	22.10	21.4	24.2	23.8	21.9	21.4	20.4	20.3	20.5

South	24.5	27.4	27.6	28.1	29.7	26.9	25.3	22.7	21.0	22.2	21.4
Paraná	5.40	6.67	8.31	8.32	9.34	9.84	8.05	7.93	7.98	8.03	7.63
Santa Catarina	2.65	2.79	2.84	2.86	3.14	3.32	3.01	2.68	3.02	3.00	3.17
Rio Grande do Sul	16.4	17.9	16.4	16.9	17.2	13.7	14.26	12.10	10.0	11.2	10.6
Center-West	27.2	20.3	17.0	14.2	11.02	11.4	11.7	11.1	11.6	11.4	11.3
Mato Grosso	1.33	1.49	2.14	2.44	2.34	3.04	3.54	3.87	4.41	4.50	4.65
Goiás	2.55	2.58	2.93	3.15	3.20	3.83	3.52	3.02	2.95	3.10	3.34
Brasília–DF	23.3	16.2	11.9	8.56	5.48	4.52	4.60	4.20	4.28	3.75	3.31

Source: IBGE (1970–1980).

years, and except for Bahía the region fared worse under Geisel than under the Médici government.

Taken together, the incentive and loan programs reveal little evidence of a substantial shift away from the traditional industrial centers. Why was there so little change? Consider the Industrial Development Council, the body charged with formulating and implementing deconcentration. The CDI was headed by Severo Gomes, the minister of industry and commerce. Gomes began as an enthusiast, arguing that:

> The indiscriminate location of industrial plants is a major cause of the disorderly and quasi-chaotic growth of some Brazilian urban centers. For a resource-poor country with the extensive territory of Brazil, the economic and social costs that result from excessive urban concentration are heavy. From the purely economic point of view, the most rational road rests, generally, in the process of accumulation and concentration of wealth. But this process, if conducted without limits, fatally and irreconcilably divides a society (Gomes 1977).

By late 1976, however, Gomes had reconsidered. He began to stress the primacy of basic industry, a sector in which "isolated factories cannot be installed all over the country."[49] In its 1977 report, the CDI reduced deconcentration to a secondary criterion, and its primary objective became the expansion of capital goods production. What really mattered, according to the new official rationale, was *intrastate* rather than interstate deconcentration:

> Even with all the support of the Government, there is no material possibility of forcing a dramatic and rapid deconcentration of the geographical reality of Brazilian industry without intolerable losses for the economy. In particular, the necessity of a rapid expansion of the capital goods industry . . . hinders a more radical decentralization, because new undertakings tend to locate in areas favoring the external economies of the firms themselves (CDI 1977).

All hope was not lost. The policy objective itself could change:

> One notes a considerable reduction in the participation of the metropolitan areas—in particular that of Greater São Paulo . . . in the locales of new projects. Such projects are almost all outside the densely urbanized regions. In the state of São Paulo there is also a clear tendency for centrifugal siting, with the majority of new factories placed

49. *Veja,* January 9, 1976.

along the great highways, at points steadily further from the capital (CDI 1977).

Was the CDI correct in its claim that plants in the most advanced states were spreading out? Between 1977 and 1982, incentives fell into two categories: those for projects in metropolitan areas and those for projects in the interior. In the three states with excessive urban concentrations (São Paulo, Rio de Janeiro, and Minas Gerais), the percentage of exemptions granted to projects in the interior ranged, except in 1978, from 57 to 79 percent of all exemptions. Intrastate deconcentration was indeed a reality. Still, was the regime's motivation purely economic?

Curiously, there was one year in which urban projects still predominated. In the election year of 1978, metropolitan areas hosted more than two-thirds of all projects, and every state received at least one. An administration seeking to maximize the short-term electoral impact of incentives would concentrate them in urban areas, and dispersing projects to every state would reward loyal local and state elites.

The politicization of incentives can be viewed more broadly. In 1977 the overall volume of fiscal incentives dropped from over 50 percent of direct taxes to only 15 percent. This drop was a result of the imposition of strict credit controls. Inflationary pressures had placed the balance of payments—the premier target of economic policy—in jeopardy, and President Geisel backed advocates of monetary restraint such as Treasury Minister Mário Henrique Simonsen.

Geisel's backing of Simonsen over "nationalist" Severo Gomes signified a change in strategy. Gomes had been appointed minister of industry and commerce in order to attract the support of *paulista* industry, and he worked tirelessly to defend domestic firms.[50] As Brazil's need for new energy sources grew, Gomes sought a government monopoly of oil exploration. Simonsen, opposing the commerce minister, supported "risk contracts" with foreign companies—contracts in which foreign companies could explore for energy and win the right to exploit their finds. Simonsen won because Brazil's need for foreign capital was ever stronger and

50. In 1975, for example, Gomes prevented Philips from buying the Brazilian appliance maker Consul, and he repeatedly defended other domestic firms against foreign buyouts.

Table 35. Interstate Distribution of Approved Loans of the National Economic Development Bank: 1970–1982

Region	1970	1971	1972	1973	1974	1975	1976	1977	1978[a]	1979	1980	1981	1982
North	1.1	4.1	0.7	1.7	0.8	0.8	0.8	0.8	1.3	2.3	1.9	14.3	15.3
Amazonas	0.30	0.17	0.42	1.3	0.54	0.62	0.22	0.26	0.22	0.80	0.34	0.11	3.15
Pará	0.16	0.53	0.15	0.27	0.10	0.08	0.45	0.39	1.04	1.54	1.30	14.2	10.8
Northeast	12.4	9.5	12.8	19.6	12.9	15.4	18.3	8.3	8.4	17.5	17.5	15.5	13.2
Maranhão	0.34	1.4	0.82	0.73	0.32	0.23	0.21	0.17	0.04	0.69	0.34	7.19	6.1
Piauí	0.01	0.01	0.23	0.65	0.30	0.17	0.06	0.05	0.03	0.17	0.37	0.41	0.35
Ceará	0.18	0.63	1.7	1.55	0.32	0.42	0.55	0.35	0.25	1.5	1.6	0.39	0.33
Rio Grande do Norte	0.01	0.08	0.14	1.14	0.59	0.51	0.22	0.17	0.32	1.37	0.49	0.39	0.33
Paraíba	0.53	1.02	0.65	0.27	0.15	0.29	0.19	0.17	0.07	0.64	0.75	0.54	0.50
Pernambuco	2.7	0.52	1.0	1.92	1.27	0.83	1.91	1.11	0.57	1.4	3.10	0.92	0.73
Alagoas	5.6	0.18	3.9	0.83	0.14	1.7	0.69	1.14	1.1	0.44	0.62	0.42	0.36
Sergipe	0.06	0.09	0.14	0.39	0.11	0.12	0.09	1.1	0.04	0.62	0.36	0.19	0.16
Bahía	2.9	5.6	4.12	12.1	9.07	11.1	13.6	4.04	6.0	10.7	9.67	4.99	4.24
Southeast	64.2	65.4	54.2	54.7	57.5	61.4	56.2	60.4	40.3	57.5	50.3	53.3	45.3
Minas Gerais	10.2	9.74	9.2	10.3	18.1	16.1	11.4	13.3	12.6	17.0	12.2	12.3	10.4
Espírito Santo	3.4	1.16	1.2	1.0	4.7	3.3	2.2	1.04	1.36	3.95	3.30	1.36	1.15
Rio de Janeiro	11.2	12.66	10.5	9.3	6.5	13.6	6.6	30.8	12.7	12.4	6.7	11.6	9.8
São Paulo	32.4	38.7	30.8	34.1	27.1	28.5	27.3	15.2	12.5	23.6	23.5	25.5	28.0

South	17.3	19.9	20.4	17.0	16.2	10.1	15.4	14.0	38.2	20.0	27.4	13.2	11.3
Paraná	1.7	2.8	4.8	3.97	7.2	2.93	5.22	9.0	33.0	7.0	15.4	8.7	7.4
Santa Catarina	2.1	2.5	3.2	4.7	2.2	2.14	1.81	1.7	0.83	2.5	2.2	1.1	0.9
Rio Grande do Sul	10.0	12.9	4.8	5.9	4.4	5.0	6.31	2.7	2.48	10.6	6.6	3.4	2.94
Center-West	1.4	1.2	6.4	2.1	1.7	1.5	3.1	1.9	0.4	2.7	2.8	3.8	3.2
Mato Grosso	1.1	0.39	2.2	1.7	1.17	0.5	0.09	0.38	0.09	0.47	0.61	1.8	1.51
Goiás	0.1	0.13	1.6	0.3	0.19	0.99	2.40	1.4	0.29	2.0	2.0	1.9	1.60
Brasília–DF	0.25	0.68	0.54	0.1	0.35	0.04	0.52	0.1	0.04	0.54	0.32	0.08	0.07

Source: IBGE (1970–1982).

Note: Regional totals include interregional projects.

[a]1978 was the year of Itaipú in Paraná.

because inflation threatened to spiral out of control. Supported only by the foreign minister, Gomes was forced out of the government at the end of 1976.

In the long run, the contradiction between the strategic priorities of the regime and the coalitions forming its political base caused the retreat of industrial deconcentration.[51] The high-priority capital goods sector initially supported Geisel enthusiastically, but by 1978 the big industrialists were disillusioned.[52] Taking PNDII at its word, capital goods producers had expanded quickly, more than doubling capacity between 1973 and 1975. By 1976 and 1977, however, the administration cared more about inflation than capital goods production. Government companies, always the largest customers for new capital goods, reduced their purchases. When capital goods producers demanded protection against foreign imports, the administration refused, claiming it needed to economize.

In effect, PNDII threatened domestic firms. If they refused to leave the São Paulo metropolitan area, foreign firms could establish plants in the hinterlands. If they did move, their capacity would be dangerously expanded. Domestic entrepreneurs must have been considerably relieved when the incentive program finally collapsed.

PNDII was not so naive that it advocated an expansion of one sector without recognizing that other sectors would suffer. The losers were to be transportation and consumer durables, especially housing. But implementing such a reduction proved impossible, because the employment-generating ability of the transport industry gave it enormous political weight. Alliances between electrical equipment and engineering firms on the one hand, and between construction companies and the financial network (especially the National Housing Bank) on the other, penetrated all levels of government. Even the powerful Geisel administration could not break them.

Complicating the picture was the increasing political strength of certain states. Seeing the possibility of attracting industry, states began to compete with each other. The government of Minas Gerais, for example, raised the ire of the *paulistas* by contributing

---

51. For an excellent parallel treatment of this topic see Lessa (1978).
52. See, for example, the "Manifesto das Oito."

enough capital and infrastructure to attract an Italian auto parts firm. Rio de Janeiro battled Pernambuco over the location of an aluminum plant, and Paraná fought São Paulo over a Michelin tire factory.

Why was the Geisel government—so clever in its political maneuvers—unable to create a strategic coalition capable of carrying out its long-term strategy? Lessa (1978) points to the "exhaustion of the referee" as the explanation. The government in Brasília, he argues, was unwilling to trouble itself resolving interstate conflicts over the location of new factories. Lessa's argument rings true, but at times the central government did avoid these conflicts. Letting the states bid against each other, the central government took no position on the establishment of the Italian firm in Minas Gerais, and it abstained as well in the dispute over a Volvo plant in Paraná.[53]

Still, interstate political struggles took their toll on a regime whose economic maneuvering room was steadily shrinking. In the end the Geisel administration must have judged that the benefits of industrial deconcentration would be long in coming, while the costs, both political and economic, were immediate. In that calculus, industrial deconcentration had no chance.

Wage Policy

The determination of wage increases occupies a distinctive position among our five policy areas.[54] Only wage policy had an immediate impact on the living standards of so many people. Only wage policy was subject to such intense public discussion during the entire post-1964 era. Wage policy, as a result, was uniquely the object of open and continuous class struggle.

In the post-1964 administrations of Presidents Castello Branco and Costa e Silva, the military leadership was intensely concerned with the process of wage setting (Ames 1973). Because inflation at the time of the coup was over 100 percent and the GNP was

53. Interview with Reis Velloso, July 1983.
54. The term "wages" refers, in common Brazilian usage, to the remunerations of blue-collar workers, while "salaries" refers to the remunerations of white-collar employees. The minimum wage, however, is called the *salário mínimo*, and wages ranging well into the middle class are set at some multiple of the minimum. I will generally use the term "wage," but it should be remembered that wages of twenty-five to thirty times the minimum would put an employee high in the upper middle class.

actually in decline, wage control was a critical near-term objective. But the regime turned out to be interested in much more than crisis management. It wanted a labor movement too weak to oppose its economic policies, and it sought to transfer income from labor to capital in order to guarantee foreign investors an attractive level of profits.

The destruction of labor's influence was accomplished partly through outright repression and partly through the use of the same corporatist structure that had long dominated the labor movement (Ames 1973; Erickson 1977). Immediately after the coup, elements friendly to the regime replaced the leaders of all the important unions. The government prohibited strikes except in very rare circumstances,[55] and it separated the social security system from the Ministry of Labor, thus eliminating a key source of union patronage.

Without the regime's political attack on the unions, its economic assault could never have succeeded. In Rio de Janeiro the real value of the minimum wage declined 9 percent by 1965, 16 percent by 1966, and more than 23 percent by 1970. The labor time required to earn the cost of a basic food ration soared from 88 hours in 1965 to 100 hours in 1969 and to 163 hours in 1974 (DIEESE 1981). Between 1970 and 1976, shares of national income declined for all except the richest 10 percent of the population. That decile, however, increased its income share by almost 8 percent (IBGE 1979:63–64).

A rigid formula applied to all collective agreements became the tool for wage reduction. The formula adjusted wages on the basis of their average value over the previous twenty-four months, with additional increases for productivity gains and for the inflation projected for the year to come. Because the formula restored wages to their previous *average* rather than their previous peak, and because the regime consistently underestimated both productivity gains and future inflation, wages could not hold their real values.

Fundamentally, the regime cut wages because its economic strategists believed Brazilian labor was overpaid. Mário Henrique Simonsen, the first Treasury minister (and occupant of the same post under Geisel), put it neatly when he commented—after four

55. The number of strikes dropped from 302 in 1963 to 25 in 1965, 12 in 1970, and none in 1971 (Erickson 1977:159).

years of wage cuts—that workers still received "beyond what is appropriate for the national economy."[56]

In the early 1970s, declining rates of inflation brought wage increases closer to increases in the cost of living, but the readjustment formula remained substantially unchanged and labor regained none of its lost ground. Since high rates of aggregate growth presumably allowed real wage gains, the Médici administration was constantly on the defensive. The regime could claim its policies were temporary, and it could even claim income was not determined by wage policy (Langoni 1972). But it could not deny that Brazil's income distribution, highly inequitable even before 1964, had worsened.

By the second half of 1973 labor militancy had begun to rise.[57] Strikes broke out in the factories of Volkswagen, Mercedes, and Chrysler, with workers demanding an immediate 10 percent increase above the wage formula. Thanks in part to a tight labor market, these strikes were successful, and in 1974 they began to multiply.

Immediately upon taking office in March 1974, Geisel indicated that labor would be kept under strict supervision.[58] At the same time, the administration began to make concessions *before* grievances could generate mass unrest. By the end of 1974 it had granted early readjustments—the chief demand of the strikers of 1973—to broad categories of workers.

With the publication of the Second National Development Plan (PNDII), an extension of the political opening to labor seemed even more likely. The First National Development Plan had explicitly postponed income redistribution until the whole economic cake grew larger (*"esperar o bolo crescer"*), but PNDII argued that it was both possible and necessary to undertake redistributive policies "while the cake grows."[59]

For many technocrats the motivation to raise workers' wages grew out of a sense of justice, but other motivations were important as well. Business now supported redistribution, because the

56. *Correio da Manhã*, April 27, 1968, p. 3.
57. For the sake of brevity I have ignored the strikes of 1968, which were harshly repressed and which led indirectly to the Fifth Institutional Act.
58. In the Villares strike, for example, police in São Paulo arrested and tortured a number of labor leaders. See Kucinski (1982).
59. See *Veja*, March 12, 1975, pp. 96–97.

internal market was experiencing inadequate demand. Sales of consumer goods had fallen sharply in the first six months of 1974, and retailers complained frequently about declining volume. It also happened that an important election was scheduled for November.[60]

In the spring of 1975 the Geisel administration proposed a reformulation of wage policy. The new formula separated the minimum wage readjustment from other wage changes and allowed a 15 percent jump in the real value of the minimum.[61] The cost of this change fell on those earning over thirty minimum wages (the upper 1 percent of wage earners). They received a full readjustment only on the part of their wages below thirty minimums.

At the end of 1974 and in the early months of 1975, the administration seemed intent on raising the real wage, but hopes of ending the squeeze soon collapsed. The problem, as always, was inflation. After April 1975, price increases accelerated, going from 1.8 percent in April to 3.7 percent in August. The August figure, representing an annual rate of 55 percent, reinforced those administration economists who believed inflation was caused by wage increases, and readjustments began a precipitous decline.[62] In April 1975 the readjustment had been 16.8 percentage points greater than inflation. By July it was only 5.6 points ahead; by July 1976 the readjustment equaled the inflation rate; and by September 1976 it was 3.3 percentage points below inflation. Once again, the regime forced workers to bear the burden of the war on inflation.

Government spokesmen were surprisingly frank about the demise of wage liberalization. The secretary of employment and wages in the Labor Ministry commented that the new policy represented not a policy of wage "strangulation" (*arrôcho*) but a "realistic measure." Claiming that the wage bill had been growing to the point where firms would begin to furlough workers, the

60. *Veja*, October 30, 1974, pp. 110–114. Geisel's first step, granted just before the election itself, was a 10 percent emergency bonus. It was expected to produce about a 3 percent increase in consumption for the Christmas season.

61. The wage formula was also changed so that wages were adjusted to compensate for changes in prices over the previous twelve months rather than the previous twenty-four, thus helping maintain the real value of wages.

62. Affonso Celso Pastore, then executive secretary of the Economic Research Institute of the University of São Paulo and later head of the Central Bank, was one advocate of this position. See *Visão*, October 13, 1975.

government had concluded it was "impossible to give workers a larger share of the increase in national productivity." In the last analysis, according to the secretary, the end of wage liberalization represented the worker's contribution to the government's anti-inflationary effort.

By the spring of 1977, the completeness of the turnaround was evident even to supporters of the administration. In 1976 the GDP had expanded by 8.7 percent. Since the labor force had grown by only 3 percent, the increase for productivity could have surpassed 5 percent. It was significantly less: The Geisel administration had decided not merely that inflation should be fought through wages, but that wage cuts should occur before inflation became a real problem. The government, in essence, had abandoned the Second National Development Plan.

João Figueiredo assumed the presidency with a mandate to broaden both the political and the social openings. A strategy that included reaching out to the working class presupposed a healthy economy, but the economic sky had begun to darken even before Figueiredo's term began. The balance of payments was ominously negative, inflation was increasing, and the foreign debt could no longer be ignored.[63] Geisel's refusal to continue wage liberalization had stimulated a new wave of strikes. In May 1978 a big walkout hit the Scania works in São Paulo. Other large strikes occurred in Rio Grande do Sul, Minas Gerais, Paraná, and Rio de Janeiro. The volume and intensity of strike activity continued to grow in 1979. In São Paulo, for example, the number of strikes jumped from 136 in 1978 to 224 in 1979 (Tavares de Almeida 1981).

The biggest dispute of the period involved the steel, mechanical, and electrical workers against the Grupo de 14—fourteen members of the Industrial Federation of the State of São Paulo. The Regional Labor Tribunal decided to grant workers only the increase officially determined by the National Wage Policy Council. The workers struck and won a 24 percent boost on top of the 39 percent granted by the tribunal. After this strike it was clear that once the labor tribunals and the Wage Policy Council had lost the power of arbitrary repression, they also lost the power of persuasion (Vieira Da Cunha 1982). Strikes were now settled without

63. The best of many treatments of this period is found in Lessa (1980).

recourse to the machinery of the Ministry of Labor, and substantial increases in real wages became common.

The president had initially responded to the strike movement with conciliation. Murilo Macedo, a skilled politician, became head of the Ministry of Labor. Negotiating with the *paulista* steelworkers, Macedo at first showed a willingness to deal. But by the middle of August 1979, when the administration had already confronted eighty-three strikes involving more than 1 million workers, Figueiredo opted for a harder line. The government defined strikes as a "national security" problem and threatened to suspend normal civil rights.

Then, without warning, the Figueiredo administration reversed course. In September 1979, Figueiredo sent the Congress a totally new wage law, a law promising, for the first time since 1964, to redistribute wages in favor of lower-paid workers. The new law (DL 6.708 of 1979) established that the size of a worker's wage in relation to the minimum wage would determine increases. Wages from one to three minimums would be readjusted 110 percent—that is, a real increment of 10 percent. Wages from three to ten minimums would be readjusted 100 percent, and wages above ten minimums would be readjusted only 80 percent. The new law also established the principle of "cascade," by which, for example, an earner of six minimum wages would receive 110 percent for the first three and 100 percent for the next three. With the cascade, workers paid up to eleven minimum wages would enjoy a real increment.[64]

To the surprise of many, the redistributiveness of the new wage formula was not merely theoretical. Between 1980 and 1981 the percentage of income going to those earning two minimum wages or less fell from 23.5 to 21.7 percent of all salaried income, so some of the poorest workers had been pushed into higher categories. Earnings of those above twenty minimum wages also declined—from 18.03 percent of all income to 15.98 percent. The gains went to workers in the two to five minimum wage range, whose share of all earnings climbed about two percentage points.[65]

64. The new law also established semiannual rather than annual readjustments, changed the index measuring the cost of living, and added a further increase based on productivity (determined separately in each sector).

65. From 25.62 to 27.55 percent. See *Veja*, May 4, 1983. The analysis was based on the census of 1980 and the PNAD household sample of 1981.

Why did the administration reverse course so unexpectedly? Cynics pointed to Delfim Neto, the newly appointed planning minister.[66] Delfim Neto's economic strategy was aggressive and growth-oriented, quite the opposite of the austerity of Mário Henrique Simonsen.[67] Moreover, many observers considered Delfim Neto, at the end of 1979 and the beginning of 1980, to be a leading civilian candidate for the presidency.[68] For Delfim Neto, a shift toward workers might produce immense political rewards.

At first glance a redistributive wage policy might seem dangerous, but the peril was really minimal. If the law failed to contain the recent wave of strikes, it would at least legitimate harsh governmental action against "ungrateful" union leaders.[69] The law would not hurt business much (it would even help some firms), because it would disallow increases far above the level of inflation. The policy might also stimulate a reversal in inflationary expectations.

A redistributive wage policy was possible only in a healthy economy. Like Delfim Neto's return to economic leadership, the redistributive formula was a profession of faith in the future. Through 1980 and 1981 the future looked bright, but when Brazil was forced in late 1982 to begin negotiations on the foreign debt with the International Monetary Fund, the new wage scheme was doomed.[70]

66. Delfim Neto began Figueiredo's term as minister of agriculture. He replaced Simonsen as minister of planning in August of 1980.

67. It was said that Simonsen never met a recession he didn't like.

68. See, for example, *Visão*, March 3, 1980, p. 22. In the debacle of 1982–1984, it was difficult to find Brazilians who could recall that Delfim Neto had once been *"presidenciável."*

69. This thinking underlay the interpretation of the new wage law offered by the labor minister. In a speech entitled "The Future of Negotiations over Labor Relations in Brazil," Murilo Macedo stressed both the need for bargaining and the role of the government as the final arbiter of social disputes (Macedo 1981). The prediction that the new law would legitimize repression was soon borne out. In April 1980 a strike developed in two steel locals in São Paulo. Apparently hoping that the strike would end of its own weight when the workers became exhausted, the labor minister began negotiations with the strike leadership. Figueiredo, however, resolved that enough was enough. Under pressure from the military, the president jailed and replaced the leadership of the two unions. See *Visão*, April 28, 1980.

70. For brevity, I have omitted one early modification to the wage formula. In 1980 it was changed to provide 80 percent increases in the ten to fifteen minimum range and 50 percent for fifteen to twenty minimums, with free negotiations above that level.

Just at the point of going to the IMF, Delfim Neto tried to force changes in the wage formula, including a return to annual hikes (from the twice-yearly raises of the 1979 law) and a limit of 70 percent of inflation on all readjustments. But Murilo Macedo defended a less drastic modification, and in the end Figueiredo backed the labor minister.[71]

The IMF was unsatisfied, and in its first mission to Brazil it proposed a modification that included Delfim Neto's 70 percent ceiling.[72] The administration could not accept such a draconian change, but its response (issued as decree DL 2.012 because the Congress would not pass it) lowered readjustments for wages below three minimums to 100 percent of inflation, with readjustments in the three to seven minimum range cut to 95 percent and those in the seven to fifteen range cut to 80 percent.[73]

Five months later the government offered another wage law, fruit of an unholy alliance between the government party (the PDS) and the Labor party (the PTB). The PDS had 235 votes in the Chamber of Deputies, 5 votes short of an absolute majority. With the PTB's 13 votes the administration would have a 248–231 edge, sufficient to pass any legislation. As the price of its adherence, the PTB demanded an improvement in DL 2.012. The administration agreed, proposing DL 2.024, which extended the 100 percent readjustment range from three minimums to seven. The difference was slight but important. Under DL 2.012 anyone making more than three minimums would not keep up with inflation. Now, with DL 2.024, only those with more than seven minimums would lose.

The IMF was less pleased. On July 7, 1983, Delfim Neto met with Jacques de Larosiere, the managing director of the IMF, and

71. *Senhor,* December 12, 1982.

72. The IMF's argument that the 1979 wage law was inflationary is at least debatable. Vieira da Cunha and others (1982) note that the large firms determining Brazilian prices generally pay more than three minimum wages—so much more, in fact, that their total wage bills dropped after 1979. Until April 1981 (when mass firings began as a result of the recession), average wages increased less than other cost indicators. Moreover, although the demand for consumer goods rose with the 110 percent increases for wage earners in the one to three minimum range, the prices of agricultural products—heavily consumed by the poor—rose less than the prices of industrial goods.

73. In the three to seven minimum range, these readjustments meant a 2.8 percent loss. For someone earning seven to ten minimums, the loss averaged 6.3 percent.

with Paul Volcker, head of the U.S. Federal Reserve. They stressed that future IMF loans depended on a satisfactory wage plan.[74] One week later Delfim Neto produced, without consulting other ministers, a new formula. With DL 2.045, all workers would receive 80 percent of the inflation index for the next twelve months, and any firm with financial problems (including government enterprises) could petition the Wage Policy Council for the right to pay even smaller increases.

The IMF seemed satisfied, but the Congress was not. The deputies first had to vote on DL 2.024, the fruit of the PDS–PTB alliance. On October 19, they rejected DL 2.024, with eleven members of the government party voting no. Realizing that the defeat of DL 2.024 spelled the end of DL 2.045 as well, the administration offered an eleventh-hour compromise. Law 2.064 would provide 100 percent readjustments for the first three minimums, 80 percent for the three to seven range, 60 percent for the seven to fifteen range, and 50 percent for wages over fifteen minimums. The proposal dropped, however, the cascade. A worker at the seven-minimum level would no longer receive 100 percent for the first three minimums and 80 percent for the next four; the new increase would simply be 80 percent for the whole wage.

Elimination of the cascade galvanized the politicians, who foresaw its enormous impact on the upper middle class. Without the cascade, a wage earner at forty minimum wages would get 30 percent of the inflation index; with the cascade, the same person would receive 58.7 percent. Fearing mortgage foreclosures if a new policy squeezed the upper middle class too hard, the National Housing Bank backed the politicians, and in the end, Delfim Neto and the technocrats were forced to concede. Another modification (DL 2.065) restored the cascade and slightly improved readjustments for those earning over eight minimums. The PDS unanimously supported the proposal, the PDS–PTB alliance held firm, and the law passed the Congress.

By the spring of 1984 the new wage law had proved no more durable than its predecessors. In April, General Motors and Volkswagen gave increases *above* the guideline. Within weeks fourteen major firms, including one large government enterprise, followed suit. By June the Wage Policy Council (CNPS) had found a legal

74. *Isto é,* July 20, 1983.

loophole in DL 2.065 and had authorized forty government enterprises to exceed its limits. The loophole was a 1983 decree permitting enterprises to grant increases above the guidelines if they reduced other expenses. When the enterprises discovered that the CNPS would accept "promises" to reduce expenses, the wage law was effectively finished.

In the end, the post-1979 wage laws were all rejected not because they gave the working class too much but because they gave the middle and upper middle classes too little. Figure 15 shows the decline in high-level salaries. By the end of 1983, salary earners who had earned thirty minimum wages in 1979 had lost 47 percent of their real income. Employees at the twenty-minimum level lost more than 25 percent.[75] In the short run the consequences for production—and therefore employment—were dramatic. An economy geared to produce goods for a very small fraction of the total population cannot suddenly reduce the incomes of that fraction. Firms were willing to break the wage law because they worried about declining sales. In the end, manipulations of the wage structure could not resolve Brazil's crisis.

In sum, then, wage policy after 1974 continued to involve values at the heart of the military regime. Gone, however, was the certainty with which the regime's technocrats applied the formulas of the first ten years of military rule. Politicians discovered they could involve themselves in policy struggles and actually affect the results. Wage policy could once again become part of survival strategies.

Geisel inherited a restive labor movement willing to test the limits of his political "relaxation." When Geisel proved unable to stick with even a modest redistribution, Figueiredo was left with labor's anger and militance. But as it became more difficult to summon the torturers, it became harder to fight inflation with wage squeezes. Figueiredo opted for a strategy reaching out to the working class, but in a deteriorating economy a redistributive program was not viable. When Brazil had to seek help from the IMF, any policy providing real gains for the working class was doomed. The new political reality—pressure for wage maintenance from

75. Moreover, the government had "purged" the inflation index so that it no longer reflected accidental elements (such as droughts) or the removal of subsidies. If these "distortions" are included, the real loss almost doubles.

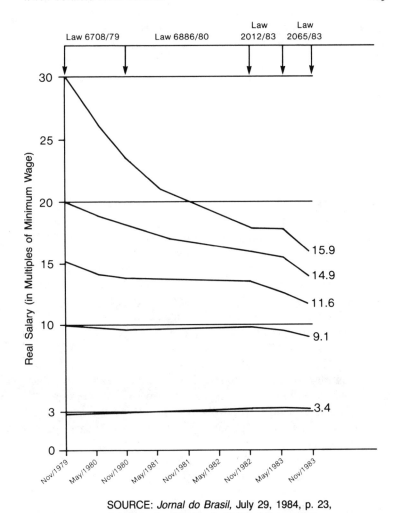

SOURCE: *Jornal do Brasil,* July 29, 1984, p. 23,
data from the São Paulo Guild of Economists.

Figure 15. Evolution of Real Salaries by Ranges:
November 1979 to November 1983

políticos and pressure for austerity from the IMF—yielded a policy redistributive only in the sense that the poorest workers lost less than the more affluent. Even this compromise soon collapsed, because Brazil's regressive income distribution determined its consumption pattern and therefore the level of employment. By squeezing the middle and upper middle classes, the redistribution of 1980–1984 wiped out the market for goods produced by the working class. Salary policy, after the spring of 1984, could no longer be a survival strategy for the military regime.

The Policy Areas Compared

Four survival strategies were available to the Geisel and Figueiredo administrations. Which were selected? Were the strategies chosen actually implemented?

The minimal "just avoid a recession" strategy can be rejected. Geisel and Figueiredo certainly wanted to avoid rapid economic decline. But this strategy assumes military leaders simply want a turmoil-free withdrawal and care little about maintaining influence after the end of military rule. Since the Geisel and Figueiredo administrations actually adopted a wide variety of policies to reach out to civil society, they surely did care about maintaining influence after the demise of the regime itself.

Geisel and Figueiredo made appeals to selected social classes, but implementing a class strategy turned out to be no simple task. Their administrations faced the usual dilemma: Could new allies be recruited without alienating old followers? A program like housing could expand to reach the upper working and lower middle classes without apparent harm to the interests of other groups. Agrarian reform, however, never got off the ground, because Geisel knew it was a red flag to the landowners. Geisel also increased welfare spending and the university share of the education budget, but he felt it necessary to boost spending at all educational levels to cushion the losses suffered by the poorer clients of primary and secondary education.

Do these policy manipulations imply an evenhandedness in Geisel's strategic perspective—a sense that the clever president had no particular targets but sought, instead, to avoid conflict and appeal to all classes? Actually, Geisel's wage policy suggests that reaching the working class was a low priority. In 1975 the president did initiate a change in the wage formula that benefited workers, but when the economic decline accelerated, he quickly jettisoned redistribution. Geisel knew austerity was implemented on the backs of workers, but he refused to challenge the economic interests that had been the mainstay of the post-1964 regime.

Figueiredo's administration represented a genuine shift in the class targets of the regime. The Ministry of Education and Culture boosted primary education, POLONORDESTE and credit policy targeted small farmers in the Northeast, and wage readjustments redistributed income. Is there less here than meets the eye? Outsiders—especially the World Bank and state-level agricultural technocrats—stimulated both POLONORDESTE and the credit shifts, and neither program directly threatened powerful interests. Spending changes in the decentralized education sector partially negated the growth of primary school spending in MEC. In wage policy, however, Figueiredo's outreach to the working class cannot be denied. The 1979 wage law, which granted raises above inflation for low- and middle-income workers and cut wages for high-income workers, changed Brazil's distribution of income. True, the policy collapsed in the economic crisis, but rapid redistribution in a declining economy is a dubious benefit for the working class, because any abrupt shift in consumption patterns increases unemployment. In any event, *intent* is the test of the hypothesis. Figueiredo must really have believed that the hostility the working class showed in the 1974 election could at least be neutralized.

Three of the five policy areas—housing, agriculture, and industrial deconcentration—reflect regional appeals, but the regime never fine-tuned these programs to its political needs. Politically marginal states did not gain at the expense of solidly progovernment and hopelessly antigovernment states. Instead, the regime aided almost all Northeastern states: It built low-income housing in every city, distributed credit to farmers everywhere, and funded deconcentration projects in every state (at least in election years). The regional strategy was more a response to the claims of powerful Northeastern supporters than a calculation of the political needs of Brasília itself.

Upon closer examination, the strength of the regional thrust diminishes. Expansion of low-cost housing owes as much to Mário Andreazza's ambitions and the political needs of Northeastern governors as it does to Figueiredo's grand design.[76] Industrial de-

76. By February 1984, when tenants of government housing had begun to

concentration died because the central government did not want the hassle of settling the states' quarrels and because the high-priority capital goods sector could not move to the hinterlands. Outsiders pushed agricultural programs harder than Brasília.

Why were regional programs so weak? Perhaps ad hoc arrangements such as intergovernmental transfers (which did flow to the Northeast) are actually fairly cheap relative to the costs of programs serving urban masses. In other words: The regime could buy the support of elites in "traditional" areas without overextending itself.

Long-range survival strategies presuppose a healthy economy. Geisel finished his term in reasonable shape, but economic pressures undermined his industrial deconcentration program and his attempts at raising wages. The roof fell in on Figueiredo: Each attempt to create a viable wage formula lasted less time than its predecessor, the IMF attacked credit subsidies, and funding cuts in the universities provoked a six-month strike.

Figueiredo's economic czars, the same technocrats who took credit for the economic miracle in the first place, betrayed him.[77] Mário Henrique Simonsen, the planning minister at the beginning of Figueiredo's administration, tried to deal with inflationary pressures in 1979 by cutting excess demand, but Figueiredo could not accept the recession a deflationary policy would cause. Simonsen resigned, and Delfim Neto moved from Agriculture to Planning. Brazil's entrepreneurs expected a return to the heady days of the economic miracle, but Delfim Neto understood the constraints placed on him:

> The objective of General Figueiredo, my superior, is to create conditions for a politically open society. He believes one must create mechanisms to dissolve the social tensions that have accumulated. . . . Because we have chosen the road of a politically open society, there will be inflation, which is a way of absorbing part of our social and economic tension. What I want to do is to reduce the rate of inflation (*Estado de São Paulo*, September 25, 1979).

protest against increases in their monthly payments greater than the increases in their wages, Andreazza changed his mind a bit. He commented that "constructing housing projects is the type of thing that doesn't get votes. . . . When the citizen enters the new house and his payments get higher, there's no way out: He ends up against the government." See *Veja*, February 22, 1984, p. 26.

77. This section owes a considerable debt to Bacha (1983) and Lessa (1980).

Delfim Neto sought merely to maintain a limited degree of growth, but in the end inflationary pressures were so strong they could not be fought without recession. Producers of wage goods had too little excess capacity, credit subsidies boosting farm production increased the public sector deficit, and, as always, the Price Council failed to hold down prices (Lessa 1980). Externally things were no better: Between 1979 and 1981 Brazil's oil import bill increased by US $4.5 billion, and annual interest payments on the foreign debt rose from US $4.2 billion to US $9.2 billion.

By May 1980 inflation was accelerating, and Delfim Neto knew his gambit had failed. When he finally decontrolled interest rates, real rates on three-month government bills rose from − 22 percent in the second quarter of 1980 to + 47 percent in the second quarter of 1981. Industrial production fell 20 percent from the third quarter of 1980 to the fourth quarter of 1981. Brazil's economy had entered a recession from which it would not recover until late 1984 (Bacha 1983:331).

On top of the buffeting of unfavorable economic winds, internal deterioration weakened Figueiredo's government. On the surface, the survival strategies launched by his administration suggest that the president was determined to seek support everywhere. In fact, his administration's multiple, even contradictory, appeals came from an absence of leadership and a fragmentation of programs.

When a regime announces its intention to withdraw from power, it is hardly surprising that its admirals seek their own lifeboats. The number of high-level members of Figueiredo's administration who aspired to the presidency or vice presidency is difficult to calculate, but at one time or another the list included Delfim Neto, Petrônio Portella (director of the Civilian Policy Staff), Andreazza, Hélio Beltrão and Jarbas Passarinho (both ministers of welfare and social assistance), Cesar Cals (minister of mines and energy), and Aureliano Chaves (the vice president). All except Chaves controlled government programs that could further their private ambitions. The search for personal advantage by a regime's principals must be inevitable in prolonged withdrawals. In the Brazilian case it was easy to pursue personal ambitions, because the complexity of the governmental apparatus made presidential control of government enterprises and decentralized agencies next to impossible.

Could a president with Geisel's skills have performed better than Figueiredo, even in the unfavorable economic climate the latter faced? Figueiredo hardly presents the appearance of a skilled leader. His unwillingness to curtail the plans of his subordinates worsened the budgetary deficit and magnified the perception of a government out of control.[78] Interviews with journalists and upper-echelon technocrats confirmed the popular image of a president who disliked politics and increasingly refused to lead.[79]

As the crisis deepened, the economic and social opening could only contract, and Figueiredo's agenda became essentially political. By 1982 he had successfully realized the granting of a general political amnesty as well as legislative and gubernatorial elections. With two years remaining in his term, Figueiredo's challenge was the selection of a successor, but that challenge was one the president seemed determined to avoid.

If the president truly detested any candidate for the government party's presidential nomination, it was surely Paulo Maluf, the ex-governor of São Paulo. Figueiredo's favorite was Andreazza, but when the president declared, in the fall of 1983, that he would no longer coordinate the PDS succession, he deprived Andreazza of the strongest weapon the minister could take to the PDS nominating convention. Figueiredo became the first president in Brazilian history to take no part in the selection of his successor. Andreazza was doomed, and Maluf won the nomination easily.

Figueiredo's successor was to be selected by indirect vote, through an electoral college rigged to favor the government party. Popular opinion overwhelmingly favored direct elections, and in late 1983 Figueiredo announced that he too preferred a direct vote. Such a vote could not be held, said the president, because the PDS would not "yield the right to elect the future president."[80] With this remark Figueiredo set himself against his own party and

78. Simonsen, for example, called Andreazza a man incapable of understanding that government has to limit expenses. Simonsen even named a monetary unit after the interior minister: the "andreazza," worth about US $50 million. See *Veja,* November 23, 1983.

79. Reliable information about Figueiredo's administration is still quite scarce. Good sources of unbiased reporting on the president's dislike of politics and his withdrawal from the exercise of leadership are the daily columns of journalist Carlos Castello Branco in *Jornal do Brasil.* I conducted interviews in the summer of 1982, the summer and fall of 1983, and the summer of 1984.

80. *Veja,* November 23, 1983. Figueiredo made these comments in Lagos, Nigeria.

helped unleash an enormous grass-roots movement for direct elections. The movement failed, but it galvanized the opposition and split the cabinet.[81]

The president's credibility suffered enormously from the economic and political crises. From a +15 in 1979, his approval-disapproval rating dropped in 1980 to −19. In 1981 and 1982, years in which the economy stabilized and elections were held, his rating rose, first to −13 and then to −1. But in 1983 it fell to −22, and by July 1984 it reached an all-time low of −44.[82] Humorist Luis Veríssimo captured popular feeling perfectly with his creation of a mythical old woman who became a national celebrity as the only person in Brazil still believing in the government.

The regime had tried to develop a basis for long-term influence without the need for coercion. If the popularity of the military when the civilians took over is any indication, it failed. Perhaps the economic crisis was a sufficient condition for failure. Since the economic crisis resulted from external shocks that were not the regime's fault, the difficulties faced by the social opening illustrate the enormous constraints on any long-range survival strategy. But the ultimate weakness of the social opening lay in its premise that the regime could substitute popularity for coercion as a currency of influence without any real redistribution of power.

The regime sought to maintain growth because it feared the social consequences of a recession on top of the deterioration in income distribution between 1964 and 1973. At the same time, the regime's inability to break the alliances supporting economic policy made it impossible to impose sacrifices on anyone, so its only alternative was a no-losers expansion that stimulated inflation. Years of rapid growth before the oil crisis had made the regime overconfident. The arrogance of the technocrats and the "Brazil Grandeur" mentality the regime itself had encouraged led to the wasteful "Pharaonic Works" absorbing US $90 billion in foreign currency. Delfim Neto's growth gambit in 1979 required heavy support from the international banking community, but the bankers lost faith in a regime no longer believed by its own sup-

81. One faction, led by Leitão de Abreu, head of the civilian cabinet, wanted to negotiate. The other, led by Octávio Medeiros, head of the secret police, preferred a show of force to minimize concessions.
82. Poll carried out by the Gallup Institute of Brazil, reported in *Veja*, August 8, 1984, p. 30.

porters and bereft of the power to repress. And, finally, the political fragmentation of the Figueiredo administration, a fragmentation that could only increase with the regime's approaching demise, reinforced the economic crisis and hindered the pursuit of long-range influence.

Conclusion: Political Survival and Comparative Politics

This concluding chapter begins by integrating and summarizing the findings of the cross-national analyses and the two Brazil applications. I then assess constraints on the strategic use of expenditure policy and consider alternative policies available to political leaders. In the final sections I advance a broader methodological claim—an argument that the analysis of survival coalitions is crucial not just to theories of short-range political strategy but to the development of long-range theory as well.

A Brief Summary of the Argument

Strategic coalition theory begins with the assertion that political executives care enormously about retaining their posts. The deepest reasons leaders want power are known only to them. Some may simply covet the trappings of office. Others may hope to bestow benefits upon a certain class, region, or ethnic group. Still others may believe they are building better futures for their nations or advancing the cause of liberty. To accomplish any of these goals, leaders have to hold onto their posts. Given the frequency of military coups, the dismal reelection record of incumbents, and the volatility of open economies, executives can rarely take political survival for granted. To the maximum degree possible, every program must be subjected to the executive's drive for security.

Like leaders in other parts of the world, Latin American executives view public expenditures as key policy instruments. Leaders in Latin America, however, use expenditures for direct fine-tuning of the polity rather than for macroeconomic stimulation. Properly targeted, expenditures benefit party activists, social classes, specific regions, or other political elites; in short, spending rewards anyone in a position to contribute to the executive's survival coalition.

Consider public spending in aggregate terms—that is, in terms of the annual totals of all central government expenditures. A wide variety of political factors affected total spending in our seventeen nations. When an election approached, expenditures rose as a way of reassuring a leader's old followers and attracting new ones. When the election passed, expenditures continued to rise if a new leader or party had been elected. The size of the margin of victory failed to affect spending one way or the other; presumably the motivation to spend created by a close election was negated by hostile legislatures and powerful civil oppositions.

The spending of military governments reflected a desire for security as powerful as that of civilian governments. When new juntas took control of national budgets, expenditures climbed sharply. As the security of military leaders increased, they retreated to austerity, and spending levels dropped.

If the political factors influencing total spending were all cyclical, expenditures would return to their original levels after each expansionary phase. They did not. The steady upward pressure had two causes. When parties with working-class or middle-class constituencies supported executives, spending grew. When leaders received good news in the form of growing holdings of international reserves, they spent more, but when the news was bad and reserves declined, executives failed to cut back, because they knew they might be able to avoid paying the costs of expansion indefinitely.

The political quality of spending seems undeniable, but aggregate expenditures remain much too blunt a political weapon. Survival requires fine-tuning of policy instruments, and such fine-tuning necessitates careful distinctions in the distribution of budgetary largesse. Latin American leaders know that different components of the budget appeal to different constituencies. Salaries are dear to the hearts of bureaucrats; public works are grist for the mills of local interests; new weapons swell the chests of generals. Leaders also know that their own vulnerability peaks during "political crises"—that is, just after coups and just before and after elections.

This strategic calculus led Latin American executives to adopt one or more of five budgetary strategies. The first strategy required pacifying the military. Regardless of their own military or civilian status, leaders vulnerable to military overthrow made certain they increased the military's share of expenditures. The military's gains came at the expense of programs in health, welfare, and even police. In the absence of a threat of revolt, military budgets declined steadily, because the soldiers' requests could not compete against the many demands for budgetary responses to national social and economic problems.

A second survival strategy centered on the recruitment of bureaucrats. This strategy was most common in countries where civil servants comprised an important fraction of the politically active population. During crises, leaders created new government jobs and boosted wages to prevent inflation from eroding bureaucratic salaries. When wage bills rose, programs with less immediate payoffs, especially programs such as public works, were losers.

Infrastructure projects became a favored instrument when regional or local interests were the targets. Executives seeking to reward a town or state knew that a well-placed dam, hospital, or school would be just the ticket. The mere suggestion of a public works project can be politically beneficial, of course, but much of the reward comes only when the project is finished. Getting a project done by the time an executive leaves office is often difficult, so public works strategies carry a political risk. As a result, leaders pursued these strategies only when they had to—that is, only during crises. Once their vulnerability to local demands lessened, their willingness to target pork barrel spending lessened as well.

Most survival strategies assume the existence of a stratum of intermediate leaders or organizations, a stratum of activists who keep a portion of the rewards and deliver the support of their followers. If intermediate leaders are absent and populations are unorganized, leaders need a direct mechanism to reach target populations. Such an instrument is found in transfer payments, including programs like social security or university scholarships. Government reports of transfer payments were rather unreliable, but leaders faced with unorganized target populations did shift funds to transfers, at the expense, especially, of the salary component of budgets.

Strategies directed at specific social classes took many forms. Leaders appealing to the upper and upper middle classes boosted the military budget to the detriment of programs benefiting the middle and working classes, especially programs in health and education. Middle-class strategies favored education while cutting both military and health budgets. In the few cases where leaders courted the working class, they boosted both public works and the military, thereby joining job creation with protection money. Executives seeking to build multistratum coalitions of middle-class and working-class groups favored education and public works. Although such multiclass approaches inevitably created destabilizing inflationary pressures, few attempts were made to buy military support. Perhaps that was a mistake, because multiclass administrations had little success in avoiding military ouster.

Theoretically, executives are free to modify the programmatic divisions of a budget without regard to changes in such economic aggregates as the gross domestic product or inflation. As it turned out, however, strategic choices were made with the economic environment clearly in mind. Executives knew they could cushion losses in budgetary shares by increasing total expenditures enough so that every program enjoyed an absolute increase. Overall increases were easier, of course, when potential budgetary resources (the GDP or export receipts) were rising. Some administrations, particularly those following multiclass strategies, lived under such stress that they increased total budgets more rapidly than their resources increased. Even during economic downturns, nothing could deter these vulnerable regimes from expansionary fiscal policies. It comes as no surprise, therefore, that the International Monetary Fund has such difficulty in imposing stringent conditions on Latin American debtors.

The links between survival strategies and expenditures centered on the notion of political crisis: the idea that leaders face moments of special vulnerability. What happened to those who overcame their crises? What happened, in other words, to the survivors? Did their strategic choices help them survive? Did their strategies affect long-term policy as well? In Chapter 3 the analysis turned to post-crisis policy, to periods in which survival was no longer the dominant problem.

The allocations of executives reaching the normal ends of their terms differed substantially from those who had been ousted. Consider just those administrations appearing vulnerable to military coups. If they increased the military budget share, they were more likely to survive. If they spent more on education and health, they were more likely to be overthrown.

Surprisingly, budgetary strategy failed to help executives (or their political parties) in subsequent elections. Spending on popular programs such as education and health advanced electoral chances a bit, but the barriers against reelection of incumbents were so strong that expenditure policy could only be a marginal aid. Executives act as if their strategies ensure success.

From the perspective of leaders, elections are costly. Compared to presidents facing only simultaneous presidential and legislative elections, those presidents facing midterm legislative elections spent more. Because midterm elections were politically risky, they generated inflationary pressures and distorted public sector allocations. Midterms did not, however, stimulate pork barrel public works programs, because in Latin America such programs would not produce tangible results quickly enough for a midterm election.

Survival strategies are short-term responses to crises, but they surely affect long-term policy outputs as well. A good example is a traditional (but still unresolved) controversy in comparative politics—the question of differences in spending on the military between military and civilian governments. In Chapter 3, Latin American administrations were classified (building on Schmitter's typology) as military, civilian noncompetitive, and civilian competitive. Three factors were found to influence military spending: vulnerability to military overthrow, rising levels of "illegitimate" participation, and constraints on total budgets.

It turned out that military administrations threatened with the possibility of an overthrow reacted very quickly with fatter military budgets. Civilian-noncompetitive regimes responded almost as strongly, but competitive regimes did not change relative shares at all. In a context of hostile legislatures and competing demands, competitive regimes confronted by a restive military too often succumbed to the temptation to increase the size of the whole budget in order to avoid cutting any program.

If the previous administration (military or nonmilitary) had experienced increases in civil violence, demonstrations, or strikes, a military government was more likely to follow. These subsequent military administrations responded by increasing the armed forces' budget. Civilian administrations, whether competitive or noncompetitive, made no equivalent response to increases in illegitimate participation. Why the divergent responses? Increases in the military budget do little in themselves to restrain civil violence, and civilian regimes face a host of competing budgetary demands. Perhaps the military responds less to the concrete threat of overthrow than to the threat to the military's self-image as the preserver of order.

The availability of budgetary resources was the third factor affecting civilians and soldiers differently. Rising budgets liberated military administrations: They spent much more on the armed forces when they could raise overall budgets. Civilian governments found the demands of other claimants too compelling to use budgetary largesse on the officer corps.

Further progress in explaining the policies of governments that overcame their survival crises requires an investigation of the post-survival preferences of executives. Since such an investigation is a separate research project in itself, Chapter 3 concluded by offering some preliminary suggestions. Purely on the basis of the similarity of their expenditure patterns, I identified four clusters of administrations. *"Reformists"* boosted social programs while cutting the military. Reformist administrations came from countries at lower levels of social mobilization and economic development. Reformists who were also politically competitive increased overall spending relative to GDP as a way of cushioning the military's losses. Perversely, this cushioning produced fiscal strain and, in the end, heightened vulnerability. A second group, the *"Repressive Militarists,"* put social programs last and military programs first. These regimes held budget increases below GDP increases, so losing programs enjoyed no cushioning; that is, they absorbed substantial absolute cuts. Since repressive regimes came from both rich and poor countries, and since they followed periods of both terrorism and peace, the rise of such regimes highlights the importance of leaders' substantive preferences. *"Defensive Liberals"* constituted a third group. Stressing both social programs and military spending, they were mostly civilian and mostly from poorer countries. Defensive liberalism was more common when the GDP was rising. Particularly in comparison to Reformists, Defensive Liberals preferred less fiscal strain; that is, they held overall spending increases below GDP increases. The final group, the *"Builders,"* favored public works at the expense of the military. These administrations were equally likely to be competitive or noncompetitive, civilian or military. Like the Defensive Liberals, these public-works-oriented administrations were more common when the GDP was rising. Growing resources enabled leaders to take the longer view of payoffs that infrastructural projects demand.

Part I of the book focused on the survival strategies of a single political actor, the executive, but we saw that the structure of political influence included other political actors pursuing their own survival strategies. Midterm electoral pressure and legislative opposition were just two of many themes suggesting that no successful executive strategy can be framed without taking the strategies of other political actors into account.

Chapter 4, which explored the budgetary process in the Brazilian Congress between 1947 and 1964, treated structures of influence in more depth. Since the Brazilian electoral system was based on proportional representation, with whole states constituting electoral districts, we might expect that legislators would have little motivation to attract spending into their states. Such expectations would be wrong. Because legislators defended electoral strongholds, or bailiwicks, within their states, they had powerful incentives to pursue allocations, particularly allocations to pork barrel programs.

Congressmen using budgetary allocations as survival strategies secured seats on powerful committees, defended amendments to budgetary proposals, and tried to win positions of leadership in the Chamber of Deputies and the Senate. Though their efforts were designed to help their strongholds rather than entire states, states gained if many budget-maximizing deputies represented them, if deputies cooperated across party lines, if state residents became ministers in presidential cabinets, and if the delegation had effective lobbying skills.

Did congressional involvement in budgetary politics lead inevitably to higher overall spending? When Brazilian presidents wanted to hold the line on spending, Congress went along. Congressmen only gave up acting as "Guardians of the Treasury" when the program of the executive became more ambitious and expansionary. Perhaps legislatures do have an inherent bias toward pushing up spending, but the Brazilian experience lays at least as much blame on the executive.

The Brazilian case highlights the importance of seeing both sides of patron–client relationships. Brazilian presidents have always been conscious of regional balance in the appointment of federal ministers, and cabinet positions have long been rewards for state and local leaders delivering important blocs of votes. At the same time, states represented in the president's cabinet were more successful in attracting budgetary largesse than states without such representation. Executives strengthened their coalitions by parceling out ministries as regional rewards, but coalition building carried an inevitable budgetary cost.

Principles sometimes got in the way of pork. The antipopulist ethos of the National Democratic Union party (UDN) kept many of its deputies from using budgetary allocations as a survival strategy; indeed, some UDN deputies took pride in preventing other deputies from pursuing their own survival strategies. Intense ideological feuds in the state of Paraná increased the turnover of the state delegation so much that Paraná's deputies rarely secured places on key committees or on the leadership. The delegation's instability increased the electoral vulnerability of its members, but lack of seniority made the deputies too weak to attract allocations.

The case of the Brazilian Congress also illuminates a difference between the survival strategies of executives and lower-level political actors. For executives, more resources are always a blessing. For lower-level actors such as legislators, more resources are a blessing only if they have access to them. When the presidential administrations of Getúlio Vargas and Juscelino Kubitschek increased spending, powerful state-level politicians dominated the Budget Committee and took control of the new resources. Weaker politicians had much better access to the arenas of budgetary decision when access was worth less.

Finally, the Brazilian case illustrates the limits of the coalition–budget relationship. Some Brazilian states, typically those ruled by oligarchies that felt safe with the status quo, avoided central government programs. Budgetary allocations threatened their strategic coalitions, because new programs might create new interests and new political competitors. Central government allocations would bring uncertainty, and that uncertainty was more threatening than the potential benefits of budgetary largesse.

The final extension of the strategic coalition model, presented in Chapter 5, centered on the Brazilian military regime between

1974 and 1984. In this chapter strategic coalition theory moved in two new directions: toward a broader notion of crisis and survival and toward a wider set of policy areas.

Three factors led to the survival crisis of the Brazilian military: the oil price increase of 1973, the regime's electoral defeat in 1974, and the popular struggle for democracy. Because the crisis grew out of the interplay between the regime's desire to create a base of support and the popular pressure for a speedy political opening, the length of the crisis was indeterminate. Since the regime's eventual withdrawal was inevitable, political survival could not mean an indefinite hold on the executive. Instead, survival meant continued influence *after* withdrawal. Put differently, survival meant affecting the structure of influence so that the fortunes of *future* civilian executives would depend on attending to the military's substantive preferences.

Because government intervention in the Brazilian economy was so vast, and because so many of the regime's group and regional targets could not be reached solely through the programs of the central ministries, the policy consequences of this expanded notion of survival extended far beyond budgetary allocations. In addition to expenditures, Chapter 5 investigated four policies: agricultural programs in the Northeast, housing for the working class and lower middle class, industrial deconcentration, and wage and salary setting.

How did the regime seek to affect the long-range structure of influence? Given that the regime was a dictatorship, we cannot hope to determine the preferences of its leaders by direct observation of decision making, by analysis of documents, or by interviews with participants. We can only infer preferences from policy outputs. Thus the fundamental question of this chapter was inductive: Given the policy evidence, what strategy (or strategies) might the regime have been pursuing?

It turns out that the regime pursued a variety of strategies at the same time, and it shifted targets during the course of its extrication. Between 1974 and 1978 (during the presidency of General Geisel), policy was mostly directed toward avoiding a recession. Geisel also made attempts to recruit Northeastern elites with programs of industrial deconcentration, to attract farmers by means of land reform and easy credit, and to appeal to urban workers through higher wages. These efforts failed because they incurred unexpected costs: Industrial deconcentration exacerbated interstate rivalries and raised capital costs; land reform aroused the ire of agrarian elites; wage hikes threatened to derail efforts to control inflation. In each case the leadership lacked the political will to push forward. The regime's leaders still believed that economic performance would be their ultimate claim to support, and the continued high rate of economic growth weakened any sense of urgency.

By the final military government, the administration of President Figueiredo, the halcyon days of the Brazilian miracle were fast becoming a dim memory. Popular support now required concrete benefits, not just vague promises of rewards in the future. Figueiredo actually responded, implementing a truly redistributive wage and salary policy, a reorientation of education spending toward primary schools, a shift in agricultural credit toward small farmers, and a significant expansion of public housing for the poor and near-poor.

Perhaps if the government had had more time, its efforts might have borne fruit. But the economic crisis overwhelmed Figueiredo's policy thrusts, and the decline in his government's administrative coherence prevented the kind of political fine-tuning that renewed support required. Rather than shape policy so that marginal states benefited at the expense of solidly progovernment or hopelessly antigovernment states, the regime was forced to distribute benefits to its supporters everywhere. Moreover, the political ambitions of powerful ministers shaped policy in ways alien to the regime's needs. In the end, the regime's survival strategies were more a response to the claims of powerful supporters and allies than a calculation of the political needs of Brasília itself.

Two additional lessons emerge from the experience of the Brazilian military. The first is that benefits for elites are less expensive than benefits for masses. Elites can be bought cheaply, even though individually they command a high price for their adherence, because they are few in number. On the other hand, when symbolic rewards fail to attract masses, a conservative government finds it difficult to deliver concrete benefits in persuasive amounts. The second lesson is that an executive's inner circle of advisers may prove his undoing rather than his bedrock support. When a regime is sinking, its admirals no longer identify their interests with those of their commander in chief. They seek their own lifeboats, and the programs they control obey a very different helmsman.

The Limits of Survival Politics

Though boosts or cuts in spending help executives hold onto their jobs, budget manipulations provide no guarantees of survival. What factors limit the ability of leaders to form survival-ensuring coalitions?

Strategic Mistakes

Executives often find it difficult to identify the factors triggering opposition. When João Goulart, Brazil's civilian president from 1962 until 1964, abandoned his centrist coalition partners—the "positive left"—and moved to the more radical "negative left," he probably sealed his own fate. Convinced that the strength of his military and labor support would discourage more cautious officers from attempting a coup, Goulart underestimated the paranoia of the right, which thought he was planning a leftist takeover (Skidmore 1967; Santos 1979).

Venezuela's Carlos Andrés Pérez was another leader who underestimated the importance of maintaining support. In the previous presidential term, different parties controlled the presidency and the legislature, and the fragmenting of authority produced an active legislature and a paralyzed executive. Pérez, however, saw himself as a charismatic figure, and when he and his party came out of the 1973 election with hefty margins, he felt unrestrained. Pérez gave only ten of the eighteen central government ministries to members of his Democratic Action party, and he relied mostly on independents loyal to him personally (Karl 1982). As the oil bonanza pushed up prices and encouraged corruption, the president's popularity plummeted. Without the support of Democratic Action loyalists, Pérez was unable to lead his party to victory in the 1978 presidential election. His defeat was enormous, personal, and, in retrospect, perfectly understandable.

Impossible Strategies

Defenders of fallen leaders often claim they faced unsolvable strategic problems. Salvador Allende, Chile's last democratic president, found himself caught between his Popular Unity coalition's radical activists, who wanted a speedier transition to socialism, and the bourgeoisie, whose hostility to serious reform was implacable. Allende was unable to construct a more inclusive multiclass coalition. At times such coalitions have been successful in Latin America: Perón made the transition in Argentina, and Paz Estenssoro managed it in Bolivia. But in Chile multiclass coalitions were no longer viable after the defeat of the Christian Democrats in 1970. Upper-middle-class groups felt no need to compromise as long as they could threaten an investment strike or call upon their allies in the military and the Nixon administration in the United States. The working class and the poor would probably have accepted a compromise guaranteeing them a steadily improving level of income, but left activists wanted nothing less than redistribution. By making claims that could only be satisfied through a reduction in the income share of the bourgeoisie, Allende's followers violated a traditional rule of the Latin American political game—the rule that new competitors must not challenge the vital interests of established players (Anderson 1967).[1] If the economy had expanded rapidly, Allende might have avoided zero-sum policies, but Chile's capitalists and their U.S. allies were hardly likely to display the kind of optimism required for private sector growth.

The Burden of Inheritance

Statistical estimations of the type undertaken in Chapter 2 assume that the various administrations within each country are mutually independent. In reality, the policies of previous executives sharply constrain the options open to a leader. Brazil's last two civilian presidents, Jánio Quadros and João Goulart, look like bumblers compared to their popular and successful predecessor, Juscelino Kubitschek. But Quadros and Goulart had a difficult time because of the policies Kubitschek adopted to gather support for the construction of Brasília, especially his enormous expansion of budgetary and wage payoffs (Kahil 1973). Kubitschek remained one of the most popular presidents in recent Brazilian history, but

___

1. Is this so different from politics in more advanced regions? In Latin America frightened elites regard even the *challenge* as illegitimate. More confident elites elsewhere know they can absorb and deflect such challenges without long-run damage.

accelerating inflation and growing debt helped make the presidencies of his successors a bitter memory.

If debts and inflationary pressures limit the sums an executive may devote to survival politics, the growth of "uncontrollable" programs hinders use of the budget itself. In the last thirty years the scope of government intervention in Latin American economies has widened, and an ever-increasing proportion of public expenditures has escaped from executive control into public enterprises or decentralized agencies. Many of these entities rely on specially earmarked taxes or on self-determined user charges; some even engage in foreign borrowing. With more than half of all public sector spending falling outside the traditional central ministries, the arsenal of budgetary weaponry has changed. The ability of executives to stimulate their economies, especially through external borrowing, has grown, but their control of individual programs has diminished.

The Economic Climate

Executives and their economic advisers often think any policy that worked in the past will continue to be successful. In the late 1950s, leaders like Kubitschek, Perón, and Rojas Pinilla came to believe rapid growth was inevitable. Albert Hirschman (1968:12) notes the delusions caused by early successes:

> The "exuberant" phase of import substitution was accompanied by flamboyant public policies which badly overestimated the tolerance of the economy for a variety of ventures, be they income redistribution by fiat, the building of a new capital, or other extravaganzas.

The general economic climate also contributed to the skyrocketing of Latin American debt. Foreign loans were seen, in David Felix's phrase, as a secure long-term alleviant of domestic financial stringencies. Anthony Sampson quotes an unnamed Latin American finance minister:

> I remember how the bankers tried to corner me at conferences to offer me loans. They wouldn't leave me alone. If you're trying to balance your budget, it's terribly tempting to borrow money instead of raising taxes; to put off the agony (Felix 1984:27).

More than one government was brought down by believing in the inexhaustibility of foreign financial flows. It is striking, moreover, how little economic expertise aided leaders. The worst disasters occurred in the countries where neoliberal economists held greatest sway: Argentina (Martinez de Hoz), Chile (de Castro), and Uruguay (Vegh Villegas). Executives' deepest holes were dug in the name of technocratic purity.

Pretenders to Power

Faced with the problem of building a survival coalition, leaders ask the cost of each actor's support. Some actors, however, simply want to hinder the leader as much as possible in order to bring him down. In 1961, Ecuador's Congress and vice president played a major role in overthrowing President Velasco. The Congress voted funds for antigovernment strikers, backed right-wing demonstrations against the government, moved to impeach Velasco's ministers, and deliberately passed disruptive budgets. The vice president (imposed on Velasco by party leaders) accused the president of trying to murder him and urged the Congress to vote impeachment (Pyne 1973).

Perhaps Ecuador's Congress is merely an extreme example of the costs of coalition formation. Still, such cases are striking for the single-mindedness of certain actors' efforts to obtain the leader's removal. Nothing can attract them to the executive's coalition, and they strive to reduce the leader's overall resources as a way of diminishing his chances of recruiting others.

Nonbudgetary Survival Strategies

The budget is a central arena of survival coalition building, but, as we saw in Chapter 5, it is just one of many policies subject to survival-directed manipulation. Do other areas of policy merit investigation?

Labor Policy

Wage and salary readjustment is probably the single policy most often linked to *electoral* timing. The administration of Argentina's President Arturo Frondizi is typical. Peronist support guaranteed Frondizi's election in 1958, but the 60 percent wage increase he decreed after the inauguration was an expensive payoff. It led to an increase of 46 percent in the money supply and a jump in the central government's deficit to almost 5 percent of the GDP. Three years later, at a time when the economy was experiencing inflationary pressures and serious balance of payments difficulties, Frondizi again granted generous wage increases, this time with an eye on the 1962 provincial elections (Mallon and Sourrouille 1975:19–24). Frondizi's policies led to the resignation of two consecutive economics ministers and, in the end, to his own ouster.

Appeals to labor go beyond wage increases. Between 1962 and 1966 the Colombian National Front government of Guillermo León Valencia faced a major crisis in labor relations. Falling real wages and rising taxes had angered Colombian labor, and when a sales tax was instituted at the end of 1964, the two major labor confederations called a national strike. The minister of war threatened a coup, and tensions started to escalate. But business groups stepped in to mediate the dispute, and a legislative package containing important concessions to labor was put together. The National Front's two-thirds rule for passage of legislation precluded congressional participation, but the president imposed the package by decree and the crisis was overcome (Hartlyn 1981).

How did Colombian labor escape the repression befalling its counterparts in bureaucratic-authoritarian regimes? Hartlyn argues that labor's very weakness facilitated compromise. Ideologically and organizationally divided, with relatively few workers unionized, Colombian labor was much less threatening than its counterparts in the Southern Cone (Hartlyn 1981:362). Colombia's experience does not suggest that elites will yield to any demand coming from nonthreatening petitioners, but it does suggest that moderate demands will be more successful when elites do not fear that more radical demands will inevitably follow.

Perhaps "radical" is the key word. Labor in Argentina is much stronger than in Colombia, but Argentine unions are not Marxist and they do not threaten capital. Argentina's post-1976 period of military rule was extremely repressive, but the military insisted that unemployment be kept low as a concession to labor and as a safeguard against unrest. (This issue is discussed further in the last section of this chapter.)

Macroeconomic Policy

In Chapter 1 (the analysis of overall central government spending), I argued that budgetary expansion is aimed at direct employment of supporters rather than economic stimulation. Economic fine-tuning is usually beyond the reach of leaders lacking comprehensive data and economic expertise. In a few countries, however, data gathering and expertise have advanced so much that fine-tuning may indeed be possible.

Mexico provides a good example of the political use of fine-tuning. John Koehler (1968) found that central government spending in Mexican administrations followed a cyclical pattern—rising in the first budget of a new president, falling for the next couple of years, then rising again in the rush to complete projects before the term's end. Given the enormous weight of the government in Mexico's economy, these cyclical spending fluctuations could be seriously destabilizing if there were no compensatory mechanisms. One such mechanism, however, was the Mexican government's control of private banks' reserve requirements. By restricting private sector credit just when the government was itself spending more, Mexican administrations forced the private sector to offset the rhythm of government spending. The result was a political–economic cycle that avoided, at least until recently, major destabilization.

This example notwithstanding, government expenditures in Latin America are more often a direct provider of benefits than a stimulus to the overall economy. The expertise necessary for a policy like Mexico's may exist in a few other advanced Latin American countries, but rarely do we see the high degree of political control required for its execution. Nonetheless, another fruitful line of investigation might be the survival-oriented manipulation of macroeconomic policy.

Political Sophistry

Casuistry—the dubious and arbitrary use of general principles to defend positions adopted on particularistic grounds—is one of the grand traditions of politics. The recent spate of transitions to liberalized regimes in Latin America has provided new opportunities to ponder casuistry's fullest flowerings. In Brazil's ten-year political opening, for example, the outgoing military regime engaged in numerous ploys to strengthen itself politically, including the indirect election of one senator in each state, the creation of a new state in a region of government strength and the fusion of two states in a region of weakness, and the creation of a ballot designed to discourage opposition voting. That these stratagems failed rather ignominiously in no way detracts from their importance as survival tactics.

The outgoing military in Ecuador followed a similar approach. In order to keep a certain populist from running for president, the junta required that all candidates have parents born in Ecuador. To prevent ex-President Velasco Ibarra from running, the junta retroactively prohibited reelection. And to strengthen candidates of the right, the junta postponed granting illiterates the right to vote until after the first civilian presidential election.

In Argentina and Peru, however, little attempt was made to structure the rules of post-transition politics. In these cases the military regime was in too much disarray to mount a political survival strategy.

Survival Coalitions in Comparative Politics

Because survival crises are a "middle-range" problem, the perspective of this book is not an alternative to class approaches, dependency theory, rational-choice political economy, or any other "grand theory" currently popular in comparative politics. At the same time, the policy consequences of crisis responses extend far beyond the crises themselves. The analysis of survival politics thus stands as an essential complement to broader theoretical perspectives. This concluding section briefly discusses six quite diverse examples of comparative political research. The initial three cases, a political economy treatment of agricultural policy in Africa, a study of the consequences of succession crises in the Soviet Union, and the debate about political business cycles in the United States and Western Europe, explicitly incorporate coalition perspectives. The final three examples, a class analysis of the links between regime and policy in Chile, a dependency treatment of Latin American economic history, and a discussion of the evolution of economic policy in certain bureaucratic-authoritarian regimes, do not explicitly incorporate strategic coalition analysis, at least at the theoretical level, but they ought to, because they cannot explain policy choice without attention to strategic factors.

In *Markets and States in Tropical Africa,* Robert Bates (1984) explains why political leaders in Africa consistently adopt policies that result in food scarcities, higher prices, food imports, and shortages of foreign exchange. Bates asks (p. 3): "Why should reasonable men adopt public policies that have harmful consequences for the societies they govern?" According to Bates, public purposes do affect the policy choices leaders make, but he stresses that "more personal motives animate political choices. Governments want to stay in power. They must appease powerful interests" (p. 4). But since agriculture is the basis of African economies, why are agriculturists so weak in advancing their political interests? Bates offers a number of explanations. One is framed in terms of the logic of collective action. Because each peasant has only a small stake in the outcome of political movements and little chance to affect them, peasants rarely join such movements. Faced with unresponsive governments, peasants opt to maximize incremental benefits or choose to use the market against the government; that is, they produce less or smuggle their production to friendlier buyers. A second explanation stresses the preference of African governments for industry over agriculture. African leaders perceive industrialization as the only route to modernization. Industry has to be fostered and protected, even if the traditional agricultural base is hurt in the process. When governments do attempt to aid farmers, they often subsidize inputs such as seeds and fertilizers. These subsidies make farming attractive to urban elites, who soon command the lion's share of the subsidies. In the end, government attempts to stimulate agriculture encourage the creation of a powerful class of elite farmers in a much better position to lobby for producer interests. In Africa, then, the agrarian–industrial conflicts inevitably accompanying the development process are actually created by government policy.

Bates's study stresses the response of farmers to harmful government policy. That focus is narrower than the perspective of survival coalitions, and it is an emphasis particularly relevant to Africa. But Bates's concern for power maximization among political leaders and for the long-term costs of policies directed at maintenance of office is fully consonant with the theory of survival coalitions.

Another illustration of concern with survival-centered coalitions is found in the debate over the policy consequences of leadership succession in the Soviet Union. Perhaps the most interesting contribution is Philip Roeder's "Do New Soviet Leaders Really Make

a Difference? Rethinking the 'Succession Connection' " (1985).[2]
Roeder's article is partly a response to research by Valerie Bunce.
Bunce had argued (1980:974) that new Soviet general secretaries
"pump up public consumption in the period immediately following succession" as a way of placating the masses. Roeder denies
that the masses are politically important. He suggests, instead, that
general secretaries actually seek allies in the political elite, framing
appeals to the military, to the party apparatus, or to the government bureaucracy. A complex cycle of policy-making styles re-
volves around the ascendance, consolidation, and decline of new
leaders. Different leaders appeal to different elite groups: Mal-
enkov sought allies in the government bureaucracy; Khrushchev
looked to the party apparatus. At times leaders seek "personal"
relationships with the masses in order to circumvent intermediate
elites, but such mass orientations occur *after* succession has been
resolved and the newly ascendant leader has consolidated his position (Roeder 1985:968).

Soviet political cycles are unlike those of Latin America—the
USSR, after all, undergoes neither competitive elections nor military coups—but the strategic calculus of leaders, the links to policy outputs, and the effects of a "political succession cycle" are
all easily recast in terms of strategic coalition theory. What remains for Roeder and other students of Soviet succession is the
issue raised here: the long-term consequences of policies initially
chosen to consolidate power.

Finally, how does research on the political business cycle relate
to a strategic approach? The notion of a political business cycle
first became popular with the work of Nordhaus (1975) and Tufte
(1978). Executives in the United States and Western Europe, they
argued, stimulate their economies near elections in order to maximize per capita income and minimize unemployment. Although
such macroeconomic stimulation must be reversed after the election, "myopic" voters ignore that prospect and reward incumbents
at the polls. Political business cycle theories provided some of the
early stimulus for this book, but in the end the divergence has
been considerable. In Latin America macroeconomic fine-tuning is
only occasionally part of executive survival strategies; in the
United States and Western Europe scholars usually assume that

2. See also the exchange between Bunce and Roeder (1986).

fine-tuning is the *only* way expenditures are used.[3] In Latin America trade-offs among *specific programs* facilitate survival and coalition building; in advanced countries researchers rarely disaggregate expenditures beyond crude categories such as consumption and transfers. In Latin America each administration has unique coalitional possibilities; in advanced countries scholars typically assume that all administrations follow the same strategy or that they have only two choices: an unchanging Republican (or Conservative) strategy and an unchanging Democratic (or Labor) strategy.[4]

Alt and Chrystal (1983) show that the evidence for the existence of political business cycles is shaky. Still, executives in advanced countries must do *something* to help their reelection chances. Why are their strategies so elusive? With abundant data facilitating elaborate statistical modeling, and with the notion that individual budgetary programs are too rigid for short-term manipulation, scholars have ignored the everyday battles waged by executives and lesser political actors. The size of the "consumption" component of the budget is rarely an object of political struggle. Instead, real fights take place over allocations to real recipients: universities, hospitals, sewage projects. And while overall ministerial expenditures do change very slowly, expenditures on individual programs are quite volatile (Gist 1977; Natchez and Bupp 1973). Finally, a programmatic emphasis also suggests that administrations cannot be described solely by party affiliation. Jimmy Carter and Walter Mondale were both Democrats, but their regional bases and substantive preferences would lead to quite different survival coalitions. Analysis of programmatic strategies and coalitions, in other words, should be part of research on survival in advanced countries as well as in Latin America.

Not all existing comparative research is consonant with the theory of survival coalitions, of course. Approaches stressing social class and corporatism remain the most common theoretical frameworks in studies of developing areas. A brief discussion of three

3. A good summary of this literature is found in Alt and Chrystal (1983). They focus on the work of Tufte (1978), Nordhaus (1975), Hibbs (1977), and Mosley (1976).

4. Some models include changes in executive popularity among their determinants of fiscal response, but even here changing popularity is assumed to have a constant effect on spending regardless of who holds power (Frey and Schneider 1978; Chrystal and Alt 1981).

applications of such frameworks will demonstrate the complementary importance of the perspective of strategic coalitions.

Class Analysis in Pluralist Chile

One of the most rigorous applications of a class approach to a developing country is Barbara Stallings's *Class Conflict and Economic Development in Chile, 1958–1973* (1978). For Stallings, there is "a direct relationship between the class alliance which controls the state apparatus, resulting economic policies which are implemented, and the outcomes" (p. 3).

How can we identify the class nature of an alliance? In Chile, according to Stallings, there were four possibilities: the voting base supporting each administration, the formal and the informal channels of influence to policymakers, and the beneficiaries of the policies carried out by the alliance in power (p. 52).[5] Relying primarily on voting patterns and channels of influence, Stallings establishes the class base of the three Chilean administrations holding power from 1958 until 1973. Industrial-finance interests and the agrarian bourgeoisie backed Jorge Alessandri (1958–1964); the modern industrial fraction of the bourgeoisie and elements of the petty bourgeois intelligentsia supported Eduardo Frei (1964–1970); blue-collar workers and, to a lesser extent, white-collar workers and the petty bourgeoisie sustained Salvador Allende (1970–1973).

In Stallings's analysis, a class may be politically dominant without being economically dominant. Otherwise, how could blue-collar workers, who were far from dominant economically, be regarded as a hegemonic class in the alliance supporting Allende? Stallings's notion of political dominance is thus somewhat closer to a strategic approach than her initial emphasis on class suggests. Nonetheless, the focus on dominance, on the ability of the class in control to implement preferred policies, sharply distinguishes her theoretical perspective.

Stallings's study provides an exceptionally thorough description of policy outputs in the three Chilean presidencies—a description revealing a far more complex pattern of policy outputs than a class logic would predict. Alessandri, for example, began a stabilization

5. The final indicator is tautological. If benefits define dominance, what evidence would falsify the hypothesis that the dominant class gets disproportionate benefits as a result of its dominance?

program intended to keep wage increases below inflation. For his program to pass in the Congress, the president needed the backing of parties like the Radicals, who drew support from government bureaucrats and white-collar workers. After his ruling alliance lost seats in the congressional election of 1961, Alessandri had to bring the Radicals into the government coalition. The price of Radical support was four cabinet positions, including the Ministry of the Economy, and subsequent wage readjustments were substantially higher.

The administration of President Frei had little more success. When organized labor opposed his plan to capture a portion of wage readjustments through a program of forced savings, the president demanded united support from the Christian Democratic party. Frei won the internal party struggle that followed, but reformists in the left wing of the party broke away and joined Allende's Popular Unity coalition. Frei's strategic miscalculation led to a long period of drift for his administration, cost the Christian Democrats any chance at the 1970 election, and heightened social class polarization during the Allende government.

Does Allende's ill-fated coalition mark the outer limit of a strategic approach? With class polarization so strong and with the prospect of a real redistribution of income so threatening to the middle class, perhaps no strategy could have prevented the bourgeois-military reaction of 1973. Even here, however, strategic considerations played a major role. Allende's problem stemmed partly from the militance of blue-collar workers, a militance that made a coalition of workers and petty bourgeoisie quite unstable. As Stallings points out (p. 237), the actions of the Popular Unity administration "implied that they thought it was necessary to buy support through increasing incomes, but the election trends call this conclusion into doubt." In strategic terms, Allende was unable to separate union leaders, who emphasized redistributive wage settlements, from the mass of workers, who would have accepted a gradual increase in their real incomes in place of redistribution.

Chile also shows signs of a political business cycle. Initially, each administration enjoyed rapid economic growth with little inflation. In this phase presidents had apparent success in implementing programs consistent with their own substantive preferences and those of the class alliances backing them. In each case, however, inflation gradually heated up and the economy began to deteriorate. A crisis followed that led to the breakdown of each government's overall program. The government then seemed to drift while various coalition members attempted a realignment. In the final phase efforts to control rising prices led to recession, with unused capacity and high unemployment. The succeeding administration was then in a good position to pump up demand without putting much pressure on prices, at least at first.

Stallings's careful discussion of policy implementation enables us to see the importance of strategic coalition problems in each Chilean presidency. No class was able to maintain political dominance throughout an entire administration. The ultimate disposition of the projects of the class alliances owed much to the structure of political access, the variety of decision-making sites, and the multiple currencies of influence.[6]

Class Logic in Dependency Theory

Probably the most sophisticated and durable work from the "dependency" school of comparativists is Fernando Henrique Cardoso and Enzo Faletto's *Dependency and Development in Latin America* (1979).[7] Cardoso and Faletto's arguments supersede the cruder formulations of early dependency theorists. Indeed, the authors claim that no single theory of dependency is possible, that different "situations" of dependency arise in different economic and historical contexts.

Cardoso and Faletto try to distinguish their approach from an analysis framed purely in terms of economic forces and social class. They suggest, for example, that in "decisive historical moments, political capacity (which includes organization, will, and ideologies) is necessary to enforce or to change a structural situation" (p. xi).[8] At other points Cardoso and Faletto claim that

6. It is striking that in spite of the different class alliances that supported Alessandri and Frei, the budgetary outputs of their administrations were quite similar. Both presidents reduced the military share of the budget more than they reduced any other program, and both increased the shares of education and agriculture.

7. The original Spanish version was published in 1971. The English version (to which the page numbers here refer) appeared in 1979.

8. This discussion of Cardoso and Faletto is in some ways close to that of Martin Staniland in *What Is Political Economy?* (1985). Staniland distinguishes "economist" from "politicist" approaches, but he lumps together politicist variants in which class interests are channeled through political institutions and variants in which political actors have interests such as survival—that is, interests not identifiable with any social class. It is the latter interpretation, of course, that my

"sectors of local classes . . . organized different forms of state, sustained distinct ideologies, or tried to implement various policies" (p. xvii).

Still, Cardoso and Faletto's view of the independence of politics is decidedly ambivalent, for they also believe that "modes of economic relations . . . set the limits of political action" (p. 15). Political institutions, moreover, "can only be fully understood in terms of the structures of domination because these express the class interests behind political organization" (p. 14).

Neither side of Cardoso and Faletto's theoretical ambivalence is consonant with an emphasis on survival coalitions, because the motivations they attribute to political leaders never reflect more than class interests. At the empirical level, however, Cardoso and Faletto uncover many examples of survival motivations and coalition building. In a discussion of postrevolutionary Mexico, for example, Cardoso and Faletto suggest that the continuing strength of prerevolutionary economic forces weakened the political power created by the 1910 revolution. Key sectors of the economy remained in foreign hands, and peasants and workers, potential supporters of the government, were dispersed and fragmented. "The only way for the government to reinforce its position against the foreign companies," they observe, "was to organize and unite the worker-peasant movements. . . . [It was] then able to challenge the foreign companies in the petroleum industry." Further, they point out that "the state, with popular support, began industrialization in Mexico" (p. 144). That is, political actors reinforced certain groups as counterweights to others, and the policies they chose benefited political elites rather than specific social classes, at least at first.

In the case of Peru, *Dependency and Development in Latin America* describes the ideological transformation of the APRA party (Alianza Popular Revolucionária Americana) between the 1930s and the 1960s. APRA represented a middle class "caught between allying itself as a junior partner with the bourgeoisie . . . and joining forces with the popular sectors" (p. 121). APRA's efforts to attain power by taking advantage of intra-elite conflicts were brutally put down, and the *apristas* were often barred from participating in elections. Gambling that a move to the right would

---

approach gives to "politicism," and it is this same interpretation that Cardoso and Faletto, at least at the theoretical level, clearly do not intend.

ensure survival, APRA risked losing popular support by seeking allies in the military and the upper class. In the end, its ideological migration failed, because the military trusted a right-wing APRA no more than its left-wing predecessor. For Cardoso and Faletto, APRA's defeat signifies that "the middle sectors lost strength" (p. 122). But since the middle sectors were growing in numbers and in economic importance, they could not have lost *economic* strength. Cardoso and Faletto can only mean the middle sectors lost political strength, and that loss could only result from the faulty strategy of APRA leaders.

Cardoso and Faletto's treatment of Brazilian industrialization provides a final example of the centrality of strategies and coalition building. The classes potentially interested in industrial development in Brazil were too weak to force favorable policies on a reluctant government. Ultimately, the government's adoption of an industrialization policy "was not just thrust on it by the force of economic circumstances—it was a political decision" (p. 140). The stimulation of certain industries "can be explained politically by the existence of masses that were mobilized without effective employment having been created to absorb them" (p. 140). If economic considerations had motivated political elites, they would have adopted a different policy (p. 139). Instead, political elites chose to consolidate their own power against the threat of urban unrest.

Between the theoretical and empirical levels, then, Cardoso and Faletto are of two minds. *Theoretically,* the language is mainly that of class analysis. Though they frequently note the importance of political considerations, the authors treat the government either as something economic groups capture or as something that weighs the different currencies of group influence. Political actors have no motivations beyond those of their economic backers. *Empirically,* however, at the concrete level of historical episodes, many of Cardoso and Faletto's interpretations rely on themes consonant with the perspective of survival-oriented coalition building. Real politicians turn out to have real, purely political, interests.

The Evolution of Economic Policy in BA Regimes

Since the beginning of the 1970s, the most significant theoretical advance in the study of Latin American politics has been the development of the "bureaucratic-authoritarian" (BA) model. Although debate over the concept has now proceeded to the point where it may no longer describe a single coherent set of phenomena, bureaucratic authoritarianism still remains the dominant characterization of the powerful military regimes that came to power in some of the most advanced Latin American nations: Brazil between 1964 and 1984, Argentina between 1966 and 1970 and again between 1976 and 1984, Chile after 1973, and Uruguay between 1973 and 1984. The main characteristics of the BA state include: exclusion of civil society (except for those at the top of large organizations such as the armed forces and major oligopolistic enterprises) from access to policymakers, domination by specialists in coercion and economic "normalization," depoliticization of social issues in favor of decision making according to supposedly objective criteria of technical rationality, suppression of democratic institutions, and increases in economic inequities.[9]

One of the key puzzles remaining in the BA debate is the model's inability to explain the evolution of economic policy in Chile, Uruguay, and post-1976 Argentina, three cases dominated by neoliberal policymakers. In this brief comment, limited to Argentina and Chile, I shall show that attention to the survival-maximizing behavior of key figures in the BA coalition can help solve the puzzle.[10]

Although BA states share important characteristics, O'Donnell did not expect them all to adopt the same policies. Economic policies would differ, in part, because the working class had posed varying degrees of threat to the interests of the bourgeoisie during the *pre*-BA period. Countries in which the working-class threat had been acute would stick much longer with orthodox policies—that is, policies emphasizing constriction of the money supply, cuts in public expenditures, and reductions in wages. While O'Donnell conceded that policy varied among high-threat Chile, Uruguay,

9. This summary fails to do justice either to contributors other than the originator of the concept, Guillermo O'Donnell, or to the evolution of his own thought. O'Donnell's first expression of these concepts, which came before authoritarian transformations occurred in Chile, Uruguay, and post-1976 Argentina, was published in *Modernization and Bureaucratic-Authoritarianism: Studies in South American Politics* (1973). This was followed by "Corporatism and the Question of the State" (1977); "Reflections on the Patterns of Change in the Bureaucratic-Authoritarian State" (1978); and "Tensions in the Bureaucratic-Authoritarian State" (1979).

10. The discussion ignores Uruguay partly in the interests of brevity and partly because less is known about the Uruguayan version of neoliberalism.

and post-1976 Argentina, he argued that all three were more orthodox than medium-threat Brazil or low-threat Argentina (1966–
1970). The evidence, however, suggests that Argentina and Chile
were not at all alike:[11]

> Public sector deficits (measured as percentages of GDP) were
> cut drastically in Chile, but they remained high in post-1976
> Argentina.[12]

> As a percentage of GDP, central government spending grew in
> Argentina; it fell in Chile.[13]

> By late 1979, Argentina's maximum tariff stood at 85 percent;
> Chile's had fallen to 10 percent.

> Unemployment climbed to over 20 percent in Chile; it remained
> below 5 percent in Argentina.

The differences between these high-threat cases are even more
dramatic when we remember that the technocrats who supposedly
made policy were advancing common economic ideologies. All
were "Chicago School" advocates of neoliberalism, particularly
neoliberalism's emphasis on control of inflation. Why were their
actual policies so different?

Chile and Argentina Compared

What is noteworthy about the Chilean case is the increasing
dominance of neoliberal technocrats even as their policies failed.[14]

11. The best criticism of O'Donnell's treatment of economic policy in the high-
threat cases is found in Remmer and Merkx (1982).
12. In Chile between 1971–1973 and 1974–1983, the average deficit fell from
12 percent of GDP to 2.93 percent of GDP. In Argentina between 1973–1975 and
1976–1983, the deficit was unchanged, averaging about 10.5 percent of GDP. The
evolution of public expenditures in Chile is a complicated issue. The most au-
thoritative treatment is Scheetz (1986). For Argentina I have relied on the World
Bank (1985).
13. In Argentina, public sector expenditures grew between 1973–1976 and
1977–1983 from 29.2 to 34.6 percent of GDP. See World Bank (1985). In Chile,
expenditures fell between 1971–1973 and 1974–1983 from 42.8 to 38.4 percent
of GDP. See Scheetz (1986).
14. This section relies on the following treatments of the Chilean case: Philip
O'Brien, "Authoritarianism and the New Economic Orthodoxy: The Political
Economy of the Chilean Regime, 1975–1983" (in O'Brien and Cammack 1985);
Karen Remmer, "Public Policy and Regime Consolidation: The First Five Years of
the Chilean Junta" (1979); and Tomás Moulian and Pilar Vergara, "Estado, Ideologia y Políticas Económicas en Chile: 1973–1978" (1981). In an interesting article
received only after this chapter was completed, Alfred Stepan highlights the im-

In April 1975, after a policy of "gradualism" had proved unable to reduce inflation to official predictions, the economic team persuaded Pinochet and the junta to accept a "shock treatment" that included an acceleration of cuts in public expenditures, a speeding up of tariff reductions, and a rapid sell-off of government enterprises. Fifteen months later, when it became clear that shock could not control inflation either, the neoliberals persuaded Pinochet to adopt an even more draconian "global monetarism." They revalued and then froze the exchange rate, reduced tariffs to almost nothing, and allowed foreign capital completely free entry. Inflation came down, but never to international levels, and unemployment remained high. Cheap imports led to a payments deficit that had to be covered with foreign loans, and the world recession contributed to a GNP decline in 1982 of more than 10 percent. When devaluation made dollar-denominated loans unbearable for the private sector, the government had to assume the debt. Through all this turmoil, economic policy remained in the hands of neoliberals. Why were they so powerful?

The power of Chile's Chicago School economists had technical, political, and institutional roots. Chicago economics got its start in Chile in 1955 when the United States government signed an agreement with the Catholic University of Chile and the University of Chicago to train Chilean graduate students. Chicago-trained economists came to dominate the economics department at the Catholic University, and they soon established ties with Chilean business groups. In the first months after the coup, the Chicago group was forced to share power with moderate Christian Democrats, but as Pinochet centralized power in his own hands, Christian Democratic economists either moved into the opposition or joined the hard-liners. By 1976 the key positions in economic policy were all controlled by the Chicago team, and they were able to install sympathizers as economic advisers in the four main military services.

The influence of the Chicago School economists was augmented by the all-or-nothing nature of their program. It alone seemed a coherent package. It alone was scientific, enjoying, after all, the

portance of the "Virginia School" of political economy (Buchanan, Tullock, and others) as an influence on Chile's neoliberals (Stepan 1985). I am also grateful to Karen Remmer for personal communications on Chile.

support of the international lending and investment community and the prestige of "godfathers" like Arnold Harberger and Milton Friedman. It alone promised a balance of payments surplus that would break Chile's dependence (and produce a surplus of hard currency for arms purchases). It alone was committed to privatization, a central objective for the frightened Chilean bourgeoisie.

Alternatives to neoliberalism existed in the form of neofascist nationalism as well as traditional Christian Democratic doctrine, but these competitors were weak. The hard-line neofascist corporatist types had nothing resembling a coherent economic program—ironically, their program resembled Allende's in its statist, redistributive, and anti-oligopoly aspects—and they were opposed by the U.S. government and the international financial institutions. The Chilean secret police (DINA) was potentially a focus of anti-Chicago opposition, but the DINA's involvement with the murder in the United States of Chilean exile Orlando Letelier had weakened it. Finally, the Christian Democrats, supporters of the coup in 1973, had moved into the opposition, but internal disputes weakened the Christian Democrats, and the armed forces distrusted them as the party that had delivered Chile to Allende and cut the military budget.

In spite of the neoliberals' enormous advantages, large factions of the military distrusted them. Why were the Chicago School economists allowed such control? Why did the military tolerate explosive levels of unemployment and accept a dramatic shrinkage in the public sector?

Before 1973 the Chilean military was regarded as one of the most professional and apolitical armed forces in Latin America. Lacking the Argentines' tradition of involvement in domestic politics, lacking the Brazilians' experience in working with civilian technocrats, lacking any training in economic management or social science, the Chilean military sought refuge in professionalism even inside the dictatorship. Military officers in the government transferred to reserve status, and they apparently did not regard themselves as representing the interests of their services. Pinochet protected the military's corporate interests, so the soldiers rarely concerned themselves with economic policy. As a result, Chilean authoritarianism approached an unfettered technocratic dominance. A variety of factors—the inexperience of the military, their

ideological distance from the Christian Democrats, the political
skill and international connections of the Chicago economists, the
trauma of the Allende years—came together to rule out alternative
coalitions.

Argentina's neoliberals never achieved a dominance equal to
their Chilean counterparts.[15] Policies that failed to control inflation
were jettisoned, but, unlike Chile, their replacements were seldom
purer versions of Chicago monetarism. A price freeze, for example,
followed gradualist stabilization. An attempt to constrict the
money supply replaced the freeze, and restrictions on foreign capital (as opposed to Chile's liberalizations) followed constriction.

The failure to cut the public sector deficit is a key to the neoliberal experience in Argentina. One cause of this failure was the
military's preoccupation with domestic insurgency, with the "dirty
war." While social expenditures declined almost 4 percent annually between 1976 and 1982, expenditures on defense and domestic security grew by more than 5 percent each year, a rate three
times that of Chile. Between 1976 and 1980, real spending just
on military personnel grew 73 percent (World Bank 1985:336–
337).

The deficit also remained high because of the political tradition
of the armed forces. Unlike the Chilean military, the Argentine
officer corps had long been involved in national politics. Because
the armed forces were determined to prevent a repetition of their
experience of 1966–1969 (when General Onganía tried to turn a
collegial junta into a permanent dictatorship), the military agreed
at the time of the 1976 coup that General Videla should serve one
five-year term, with subsequent presidencies rotating among the
military services. The generals also agreed to "feudalize" the state
apparatus, placing certain ministries under the permanent control
of certain branches of the military. The interior and labor ministers, for example, were always army officers. Military officers in
government remained part of a hierarchy stretching back to their

15. Among the works especially useful in analyzing the Argentine case were
William C. Smith, "Reflections on the Political Economy of Authoritarian Rule
and Capitalist Reorganization in Contemporary Argentina" (1985); Andrés Fontana, "Forças Armadas e Ideologia Neoconservadora: O 'Encolhimento' do Estado
na Argentina (1976–1981)" (1981); and Adolfo Canitrot, "Teoría y Práctica del
Liberalismo: Política Antiinflacionária y Apertura Económica en la Argentina,
1976–1981" (1981). I am also grateful to William Smith for a personal communication.

commanders in chief, and they controlled their domains like private fiefs. As Fontana notes:

> Each one of the Armed Forces considered the area under its control as a private patrimony to be run at its discretion, without interference by any outside power. In turn, most high level public agencies, such as ministries, provincial and municipal governments, public autarchies, and state enterprises, were headed by military officials, either on active duty or in the reserve (1981:356–357).

With this deep corporate interest in the governmental apparatus, it comes as no surprise that the armed forces resisted proposals to sell off inefficient government companies or cut public employment. In 1978, for example, when a Japanese group proposed an experimental takeover of an unprofitable railway, the general in charge of Military Industries (a government holding company) vetoed the plan. The military blocked attempts to denationalize military-controlled mining and metal-processing plants (*LAER*, November 17, 1978:355), and they insisted on exemptions from tariff reductions for their own arms industry and for strategic sectors like steel and electronics (*LAER*, November 30, 1979:54–55).

Unable to make any progress in shrinking the government, Economy Minister José Martinez de Hoz had only one alternative: to dampen aggregate demand by inducing unemployment. Once again the armed forces vetoed the policy. The military feared strikes, of course, but many officers viewed workers as potential partners, allies to be subordinated but protected. If workers were to be bulwarks against Marxism, unemployment had to be kept low.

In sum, then, Argentine and Chilean neoliberalism generated very different economic policies. As a theoretical perspective, bureaucratic authoritarianism cannot explain these differences, because it only goes as far as defining the dominant coalition—a coalition apparently composed, in each case, of the same players. Equivalent sets of players, however, failed to produce equivalent policies, because the players bargained with different histories, resources, and objectives.

Strategic coalition theory helps illuminate the neoliberals' dominance in Chile as compared to their weakness in Argentina. From Pinochet's viewpoint, there was no serious alternative to neoliberal dominance. Chile's politically inexperienced generals refused to involve themselves in policy beyond questions of weapons, salaries, and repression, and the neoliberals prevented alternative economic programs from emerging. From Videla's viewpoint, however, the situation looked quite different. Argentina's military had a tradition of political involvement, its interests were very broad, and neoliberalism competed with many economic theories.

Strategy and Survival
in an Uncertain World

These examples of comparative political research demonstrate the indispensability of strategic coalition analysis as a complement to the "grand theories" dominating the study of developing areas. We cannot reduce policy outputs to the interests of the social classes backing political executives or to the class origins of executives themselves. Political leaders have their own interests, and the evolution of policy responds to the interplay of these interests with those of classes, regions, and other political actors. Rarely is a single social class or group truly dominant in the sense that it can avoid concessions to other classes or groups. Everyone has to bargain, coalesce, and compromise. Executive authority is never absolute; indeed, the executive's position itself is frequently in doubt. In such environments tactical skill may be as important as wealth, popularity, or control of the means of coercion, and the outcomes of the process can seldom be predicted with much certainty.

Leaders pursue many substantive goals, but none are achievable unless they maintain their positions. In an environment where military interventions are commonplace, where incumbent parties rarely win elections, and where economic fluctuations are severe, survival in office is no easy task, either for civilian or military governments. Leaders must husband their resources and develop strategies ensuring their positions.

For leaders, choosing a survival strategy is a question of constant evaluation and reevaluation of the political and economic environment. Who can be brought into a support coalition? At what price? Will new allies result in the loss of old supporters? Must the military be paid off? If the budgetary share of a powerful interest is cut, should the loss be cushioned by expanding total expenditures? All these questions have to be answered in an economic context plagued by instability and debilitating inflation.

Political executives pursue substantive policy objectives when they feel secure in office, but at moments of political crisis the balance between survival and substance tips toward survival. Political crises in developing countries are so severe and so frequent that whether leaders survive or fall, the effects of the short-term strategies they adopt are felt for the remainder of their terms in office and for many years to come. To understand the ultimate evolution of significant areas of policy, we must comprehend the strategic responses of leaders facing the challenge of survival in an uncertain and ever-shifting political world.

Appendix A: Technical Data for Chapter 1

Except in Chapter 4, the analyses of this book always measure central government spending in terms of final expenditures, those the IMF refers to as "closed accounts." The terms "budget," "expenditure," and "spending" are used interchangeably. The expenditure data have been gathered, disaggregated, and coded over a period of years. They come from reports of controllers general, treasury ministries, central banks, and similar sources. Secondary sources such as *América en Cifras* have not been used for any country. There are a number of special cases. For Brazil between 1950 and 1967 I used Margaret Daly Hayes' line-by-line recoding of the entire Brazilian budget. For Argentina I reorganized all the decentralized agencies into appropriate programs. In Ecuador I relied for certain years on hand-tabulated material provided by the controller general. A partial list of sources is found at the end of this appendix.

How good are these data? We can never really know. Undoubtedly the classification of expenditures into different programs is occasionally wrong, and undoubtedly a substantial portion of some ministries' expenditures are occasionally siphoned off in graft. On the whole, however, most of the money got into the appropriate programs most of the time. I assume that cases of extreme corruption are randomly distributed by countries, ministries, and years. If this assumption is correct, then corruption contributes no systematic bias to the estimates. In the end, the only serious defense against a charge that "Latin American statistics are all meaningless" lies in the results these data generate. What story based on corruption is consistent with the estimates presented here?

Operationalizing the Variables

A series of "dummy" variables, one for each year of the cycle, operationalized the various electoral cycle hypotheses. If, for example, a country had two elections, in 1950 and 1960, then those two years were coded 1 on the "election" variable and 0 on the "postelection" variable. The years 1951 and 1961 were coded 0 on "election" and 1 on "postelection." The third variable, "all other years," is left out of the equations for technical reasons. Provisional governments not participating in the electoral contest (and therefore lacking spending incentives) were assigned 0. Reelected incumbents and newly elected nonincumbents have similar incentives to spend, so they were grouped together. Incentives to spend were attributed to presidents if their parties participated in the election, even if the incumbents could not or did not seek reelection.

An administration assuming power early in the year can shift budget priorities in that year, but an administration taking office late in the year can only affect spending in the next year. If an election occurred before May 30, the previous year was therefore coded as the *election* year and the year in which it actually occurred was coded as the first *postelection* year.

The military coup cycle was also operationalized with a series of dummies:

Coup$_t$ (the year in which the coup occurs)

Postcoup$_t$ (the first year after the coup)

Postcoup $+$ 1$_t$ (the second year after the coup)

Postcoup $+$ 2$_t$ (the third year after the coup)

Postcoup $+$ 3$_t$ (the fourth year after the coup)

If a coup occurred before June 1, the previous year was considered to be the year of the coup, and the year in which it actually occurred was defined as the first postcoup year. If the coup occurred after June 1, that year was coded as the year of the coup.

The nonlinear hypothesis predicting the closeness of the electoral margin was operationalized with a quadratic of the form $y = x + x^2$, where y is public spending and x is the difference between the two leading contenders. A nonlinear story is as follows: When elections are extremely close, the discretion of executives over expenditures might be so limited that spending changes are zero or even negative. When the electoral margin widens a bit, constraints lessen even though insecurity remains. Then, as margins become very large, low incentives again depress spending.

Other nonmonetary variables were operationalized with dummy variables in the same manner as those cited above.

All variables were measured in calendar years. Occasional expenditure reports with fiscal years starting midyear were converted to calendar years. It should be noted that the conversion to constant currency is somewhat problematic, due to difficulties in the construction and interpretation of cost of living indices.

Left-Out Variables

Loans to Latin American nations from the United States were included in preliminary estimations. These loans yielded a coefficient near zero.

This result is not surprising, since loans that must be repaid should be at least partially discounted in the plans of budget makers. Ideally we would like to know the effect of loans and grants on other kinds of spending. External funds might substitute for domestic resources, or they might increase the use of domestic resources, because programs begun with outside money must be maintained. Unfortunately, Latin American expenditure reports are rarely precise as to the inclusion or exclusion of all aid. Consequently, caution is advised in attributing causal significance to the grant–spending relationship. This variable simply accounts for a portion of the variance in total spending.

One important aspect of the international economic environment has been excluded from this analysis. Foreign private investment is important to Latin American economies, but it does not directly enter the revenue calculations of budget makers until it becomes part of the domestic resource base. To count foreign investment as a resource would be to double-count, because private investment is not a separate taxable resource distinct from the revenue base.

Regression and the Interpretation of Results

Due to certain statistical problems, the ordinary-least-squares (OLS) approach could not be used. Instead, it was necessary to estimate the model with an instrumental-variables, generalized-least-squares (GLS) regression. If a model including a lagged dependent variable on the right side of the equation is estimated with OLS in the presence of autocorrelated error, the usual result is an inflation of the coefficient of the lagged variable and a deflation of other coefficients. Interested readers should consult Hibbs (1974b). Hibbs (1974a) also provides a good example of the fixed-parameters, dummy-variables approach to pooling. Estimation in Chapter 1 relied on the Scientific Analysis System (SAS) to create an estimate of the dependent variable in the previous year. Then the Parks routine in SAS TSCSREG produced the GLS estimates.

One caveat about the interpretation of individual results: Due to the conjunction of two continuous variables (previous spending and resources) with the dichotomous dummy variables, the relative weight of specific variables in the overall explanation of total spending cannot be inferred from the differences in the sizes of their coefficients or t scores. The coefficients do measure the differential importance of economic versus bureaucratic constraints, but they cannot, for example, measure the substantive importance of the electoral cycle versus the economic constraints, because elections occur relatively infrequently. In other words, the coefficients of the political variables measure the effects on spending when a certain condition exists, but since no single political variable occurred in more than one-third of all cases, they contribute relatively little to the *overall* explanation of total spending. Note also that if the data are partitioned into pre-1965 and post-1964 cohorts, the model works about as well in each set of years, given that variances generally increase with decreasing data points. Finally, *t* scores are somewhat unsuitable for hypothesis testing in this model due to certain statistical anomalies. They are presented simply as rough guides to the strength of coefficients. A *t* of 1.65 would indicate significance at the 0.05 level.

The discussion in the text uses both residuals and comparisons of predicted and actual values. Regression models allow a comparison of the actual behavior of any case with its predicted behavior. Predicted values can be calculated for each year by adding the intercept term to the coefficients for each variable in the model multiplied by the actual value of the variable for that year for a particular country. This predicted value can then be compared to the actual value. If the prediction is less than the actual value, the model underpredicts; if the prediction is greater than the actual value, the model overpredicts. The difference between the actual and predicted values is the residual.

Data Sources

Argentina. Ministerio de Hacienda. *Memoria.*
Bolivia. Banco Central de Bolivia. *Memoria Anual.*
Brazil. Contadoria Geral da República. *Balanço Geral da União.*
———. IBGE. *Anuário Estatístico.*
Chile. Ministerio de Hacienda. *Cuentas Fiscales de Chile.*
———. Contraloría General. *Memoria.*
Colombia. Contraloría General de la República. *Informe Financiero de Contraloría.*
———. Contraloría General de la República. *Cifras Fiscales del Gobierno Nacional y las Entidades Descentralizadas Nacionales.*
Costa Rica. Banco Central. *Memoria Anual.*
———. Contraloría General. *Memoria.*
———. Ministerio de Economía y Hacienda. *Memoria Anual.*
———. Dirección General de Estadística y Censos. *Anuario Estadístico de Costa Rica.*
Ecuador. Contraloría General de la Nación. *Informe.*
———. Banco Central del Ecuador. *Memoria.*
———. Ministerio del Tesoro. Organo de Información Trimestral. *Boletín.*
El Salvador. Ministerio de Economía. *Anuario Estadístico.*
———. Ministerio de Hacienda. *Liquidaciones del Presupuestos Fiscales del Departamento de Auditoría de la Corte de Cuentas de la República.*

Guatemala. Banco de Guatemala. *Memoria.*

———. Ministerio de Economía. Dirección General de Estadística. *Guatemala en Cifras.*

———. Banco de Guatemala. *Memoria Anual.*

Honduras. Secretaría de Economía y Hacienda. Contaduría General de la República. *Informe.*

Mexico. Secretaría de Economía. Dirección General de Estadística. *Anuario Estadístico de los Estados Unidos Mexicanos.*

———. Secretaría de Hacienda y Crédito Público. Contaduría de la Federación. *Cuenta Pública.*

———. Secretaría de la Presidencia. *Inversion Pública Federal.*

Nicaragua. Ministerio de Hacienda y Crédito Público. Tribunal de Cuentas. *Memoria.*

Panama. Contraloría General de la República. *Informe.*

———. Contraloría General de la República. *Panamá en Cifras.*

Paraguay. Banco Central del Paraguay. *Memoria.*

———. Ministerio de Hacienda. Dirección General de Presupuesto. *Informe.*

Peru. Ministerio de Hacienda y Comercio. Dirección Nacional de Estadística y Censos. *Anuario Estadístico del Peru.*

———. Ministerio de Hacienda. Contraloría General de la República. *Balance y Cuenta General de la República.*

———. Ministerio de Economía y Finanzas. Dirección General de la República. *Cuenta General de la República.*

Uruguay. 1969. Universidad de la República. Facultad de Ciencias Económicas y de Administración. Instituto de Economía. *Uruguay: Estadísticas Básicas.*

———. Contaduría General. *Clasificación Funcional de los Gastos Presupuestales del Uruguay.*

Venezuela. *Anuario Estadístico.*

———. Contraloría General. *Informe al Congreso.*

———. Ministerio de Fomento. *Boletín Mensual de Estadística.*

Appendix B: Technical Data
for Chapter 2

The assertion that the five strategies cited in Chapter 2 exhaust the possible responses of Latin American executives raises some logical problems. The hypothesis-testing procedure first classified each case into one of the five strategies. Regression analysis measured the effect of the existence of that condition on various budgetary programs. Acceptance of the null hypothesis implies that executives who ought to follow a given strategy in fact do not. The regressions determine whether any other strategies, or some subset, are followed. But if some entirely different strategy is in use, it could escape detection. Careful manipulation of the data might reveal additional strategies, but fundamentally the argument that these five strategies exhaust the reality of contemporary Latin America rests on my understanding of the area and the knowledge of other scholars. Note also that strategies are not assumed to remain constant throughout a given administration.

Earlier drafts of Chapter 2 discussed a sixth strategy—a strategy calling for an expanding total budget with no changes in the shares of individual programs. There were too few cases of this strategy to allow empirical testing, but it can be outlined as a guide to future investigation. Suppose a party or coalition maintains power through a series of competitive elections. Following any security-maximizing strategy, the executive increases the shares of key programs at each crisis. After the crisis these shares return to their earlier levels. But if politicization is very high and defection of followers to opponents is very easy, it will be difficult to reduce the just-increased shares. Cutting the salary budget, for example, would immediately lower bureaucratic wages or reduce employment. If the executive chooses to preserve the increments granted during crises, the effect is like a ratchet, with the shares of critical programs growing to new heights at each crisis. Over time, however, such increments will decrease. Some minimal level must be maintained in each program, and advocates of declining programs fight harder as their shares diminish. The returns to executive security from budget increases shrink, and the costs of an inefficient pattern of allocations grow. In the end, competition reaches an equilibrium. The whole budget still rises, but shares remain fixed. This sort of equilibrium might characterize Uruguay in the 1950s and 1960s. See Weinstein (1975).

Trends, Transformations, and Interpretations

Sometimes trends appear in expenditure shares over time. In general, I did not detrend the data, because observed trends could be consequences of variables included in the model. If a trend might not be captured and could affect results, it is so noted in the text.

On theoretical and statistical grounds a semilog transformation was performed—that is, a logarithmic transformation of the dependent variable alone—after adding a constant so that negative numbers were eliminated. Hence

$$\text{Mil–Works}_t = \ln \Delta A_t - \ln \Delta B_t = \ln \frac{\Delta A_t}{\Delta B_t}$$

where A_t and B_t are the percentage changes in the respective programs from time $t - 1$ to time t. A semilog transformation of this type means that the coefficient of an independent variable ($\times$ 100) is approximately equal to the percentage increase in the change in the dependent variable per unit increase in the independent variable. Since the strategy dummies take values of 0 or 1, the coefficient ($\times$ 100) of the strategy dummy indicates the percentage increase in the expenditure share when that strategy is optimal.

With the dependent variables formulated in this way, a simple interpretation of the estimated coefficients is difficult, because the effect of a given coefficient on the difference in the rates of change of a pair of programs depends on the relative size of the original programs. It is still possible to convert the estimated coefficients into substantively meaningful differences in rates of change. In general, the true difference between growth rates (in percentage points) is about twice the coefficient ($\times$ 100). Thus an estimated coefficient of 0.10 implies a difference in rates of growth of about twenty percentage points.

Coding the Strategies

The text identified the administrations for which the social class strategies were optimal. The lists that follow detail the coding of the remaining approaches. The citations appended to the first list also identify scholarly works found particularly useful in coding that country on all administrations and strategies. For the sake of brevity I have omitted changes occurring in strategic approaches during the tenure of administrations.

Note that only administrations for which expenditure data were available are listed.

Military Pacification

Argentina: Perón (1946–1955), Frondizi, Illía. See Cardoso and Faletto (1979), Kenworthy (1970), O'Donnell (1973), Ranis (1968), Wynia (1978), and Zuvekas (1968). *Bolivia:* Siles Zuazo, Paz Estenssoro (1960–1964), Barrientos–Banzer. See Kenworthy (1970), Malloy (1970), Mitchell (1977), Van Niekerk (1976). *Brazil:* Vargas (1951–1954), Kubitschek, Quadros, Goulart, Castello Branco, Geisel. See Ames (1973), Cardoso and Faletto (1979), Chaloult (1978), Diniz (1978), Erickson (1977), Graham (1968), Jenks (1978), Kenworthy (1970), Nunberg (1986), Skidmore (1967). *Chile:* Allende, Pinochet. See Bowers (1958), Cleaves (1969), Ffrench-Davis (1973), Hughes and Mijeski (1973), Kenworthy (1970), Levy (1979), Moran (1974), Stallings (1978), Valenzuela and Wilde (1979) O'Brien and Cammack (1985). *Colombia:* Ospina Pérez–Rojas Pinilla. See Hartlyn (1981), Agor (1971), Alexander (1973), Campos and McCamant (1972), Dix (1967), Hoskin, Leal, and Kline (1976), Payne (1968), Rothenberg (1973), Vidal (1966). *Ecuador:* Velasco (all), Carlos Julio Arosemena, Rodríguez Lara. See Fitch (1977), Martz (1972), Pyne (1973), Hurtado (1980). *Peru:* Bustamente, Odría (1949–1952), Belaúnde (late in administration). See Alexander (1973), Anderson (1967), Cotler (1970), Gilbert (1977), Hilliker (1971), Jaquette (1971), Payne (1965), Pike (1967). *Uruguay:* none for 1955–1966. See Taylor (1960), Weinstein (1975). *Venezuela:* Junta (1949–1952), Betancourt (1959–1963). See Agor (1971), Anderson (1967), Burggraaff (1972), Levine (1973), Myers (1973), Powell (1971), Ray (1969), Tugwell (1975). *Costa Rica:* none. See Ameringer (1978), Anderson (1962), Arias Sánchez (1971, 1976), Bell (1971), Denton (1971), Ebel (1972), Hughes and Mijeski (1973), Rothenberg (1973). *Guatemala:* all administrations. See Anderson (1962), Ebel (1972), Jonas and Tobis (1974), Melville and Melville (1971), Weaver (1971), Wiarda and Kline (1979). *Honduras:* all administrations. See Anderson (1962), Ebel (1972), Wiarda and Kline (1979). *Mexico:* none. See Ames (1970), Camacho (1974), Hansen (1971), Koehler (1968), Purcell and Purcell (1980). *Nicaragua:* Román y Reyes and Somoza (1947–1956). See Anderson (1962), Millett (1977). *Panama:* all administrations. See Pippin (1964), Soler (1972), Souza and others (1970), Wiarda and Kline (1979). *El Salvador:* Osorio, Lemus. See Anderson (1962), Ebel (1972), Wiarda and Kline (1979).

Bureaucratic Recruitment

Bolivia: Paz (1953–1956), Siles Zuazo, Paz (1961–1964). *Brazil:* Vargas (1951–1954), Kubitschek, Quadros, Goulart. *Colombia:* administrations of the National Front. *Ecuador:* Velasco Ibarra (1969–1971). *Peru:* Bustamente, Prado, Belaúnde. *Venezuela:* Betancourt, Leoni, Caldera. *Costa Rica:* Figueres, Echandi, Orlich, Trejos, Figueres. *Honduras:* Villeda Morales. *Panama:* Arosemena, Remón, Arias Espinosa, de la Guardia, Robles. *El Salvador:* Sánchez Hernández, Molina.

Regional Interests

Bolivia: Barrientos. *Brazil:* Kubitschek. *Colombia:* Rojas Pinilla, all National Front administrations. *Ecuador:* Galo Plaza (due to earthquake), Velasco, Carlos Julio Arosemena, Junta (1963–1966). *Peru:* Belaúnde, Velasco Alvarado. *Venezuela:* Caldera. *Costa Rica:* Figueres, Orlich, Figueres. *Guatemala:* Arbenz, Castillo Armas, Méndez Montenegro. *Honduras:* Gálvez, Lozano Días, Villeda Morales, López Arellano. *Nicaragua:* Luis Somoza. *Panama:* Chiari, Torrijos. *El Salvador:* Osorio, Lemus, Rivera Carballo.

Transfers

Argentina: Perón (post-1950). *Brazil:* Quadros. *Chile:* Carlos Ibañez. *Ecuador:* Velasco Ibarra (1969–1971). *Peru:* Odría. *Panama:* de la Guardia, Arnulfo Arias.

Appendix C: Technical Data
for Chapter 4

The theoretical model presented in the second section of Chapter 4 did not limit its predictions to factors for which evidence was known to be available. The information required for empirical verification can be summarized in five categories:

1. *Individual Incentives:* permeability of electoral zone, rank in party list, party ideology, number of terms
2. *Delegation Characteristics:* turnover, leadership positions, committee and occupational distributions
3. *Attitudes:* deputies' perceptions of their own behavior
4. *Behavior:* deputies' activities directed toward maximizing expenditures in their zones
5. *Budgets and Expenditures:* annual proposed budgets and final expenditures for each state and program

Such readily available information as ranks in party lists, party membership, and number of terms served were all used. Electoral results by county (necessary to establish the boundaries of bailiwicks) were almost never available, so the surrogate permeability variable discussed in the text was used as a preliminary attempt to address the question.

In order to tap legislators' self-perceptions, I mailed a questionnaire to all deputies serving in the Chamber of Deputies between 1947 and 1967. This survey, undertaken with the collaboration of Prof. David Fleischer of the Universidade de Brasília, was implemented between May and August 1983. The questionnaire dealt with such topics as campaign practices, vote concentration, committees, strategies, interparty state-level cooperation, leadership roles, and amending frequency. The number of deputies replying was 103. I then conducted extensive personal interviews with 28 deputies from fourteen states, and I supplemented these interviews with conversations with local academics in Ceará, Maranhão, Paraíba, Rio Grande do Norte, Bahía, and Santa Catarina.

Documentary information about budgetary behavior came from the

Record of the National Congress (DCN). The DCN contains speeches and amendments, including budget amendments by author, program, and outcome. It is, however, woefully incomplete, lacking either an index or a consistent format, leaving out many programs altogether, and presenting, for many years, only fragments. Since the DCN is the only information source on those budgetary activities occurring between the first presidential proposals and actual expenditures, and since executive agencies published state-by-state totals only occasionally (rarely disaggregated below the ministerial level), it is impossible to examine every program over which congressmen fought. The available data are not biased; they are simply very sparse. Given these limitations, even a simple multivariate estimation is possible only at the state level.

References

Abranches, Sérgio Hudson de. 1978. "The Divided Leviathan: State and Economic Policy Formation in Authoritarian Brazil." Ph.D. dissertation, Cornell University.

Agor, Weston. 1971. *Latin American Legislatures: Their Role and Influence.* New York: Praeger.

Albuquerque, Roberto Cavalcanti de. n.d. "A execução do planejamento: o que se obteve em dois anos com o II PND." *Política.*

Alexander, Robert. 1973. *Latin American Political Parties.* New York: Praeger.

Allison, Graham. 1971. *Essence of Decision: Explaining the Cuban Missile Crisis.* Boston: Little, Brown.

Almond, Gabriel, Scott Flanagan, and Robert Mundt, eds. 1973. *Crisis, Choice and Change.* Boston: Little, Brown.

Alt, James, and K. Alec Chrystal. 1983. *Political Economics.* Berkeley: University of California Press.

Ameringer, Charles. 1978. *Don Pepe.* Albuquerque: University of New Mexico Press.

Ames, Barry. 1970. "Bases of Support for Mexico's Dominant Party." *American Political Science Review* 63 (March): 153–177.

———. 1973. *Rhetoric and Reality in a Militarized Regime: Brazil After 1964.* Beverly Hills: Sage.

———. 1977. "The Politics of Public Spending in Latin America." *American Journal of Political Science* 21(1):149–176.

Ames, Barry, and Edward Goff. 1975. "Education and Defense Expenditures in Latin America: 1946–68." In Craig Liske, William Loehr, and John McCamant, eds., *Comparative Public Policy: Issues, Theories, and Methods.* Beverly Hills: Sage.

Anderson, Charles. 1962. "Central American Political Parties: A Functional Approach." *Western Political Quarterly* 15:125–139.

———. 1967. *Politics and Economic Change in Latin America.* Princeton: D. Van Nostrand.

Arias Sánchez, Oscar. 1971. *Grupos de Presión en Costa Rica.* San José: Editorial Costa Rica.

———. 1976. *Quien Gobierna en Costa Rica?* San José: Educa.

Assis, José Carlos de. 1983. *As Chaves do Tesouro.* Rio de Janeiro: Paz e Terra.

Azevedo, Sérgio, and Luis Aureliano Gama de Andrade. 1981. *Habitação e Poder.* Rio de Janeiro: Zahar.

Baaklini, Abdo. 1977. "Legislative Reforms in the Brazilian Chamber of Deputies, 1964–1975." In Abdo Baaklini and James Heaphey, eds., *Comparative Legislative Reforms and Innovations.* Albany: Comparative Development Studies Center, State University of New York at Albany.

Bacha, Edmar. 1983. "Vicissitudes of Recent Stabilization Attempts in Brazil and the IMF Alternative." In John Williamson, ed., *IMF Conditionality.* Cambridge: MIT Press.

Bagley, Bruce. 1986. *Mexico in Crisis: The Parameters of Accommodation.* Washington, D.C.: Foreign Policy Institute, School of Advanced International Studies, Johns Hopkins University.

Baloyra, Enrique. 1977. "Democratic versus Dictatorial Budgeting: The Case of Cuba with Reference to Venezuela and Mexico." In James Wilkie, ed., *Money and Politics in Latin America.* Los Angeles: UCLA Latin American Center.

Banks, Arthur. 1971. *Cross-Polity Time-Series Data.* Cambridge: MIT Press.

Barkan, Joel. 1979. "Bringing Home the Pork: Legislative Behavior, Rural Development, and Political Change in East Africa." In Joel Smith and Lloyd Musolf, eds., *Legislatures in Development: Dynamics of Change in New and Old States.* Durham: Duke University Press.

Bates, Robert. 1984. *Markets and States in Tropical Africa: The Political Basis of Agricultural Policies.* Berkeley: University of California Press.

Bell, John Patrick. 1971. *Crisis in Costa Rica.* Austin: University of Texas Press.

Benevides, Maria Victoria Mesquita de. 1976. *O Governo Kubitschek: Desenvolvimento Econômico e Estabilidade Política, 1956–1961.* Rio de Janeiro: Paz e Terra.

———. 1981. *A UDN e O Udenismo.* Rio de Janeiro: Paz e Terra.

Bowers, Charles. 1958. *Chile Through Embassy Windows: 1939–1953.* New York: Simon & Schuster.

Brazil. Banco do Nordeste. 1958. *Banco do Nordeste.* Fortaleza: BNB. Setor de Documentação e Biblioteca.

———. BNH. 1979. *Ação da Area de Programas de Natureza Social.*

———. BNH. 1981. *Relatório.* Depto. de Planejamento e Coordenação (Dplan).

———. BNH. n.d. *Carteira de Operações de Natureza Social.*

———. CDI. 1971–1982. *Relatórios.*

———. Congresso Nacional. 1947–1963. *Diário do Congresso Nacional.*

―――. Contadoria Geral da República. 1932–1964. *Balanço Geral da União*.

―――. IBGE. 1970–1982. *Anuário Estatístico do Brasil*. Rio de Janeiro: Instituto Brasileiro de Geografia e Estatística.

―――. IBGE. 1979. *Indicadores Sociais, Tabelas Selecionadas*.

―――. Ministério da Fazenda. 1970–1982. *Anuário Econômico-Fiscal*.

―――. Ministério da Fazenda. 1970–1982. *Balanço Geral*.

―――. PNDII. n.d. *II Plano Nacional de Desenvolvimento*.

―――. Tribunal de Contas. 1945–1954. *Relatório*.

―――. Tribunal Superior Eleitoral. 1973. *Dados Estatísticos*. 7 vols. n.p. Depto. de Imprensa Nacional.

Bray, Donald. 1967. "Peronism in Chile." *Hispanic American Historical Review* 47(1):38–49.

Bunce, Valerie. 1980. "The Succession Connection: Policy Cycles and Political Change in the Soviet Union and Eastern Europe." *American Political Science Review* 74:966–977.

Bunce, Valerie, and Philip Roeder. 1986. "The Effects of Leadership Succession in the Soviet Union." *American Political Science Review* 80:215–224.

Burggraaff, Winfield. 1972. *The Venezuelan Armed Forces in Politics, 1935–1959*. Columbia: University of Missouri Press.

Café Filho, João. 1966. *Do Sindicato ao Catete*. Rio de Janeiro: José Olympio.

Caldeira, José Ribamar de. 1978. "Estabilidade Social e Crise Política: O Caso do Maranhão." *Revista Brasileira de Estudos Políticos* 46:55–102.

Camacho, Manuel. 1974. "El Poder: Estado o 'Feudos' Políticos." *Foro Internacional* 14(3):331–351.

Cammack, Paul. 1982. "Clientelism and Military Government in Brazil." In Christopher Clapham, ed., *Private Patronage and Public Power*. New York: St. Martin's Press.

Campos, Judith, and John McCamant. 1972. *Cleavage Shift in Colombia: Analysis of the 1970 Elections*. Beverly Hills: Sage.

Cancio Villa-Amil, Mariano. 1883. *Su Presupuesto de Gastos*. Madrid: Imprenta de R. Moreno y R. Rojas.

Canitrot, Adolfo. 1981. "Teoría y Práctica del Liberalismo: Política Antiinflacionária y Apertura Económica en la Argentina, 1976–1981." *Desarrollo Económico* 21:131–189.

Cardoso, Fernando H., and Enzo Faletto. 1979. *Dependency and Development in Latin America*. Berkeley: University of California Press.

Cardoso, Fernando H., and Bolívar Lamounier. 1975. *Os Partidos e as Eleições no Brasil*. Rio de Janeiro: Paz e Terra.

Carpenter, Robert, and Clark Reynolds. 1975. "Housing Finance in Brazil: Towards a New Distribution of Wealth." In Wayne Cornelius and Felicity Trueblood, eds., *Urbanization and Inequality: The Political Economy of Urban and Rural Development in Latin America.* Vol. 5. Beverly Hills: Sage.

Carvalho, José Murilo de. 1966. "Barbacena: A Família, a Política e uma Hipótese." *Revista Brasileira de Estudos Políticos* 20:125–193.

———. 1973. "Mecanismo Conflitual de Decisão na Câmara dos Deputados: O Significado Político da Votação Nominal no Período 1956–1960. Dados Preliminares." *Dados* 11:194–205.

Carvalho, Rejane Vasconcelos Accioly. 1982. *Justiça Social e Acumulação Capitalista (O Proterra).* Fortaleza: Edições Universidade Federal do Ceará.

Chalmers, Douglas. 1972. "Parties and Society in Latin America." *Studies in Comparative International Development* 7(2) Summer:102–128.

Chaloult, Yves. 1978. *Estado Acumulação e Colonialismo Interno.* Petrópolis: Editôra Vozes Ltda.

Chrystal, K. Alec, and James Alt. 1981. "Some Problems in Formulating and Testing a Politico-Economic Model of the U.K." *Economic Journal* 91:730–736.

Cintra, Antônio Octávio. 1979. "Traditional Brazilian Politics: An Interpretation of Relations Between Center and Periphery." In Neuma Aguiar, ed., *The Structure of Brazilian Development.* New Brunswick, N.J.: Transaction Books.

Cleaves, Peter. 1969. *Developmental Process in Chilean Local Government.* Politics of Modernization Series, no. 8. Berkeley: Institute of International Studies, University of California.

———. 1974. *Bureaucratic Politics and Administration in Chile.* Berkeley: University of California Press.

Cohen, Youssef. 1982. " 'The Benevolent Leviathan': Political Consciousness Among Urban Workers Under State Corporatism." *American Political Science Review* 76:46–59.

Coleman, Kenneth, and John Wanat. 1973. "Models of Political Influence on Federal Budgetary Allocations to Mexican States." Paper delivered at the American Political Science Association meeting, September 4–8, New Orleans.

Collier, David, and R. E. Messick. 1973. "Functional Prerequisites Versus Diffusion: Testing Alternative Explanations of Social Security Adoption." Paper delivered at the 1973 annual meeting of the Midwest Political Science Association, Chicago.

Conselho Nacional da Indústria (CNI). n.d. "Anais-Seminário Internacional sobre Negociações e Relações de Trabalho." Rio de Janeiro: Instituto Euvaldi Lodi.

Contador, Claudio. 1975. *Tecnologia e Desenvolvimento Agrícola.* Serie Monográfica, no. 17. Rio de Janeiro: IPEA.

Cotler, Julio. 1970. "The Mechanics of International Domination and Social Change in Peru." In I. Horowitz, ed., *Masses in Latin America.* New York: Oxford University Press.

Cuniff, Roger. 1975. "The Birth of the Drought Industry: Imperial and Provincial Response to the Great Drought in Northeast Brazil—1877–1900." *Revista de Ciências Sociais* (Fortaleza) 6:265–282.

Daland, Robert. 1972. "The Paradox of Brazilian Planning." Unpublished manuscript, University of North Carolina, Chapel Hill.

Da Mata, M. 1982. "Crédito Rural: Caracterização do Sistema e Estimativas dos Subsídios Implícitos." *Revista Brasileira de Economia* 36:3.

Denton, Charles. 1971. *Patterns of Costa Rican Politics.* Boston: Allyn & Bacon.

DiBacco, Thomas. 1977. *Presidential Power in Latin American Politics.* New York: Praeger.

DIEESE. 1975. *Informe Estatístico.* São Paulo: DIEESE.

———. 1981. *Pesquisa de Padrão de Vida e Emprego. Relatório Preliminar.* São Paulo: DIEESE.

Diniz, Eli. 1978. *Empresário, Estado e Capitalismo no Brasil: 1930–1945.* São Paulo: Paz e Terra.

Dix, Robert. 1967. *Colombia: The Political Dimensions of Change.* New Haven: Yale University Press.

———. 1984. "Incumbency and Electoral Turnover in Latin America." *Journal of Interamerican Studies and World Affairs* 26:435–448.

Duff, Ernest, and John McCamant. 1976. *Violence and Repression.* New York: Free Press.

Ebel, Roland. 1972. "Governing the City-State: Notes on the Politics of the Small Latin American Countries." *Journal of Interamerican Studies and World Affairs* 14:325–346.

Echols, John, and Barry Rundquist. 1979. "Relating Political Power to Political Benefits: A Working Paper." Paper presented at the American Political Science Association convention, August 31, Washington, D.C.

Ercilla. 1981. (June 3).

Erickson, Kenneth. 1977. *The Brazilian Corporative State and Working-Class Politics.* Berkeley: University of California Press.

Fausto, Boris. 1970. *A Revolução de 1930: Historiografia e História.* São Paulo: Editôra Brasiliense.

Felix, David. 1984. "On Financial Blowups and Authoritarian Regimes in Latin America." Working paper 60. St. Louis: Washington University.

Fenno, Richard. 1966. *The Power of the Purse: Appropriations Politics in Congress.* Boston: Little, Brown.

Fenton, John. 1966. *Midwest Politics.* New York: Holt, Rinehart and Winston.

Ffrench-Davis, Ricardo. 1973. *Políticas Económicas en Chile: 1952–1970.* Santiago: Centro de Estudios de Planificación Nacional.

Fitch, John. 1977. *The Military Coup d'Etat as a Political Process.* Baltimore: Johns Hopkins University Press.

Fleischer, David. 1973. "O Trampolim Político: Mudanças nos Padrões de Recrutamento Político em Minas Gerais." *Revista de Administração Pública* 7:99–116.

———. 1976. "Concentração e Dispersão Eleitoral: Um Estudo da Distribuição Geográfica do Voto em Minas Gerais (1966–1974)." *Revista Brasileira de Estudos Políticos* 43 (July):333–360.

———. 1977. "A Bancada Federal Mineira." *Revista Brasileira de Estudos Políticos* 45 (July):7–58.

———. 1981. *Os Partidos Políticos no Brasil.* Brasília: Editôra Universidade de Brasília.

Fontana, Andrés. 1981. "Forças Armadas e Ideologia Neoconservadora: O 'Encolhimento' do Estado na Argentina (1976–1981)." *Dados* 27:347–359.

Frey, Bruno, and Friedrich Schneider. 1978. "An Empirical Study of Politico-Economic Interaction in the United States." *Review of Economics and Statistics* 60:174–183.

Fundação Getúlio Vargas. 1978, 1980. *Regionalização das Transações do Setor Público 1970, 1975.* Rio de Janeiro: Instituto Brasileiro de Economia, Divisão de Contabilidade Social, Centro de Estudos Fiscais.

Geddes, Barbara, and John Zaller. 1985. "Sources of Popular Support for Authoritarian Regimes." Paper presented at the 1983 meeting of the American Political Science Association, Chicago.

Geisel, Ernesto. 1974–1979. *Discursos.* Brasília: Assessoria de Imprensa e Relações Públicas da Presidência da República.

Gilbert, Dennis. 1977. *The Oligarchy and the Old Regime in Peru.* Ithaca: Latin American Studies Program Dissertation Series, Cornell University.

Gist, John. 1977. "Increment and Base in the Congressional Appropriations Process." *American Journal of Political Science* 21:341–352.

———. 1979. "'Stability' and 'Competition' in Budgetary Theory." *American Political Science Review* 76:859–872.

Góes, Walder de. 1978. *O Brasil de General Geisel.* Rio de Janeiro: Nova Fronteira.

Gomes, Severo. 1977. *Tempos de Mudar.* Porto Alegre: Editôra Globo.

Goodman, Allan. 1975. "Correlates of Legislative Constituency Service in South Vietnam." In G. Boynton and C. Kim, eds., *Legislative Systems in Developing Countries*. Durham: Duke University Press.

Graham, Lawrence. 1968. *Civil Service Reform in Brazil: Principles versus Practice*. Austin: University of Texas Press.

Greenfield, Sidney. 1977. "Patronage, Politics, and the Articulation of Local Community and National Society." *Journal of Interamerican Studies and World Affairs* 19:139–172.

Groennings, Sven, E. W. Kelly, and Michael Leiserson, eds. 1970. *The Study of Coalition Behavior*. New York: Holt, Rinehart and Winston.

Guimarães, César. 1979. *Expansão do Estado e Intermediação de Interesses no Brasil*. Rio de Janeiro: IUPERJ.

Hansen, Roger. 1971. *The Politics of Mexican Development*. Baltimore: Johns Hopkins University Press.

Hartlyn, Jonathan. 1981. "Consociational Politics in Colombia: Confrontation and Accommodation in Comparative Perspective." Unpublished Ph.D. dissertation, Yale University.

Hayes, Margaret. 1975. "Policy Consequences of Military Participation in Politics: An Analysis of Trade-offs in Brazilian Federal Expenditures." In Craig Liske, William Loehr, and John McCamant, eds., *Comparative Public Policy: Issues, Theories, and Methods*. Beverly Hills: Sage.

Hayter, Teresa. 1971. *Aid as Imperialism*. Harmondsworth, England: Penguin Books.

Hibbs, Douglas. 1974a. "Industrial Conflict in Advanced Industrial Societies." Cambridge: MIT Center for International Studies.

———. 1974b. "Problems of Statistical Estimation and Causal Inference in Time-Series Regression Models." In H. Costner, ed., *Sociological Methodology 1973–1974*. San Francisco: Jossey-Bass.

———. 1977. "Political Parties and Macroeconomic Policy." *American Political Science Review* 71:1467–1487.

Hilliker, Grant. 1971. *The Politics of Reform in Peru*. Baltimore: Johns Hopkins University Press.

Hirschman, Albert. 1968. "The Political Economy of Import-Substituting Industrialization in Latin America." *Quarterly Journal of Economics* 82:1–32.

———. 1978. "The Social and Political Matrix of Inflation: Elaborations on the Latin American Experience." Princeton: Institute for Advanced Studies. Mimeo.

Hopkins, Raymond. 1979. "The Influence of the Legislature on Development Strategy: The Case of Kenya and Tanzania." In Joel Smith and Lloyd Musolf, eds., *Legislatures in Development: Dynamics of Change in New and Old States*. Durham: Duke University Press.

Hoskin, Gary, Franciso Leal, and Harvey Kline, eds. 1976. *Legislative Behavior in Colombia*. Buffalo: Council on International Studies.

Hughes, Steven, and Kenneth Mijeski. 1973. *Legislative-Executive Policy-Making: The Cases of Chile and Costa Rica*. Beverly Hills: Sage.

Hurtado, Osvaldo. 1980. *Political Power in Ecuador*. Albuquerque: University of New Mexico Press.

Instituto Americano de Estatística. 1971. *América en Cifras*. Washington, D.C.: Secretaría General de la Organización de los Estados Americanos.

International Monetary Fund. 1970–1984. *International Financial Statistics*. Washington, D.C.: IMF.

Jaquette, Jane. 1971. *The Politics of Development in Peru*. Ithaca: Latin American Studies Program Dissertation Series, Cornell University.

Jenks, Margaret. 1978. "Political Parties in Authoritarian Brazil." Unpublished Ph.D. dissertation, Duke University.

Jennings, Edward. 1979. "Competition, Constituencies, and Welfare Policies in American States." *American Political Science Review* 73:414–429.

Jonas, Susan, and David Tobis. 1974. *Guatemala*. Berkeley: NACLA.

Kahil, Raouf. 1973. *Inflation and Economic Development in Brazil, 1946–1963*. Oxford: Clarendon Press.

Karl, Terry. 1982. "The Political Economy of Petrodollars: Oil Democracy in Venezuela." Unpublished Ph.D. dissertation, Stanford University.

Kelly, Margaret. 1982. "Fiscal Adjustment and Fund-Supported Programs, 1971–1980." *IMF Staff Papers* 29:561–602.

Kenworthy, Eldon. 1970. "Coalitions in the Political Development of Latin America." In S. Groennings, E. Kelly, and M. Leiserson, eds., *The Study of Coalition Behavior*. New York: Holt, Rinehart and Winston.

Kim, C., and B. Woo. 1975. "Political Representation in the Korean National Assembly." In G. Boynton and C. Kim, eds., *Legislative Systems in Developing Countries*. Durham: Duke University Press.

Kinzo, Maria d'Alva. 1980. *Representação Política e Sistema Eleitoral no Brasil*. São Paulo: Símbolo.

Kirschen, E., and others. 1964. *Economic Policy in Our Time*. Vol. 1: *General Theory*. Amsterdam: North-Holland.

Kline, Harvey. 1974. "Interest Groups in the Colombian Congress." *Journal of InterAmerican Studies* 16:274–300.

Koehler, John. 1968. "Economic Policy-making with Limited Information: The Process of Macro-control in Mexico." Memorandum RM-5682-RC. Santa Monica: Rand Corporation.

Kramer, Gerald. 1971. "Short-term Fluctuations in U.S. Voting Behavior, 1896–1964." *American Political Science Review* 65:131–143.

Kucinski, Bernardo. 1982. *Abertura: A História de uma Crise*. São Paulo: Editôra Brasil Debates.

Kuczynski, Pedro-Pablo. 1977. *Peruvian Democracy Under Economic Stress*. Princeton: Princeton University Press.

Lamounier, Bolívar, and José Eduardo Faria. 1981. *O Futuro da Abertura: Um Debate*. São Paulo: Cortez.

Langoni, Carlos. 1972. "Distribuição de Renda e Desenvolvimento Econômico do Brasil." *Estudos Econômicos* 2:5.

Latin America. 1967. London: Latin America Newsletters, Ltd.

Latin America Economic Report (LAER). 1973–1979. London: Latin America Newsletters, Ltd.

Latin America Regional Report: Southern Cone. 1979–1982. London: Latin America Newsletters, Ltd.

Lessa, Carlos. 1975. *Quinze Anos de Política Econômica*. Cadernos do Instituto de Filosofia e Ciências Humanas. Campinas: Universidade Estadual de Campinas.

————. 1978. "A Estratégia de Desenvolvimento 1974–1975—Sonho e Fracasso." Rio de Janeiro: UFRJ.

————. 1980. "A Administração da Crise." *Cadernos de Economia Brasileira* 1:1–17.

Levine, Daniel. 1973. *Conflict and Political Change in Venezuela*. Princeton: Princeton University Press.

Levy, Daniel. 1979. "Higher Education Policy in Bureaucratic-Authoritarian Regimes: Comparative Perspectives on the Chilean Case." Paper prepared for the 1979 meeting of the Latin American Studies Association, Pittsburgh, April 5–7.

Lima Junior, Olavo Brasil de. 1977. "Mudança Política e Processo Decisório: Análise da Política Orçamentária Brasileira." *Dados* 14:141–163.

Lindblom, Charles. 1977. *Politics and Markets: The World's Political and Economic Systems*. New York: Basic Books.

Lipset, Seymour Martin. 1968. *Agrarian Socialism*. Garden City: Doubleday.

Lowi, Theodore. 1964. "American Business, Public Policy, Case Studies and Political Theory." *World Politics* 16:677–715.

Macedo, M. 1981. "O Futuro das Negociações e das Relações do Trabalho no Brasil." *Anais-Seminário Internacional sobre Negociações e Relações de Trabalho*. Rio de Janeiro: Instituto Euvaldo Lodi (CNI).

Mallon, Richard, and Juan Sourrouille. 1975. *Economic Policymaking in a Conflict Society: The Argentine Case.* Cambridge: Harvard University Press.

Malloy, John. 1970. *Bolivia: The Uncompleted Revolution.* Pittsburgh: University of Pittsburgh Press.

———, ed. 1977. *Authoritarianism and Corporatism in Latin America.* Pittsburgh: University of Pittsburgh Press.

Malloy, John, and Richard Thorn, eds. 1971. *Beyond the Revolution: Bolivia Since 1952.* Pittsburgh: University of Pittsburgh Press.

Martz, John. 1972. *Ecuador: Conflicting Political Culture and the Quest for Progress.* Boston: Allyn & Bacon.

Mayhew, David. 1974. *Congress: The Electoral Connection.* New Haven: Yale University Press.

McDonald, Ronald. 1971. *Party Systems and Elections in Latin America.* Chicago: Markham.

McDonough, Peter. 1981. *Power and Ideology in Brazil.* Princeton: Princeton University Press.

Melville, Thomas, and Marjorie Melville. 1971. *The Politics of Land Ownership.* New York: Free Press.

Mendes, Cândido. 1975. *O Legislativo e a Tecnocracia.* Rio de Janeiro: Imago Editorial/Conjunto Universitário Cândido Mendes.

———. n.d. "O Discurso Político como Indicador nos Sistemas de Elite de Poder na América Latina." In Cândido Mendes, ed., *Crise e Mudança Social.* Rio de Janeiro: Eldorado.

Merkx, Gilbert. 1969. "Sectoral Clashes and Political Change: The Argentine Experience." *Latin American Research Review* 4:89–114.

Mesa Lago, Carmelo. 1978. *Social Security in Latin America.* Pittsburgh: University of Pittsburgh Press.

Millett, Richard. 1977. *Guardians of the Dynasty.* Maryknoll, New York: Orbis Books.

Mitchell, Christopher. 1977. *The Legacy of Populism in Bolivia.* New York: Praeger.

Montenegro, Abelardo. 1960. "Tentativa de Interpretação das Eleições de 1958 no Ceará." *Revista Brasileira de Estudos Políticos* 8:39–49.

Moran, Theodore. 1974. *Multinational Corporations and the Politics of Dependence: Copper in Chile.* Princeton: Princeton University Press.

Mosley, Phillip. 1976. "Towards a Satisficing Theory of Economic Policy." *Economic Journal* 1:137–173.

Moulian, Tomás, and Pilar Vergara. 1981. "Estado, Ideologia y Políticas Económicas en Chile: 1973–1978." *Revista Mexicana de Sociología* 43:845–903.

Muller, Geraldo. 1982. "Estado e Classes Sociais na Agricultura." *Estudos Econômicos.* 12:81–94.

Myers, David. 1973. *Democratic Campaigning in Venezuela*. Caracas: Fundación La Salle de Ciencias Naturales.

Natchez, P., and I. Bupp. 1973. "Policy and Priority in the Budgetary Process." *American Political Science Review* 66:951–973.

Needler, Martin. 1974. "The Causality of the Latin American Coup d'Etat: Some Numbers, Some Speculations." In Gerald Dorfman and Steffan Schmidt, eds., *Soldiers in Politics*. Los Altos, Calif.: Geron-X.

Nordhaus, William. 1975. "The Political Business Cycle." *Review of Economic Studies* 42:169–190.

Nunberg, Barbara. 1986. "Structural Change and State Policy: The Politics of Sugar in Brazil Since 1964." *Latin American Research Review* 21:53–92.

Nunes, Edson Oliveira de. 1978. "Legislativo, Política e Recrutamento de Elites no Brasil." *Dados* 17:53–78.

O'Brien, Philip, and Paul Cammack. 1985. *Generals in Retreat*. Manchester: Manchester University Press.

O'Brien, Philip, and John Roddick. 1983. *Chile: The Pinochet Decade*. London: Latin America Bureau.

O'Donnell, Guillermo. 1973. *Modernization and Bureaucratic-Authoritarianism: Studies in South American Politics*. Berkeley: University of California, Institute of International Studies.

———. 1977. "Corporatism and the Question of the State." In J. Malloy, ed., *Authoritarianism and Corporatism in Latin America*. Pittsburgh: University of Pittsburgh Press.

———. 1978. "Reflections on the Patterns of Change in the Bureaucratic-Authoritarian State." *Latin American Research Review* 12:3–38.

———. 1979. "Tensions in the Bureaucratic-Authoritarian State." In David Collier, ed., *The New Authoritarianism in Latin America*. Princeton: Princeton University Press.

Packenham, Robert. 1971. "Functions of the Brazilian National Congress." In Weston Agor, ed., *Latin American Legislatures: Their Role and Influence*. New York: Praeger.

Parrish, Charles. 1970. *Bureaucracy, Democracy and Development: Some Considerations Based on the Chilean Case*. LADAC Occasional Papers. Austin: Latin American Development Administration Committee, University of Texas.

Payer, Cheryl. 1974. *The Debt Trap: The IMF and the Third World*. New York: Monthly Review Press.

Payne, James. 1965. *Labor and Politics in Peru*. New Haven: Yale University Press.

———. 1968. *Patterns of Conflict in Colombia*. New Haven: Yale University Press.

Peroff, Kathleen, and Margaret Podolak-Warren. 1979. "Does Spending on Defense Cut Spending on Health?" *British Journal of Political Science* 9:21–39.

Pike, Frederick. 1967. *The Modern History of Peru.* New York: Praeger.

Pippin, Larry. 1964. *The Remón Era.* Stanford: Institute of Hispanic American and Luso-Brazilian Studies.

Powell, John D. 1971. *Political Mobilization of the Venezuelan Peasant.* Cambridge: Harvard University Press.

Pressman, Jeffrey. 1980. "Setting Limits in a Decentralized System." In Dennis Sullivan and others, eds., *How America Is Ruled.* New York: Wiley.

Purcell, Susan K., and John F. H. Purcell. 1980. "State and Society in Mexico." *World Politics* 32:194–227.

Putnam, Robert. 1967. "Toward Explaining Military Intervention in Latin America." *World Politics* 20:83–100.

Pyne, Peter. 1973. "The Role of the Congress in the Ecuadorian Political System and Its Contribution to the Overthrow of President Velasco Ibarra in 1961." Occasional Paper no. 7. Glasgow: Institute of Latin American Studies.

Ranis, Peter. 1968. "A Two-Dimensional Typology of Latin American Political Parties." *Journal of Politics* 30:798–832.

Ray, Talton. 1969. *The Politics of the Barrios of Venezuela.* Berkeley: University of California Press.

Reichmann, Thomas, and Richard Stillson. 1978. "Experience with Problems of Balance of Payments Adjustment: Stand-by Arrangements in the Higher Credit Tranches." *IMF Staff Papers* 25:293–309.

Reis Velloso, João Paulo dos. 1978. *Brasil: A Solução Positiva.* São Paulo: Abril-Tec.

Remmer, Karen. 1978. "Evaluating the Policy Impact of Military Regimes in Latin America." *Latin American Research Review* 13:39–54.

———. 1979. "Public Policy and Regime Consolidation: The First Five Years of the Chilean Junta." *Journal of Developing Areas* 13:441–462.

Remmer, Karen, and Gilbert Merkx. 1982. "Bureaucratic-Authoritarianism Revisited." *Latin American Research Review* 17:3–40.

Rezende, Fernando. 1982a. "Autonomia Política e Dependência Financeira: Uma Análise das Transformações Recentes nas Relações Intergovernamentais e seus Reflexos sobre a Situação Financeira dos Estados." Textos para Discussão Interna, no. 47. Rio de Janeiro: IPEA.

———. 1982b. "Crédito Rural Subsidiado e Preço da Terra no Brasil." *Estudos Econômicos* 12:117–138.

Roeder, Philip. 1985. "Do New Soviet Leaders Really Make a Difference?

Rethinking the 'Succession Connection.' " *American Political Science Review* 79:958–976.

Ronning, C. Neil, and H. Keith. 1976. "Shrinking the Political Arena: Military Government in Brazil Since 1964." In H. Keith and R. Hayes, eds., *Perspectives on Armed Politics in Brazil*. Tempe: Arizona State University Press.

Rosenberg, Mark B. 1976. "The Politics of Health Care in Costa Rica." Unpublished Ph.D. dissertation, University of Pittsburgh.

Rothenberg, Irene F. 1973. "Centralization Patterns and Policy Outcomes in Colombia." Unpublished Ph.D. dissertation, University of Illinois, Urbana.

Ruddle, Kenneth, and Kenneth Barrows. 1974. *Statistical Abstract of Latin America*. Los Angeles: UCLA Latin American Center.

Ruddle, Kenneth, and Phillip Gillette. 1972. *Latin American Political Statistics*. Los Angeles: UCLA Latin American Center.

Russett, Bruce, and others. 1964. *World Handbook of Political and Social Indicators*. New Haven: Yale University Press.

Sacks, Paul. 1976. *The Donegal Mafia: An Irish Political Machine*. New Haven: Yale University Press.

Sampaio, Yony, Luís Sampaio, and Sílvio Maranhão. 1980. *Desenvolvimento Rural no Nordeste*. Recife: CME-PIMES, Universidade Federal de Pernambuco.

Santos, José Nicolau dos. 1964. "Comportamento Eleitoral do Paraná nas Eleições de 1962." *Revista Brasileira de Estudos Políticos* 16:227–250.

Santos, Wanderley Guilherme dos. 1979. "The Calculus of Conflict: Impasse in Brazilian Politics and the Crisis of 1964." Unpublished Ph.D. dissertation, Stanford University.

Sartori, Giovanni. 1976. *Parties and Party Systems: A Framework for Analysis*. Cambridge: Cambridge University Press.

Scheetz, Thomas. 1986. "Public Sector Expenditures and Financial Crisis in Chile." Paper presented at the seminar "Inflation in Latin America," April 4–5, University of Illinois, Urbana.

Schmitter, Philippe. 1971a. "Military Intervention, Political Competitiveness, and Public Policy in Latin America." In Morris Janowitz and Jacques Van Doorn, eds., *On Military Intervention*. Rotterdam: Rotterdam University Press.

———. 1971b. *Interest Conflict and Political Change in Brazil*. Stanford: Stanford University Press.

Schwartzman, Simon. 1970. "Representação e Cooptação Política no Brasil." *Dados* 7:9–41.

Scott, James. 1972. "Patron-Client Politics and Political Change in Southeast Asia." *American Political Science Review* 66:91–113.

Selowsky, Marcelo. 1979. *Who Benefits from Government Expenditures?* New York: Oxford University Press.

Shepsle, Kenneth, and Barry Weingast. 1981. "Political Preferences for the Pork Barrel: A Generalization." *American Journal of Political Science* 25:96–111.

Siegel, Gilbert. 1974. "The Vicissitudes of Governmental Reform in Brazil: A Study of the DASP." Ann Arbor: University Microfilms.

Sinding, Steven. 1972. "The Impact of Political Participation on Public Expenditures: The Case of Chile." Unpublished manuscript, University of North Carolina.

Skidmore, Thomas. 1967. *Politics in Brazil.* New York: Oxford University Press.

Smith, William C. 1980. "Crisis of the State and Military-Authoritarian Rule in Argentina." Ph.D. dissertation, Stanford University.

———. 1985. "Reflections on the Political Economy of Authoritarian Rule and Capitalist Reorganization in Contemporary Argentina." In Philip O'Brien and Paul Cammack, eds., *Generals in Retreat.* Manchester: Manchester University Press.

Soares, Glaucio Ary Dillon. 1964. "Alianças e Coligações Eleitorais: Notas para uma Teoria." *Revista Brasileira de Estudos Políticos* 17:95–124.

———. 1971. "El Sistema Electoral y la Representación de los Grupos Sociales en el Brasil, 1945–1962." *Revista Latino-americana de Ciencia Política* 2:5–23.

———. 1973. *Sociedade e Política no Brasil.* São Paulo: Difusão Europeia do Livro.

———. 1978. "After the Miracle." *Luso-Brazilian Review* 15:278–301.

Soler, Ricuarte. 1972. *Formas Ideológicas de la Nación Panameño.* San José, Costa Rica: Editorial Universitaria Centroamericana.

Souza, Maria do Carmo C. 1976. *Estado e Partidos Políticos no Brasil (1930 a 1964).* São Paulo: Editôra Alfa-Omega.

Souza, Rubén Dario, and others. 1970. *Panamá 1930–70.* Santiago: n.p.

Stallings, Barbara. 1978. *Class Conflict and Economic Development in Chile, 1958–1973.* Stanford: Stanford University Press.

Staniland, Martin. 1985. *What Is Political Economy?* New Haven: Yale University Press.

Stepan, Alfred. 1971. *The Military in Politics: Changing Patterns in Brazil.* Princeton: Princeton University Press.

———. 1985. "State Power and the Strength of Civil Society in the Southern Cone of Latin America." In Peter B. Evans, Dietrich Rueschemeyer, and Theda Skocpol, eds., *Bringing the State Back In.* Cambridge: Cambridge University Press.

Tavares de Almeida, Maria Helena. 1981. "Tendéncias Recentes da Negociação Coletiva no Brasil." In *Trabalho e Cultura no Brasil*. Rio de Janeiro: ANPPCS/CNPq.

Taylor, Charles, and Michael Hudson. 1983. *World Handbook of Political and Social Indicators*. 2nd ed. New Haven: Yale University Press.

Taylor, Philip. 1960. *The Government and Politics of Uruguay*. New Orleans: Tulane University Press.

Tolipan, Ricardo, and Arthur Carlos Tinelli. 1975. *A Controvérsia sobre Distribuição de Renda e Desenvolvimento*. Rio de Janeiro: Zahar.

Tufte, Edward. 1978. *Political Control of the Economy*. Princeton: Princeton University Press.

Tugwell, Franklin. 1975. *The Politics of Oil in Venezuela*. Stanford: Stanford University Press.

Valenzuela, Arturo, and Alexander Wilde. 1979. "Presidential Politics and the Decline of the Chilean Congress." In Joel Smith and Lloyd Musolf, eds., *Legislatures in Development: Dynamics of Change in New and Old States*. Durham: Duke University Press.

Van Niekerk, A. E. 1976. *Populism and Political Development in Latin America*. The Hague: Rotterdam University Press.

Velasco e Cruz, Sebastião, and Carlos Estevam Martins. 1983. "De Castelo a Figueiredo: Uma Incursão na pre-História da Abertura." In *Sociedade e Política no Brasil pos-1964*. São Paulo: Brasiliense.

Venezuela. 1971. *Informe Económico: Banco Central de Venezuela*. Caracas: Banco Central de Venezuela.

Vidal, Jaime Perdomo. 1966. *Derecho Administrativo General*. Bogotá: Editorial Ternis.

Vieira Da Cunha, Paulo, and others. 1982. "Política Salarial, Inflação e Emprego." In Maria da Conceição Tavares and M. D. Dias, eds., *A Economia Política da Crise*. Rio de Janeiro: Vozes-Achiame.

Villanueva, V. 1969. *Nueva Mentalidad Militar en el Peru?* Lima: Editorial Juan Mejia Baca.

Wallerstein, Emmanuel. 1974. *Modern World System*. New York: Academic Press.

Weaver, Jerry. 1971. *Bureaucracy During a Period of Social Change: The Guatemalan Case*. Austin, Texas: Institute of Latin American Studies.

Webb, Richard. 1977. *Government Policy and the Distribution of Income in Peru, 1963–73*. Cambridge: Harvard University Press.

Weinstein, Martin. 1975. *Uruguay: The Politics of Failure*. Westport, Conn.: Greenwood Press.

Wiarda, Howard J., and Harvey Kline, eds. 1979. *Latin American Politics and Development*. Boston: Houghton Mifflin.

Wildavsky, Aaron. 1964. *The Politics of the Budgetary Process*. Boston: Little, Brown.

Wilkie, James. 1971. "Public Expenditure Since 1952." In James Malloy and Richard Thorn, eds., *Beyond the Revolution: Bolivia Since 1952.* Pittsburgh: University of Pittsburgh Press.

Wolf, Eric R., and E. C. Hansen. 1967. "Caudillo Politics: A Structural Analysis." *Comparative Studies in Society and History* 9:168–179.

World Bank. 1975. *Rural Development Issues and Options in Northeast Brazil.* Washington, D.C.: World Bank.

———. 1981. *A Review of Agricultural Policies in Brazil.* Washington, D.C.: World Bank.

———. 1985. *Argentina: Economic Memorandum.* Vol. 2. Washington, D.C.: World Bank.

Wriggins, W. Howard. 1969. *The Ruler's Imperative.* New York: Columbia University Press.

Wynia, Gary. 1978. *Argentina in the Postwar Era.* Albuquerque: University of New Mexico Press.

Zuk, Gary, and William Thompson. 1982. "The Post-Coup Military Spending Question: A Pooled Cross-Sectional Time Series Analysis." *American Political Science Review* 76:60–74.

Zuvekas, Clarence. 1967. "Argentine Economic Policies Under the Frondizi Government, 1958–62." Unpublished Ph.D. dissertation, Washington University, St. Louis.

———. 1968. "Argentine Economic Policy 1958–62: The Frondizi Government's Development Plan." *InterAmerican Economic Affairs* 22:45–74.

Index

Abertura: as appeal to elites, 150; and avoiding recession, 150; combining survival strategies, 154; comparing policies as regional strategies, 205; comparing policies as social strategies, 205; decline in growth after second oil shock, 207; irreconcilable strategies, 154; liberalization and economic crisis, 149; as mass support strategy, 151; as opportunistic response, 145; policy options for mass support, 151; problems in implementing an appeal to elites, 150–51; as regional strategy, 152, 206; regional strategy vs. local pressure, 153; as response to Geisel's need for support, 145; as return to barracks, 149, 204; skill of Geisel and Golbery, 145; social components after 1974, 148; strategic dilemmas of class appeals, 204

Acre, 152

Administration: as case, 2; distinguished from regime, 2; definition, 2; in ordinary discourse, 2

Administrative Department of the Public Service, Brazil, 106

Africa. *See* Coalitions in Africa

Alagoas, and rural credit shares, 157

Aleixo, Pedro, 120

Alemán, Miguel, 96

Alessandri, Jorge: budgetary outputs, 233 n.6; political base, 231; political strategy, 232

Alianza Popular Revolucionaria Americana. *See* APRA

Allende, Salvador: breaking rule of political game, 222; impossible strategies, 221–22; political base, 231; political strategy, 232; role of Congress in overthrow, 103; and subordinate-class strategy, 60

Allison, Graham, 141n

Alt, James, 230

Alves, Aluísio, 134 n.34

Amazonas, and rural credit shares, 157

Ames, Barry, 16

Anderson, Charles, 13

Andreazza, Mário: Figueiredo's favorite, 208; housing policy, 171–72; political ambitions, 205; presidential candidate, 207; unhappiness with housing payoffs, 206 n.76

Andrés Pérez, Carlos, 221

APRA, and coalition approach, 234–35

Arana, Carlos, and dominant-class strategy, 58

Arbenz, Jacobo, 21; as defensive liberal, 95; and subordinate-class strategy, 60

Archer, Renato, 135

ARENA (Aliança Renovadora Nacional), 132 n.29, 144, 148, 152 n.17, 153

Arévalo, Juan José: overspender in total spending model, 29; and subordinate-class strategy, 60

Argentina: BA regime 1966–1970 and

Compositor: Auto-Graphics, Inc.
Printer: Braun-Brumfield, Inc.
Binder: Braun-Brumfield, Inc.
Text: 10/12 Sabon
Display: Sabon